JUNGIAN PERSPEC

CLINICAL SUPERVISION

Jungian Perspectives
on Clinical
Supervision

Edited by Paul Kugler

DAIMON

ISBN 3-85630-552-1

Cover illustration from: Michael Maier, *Tripus Aureus*, Frankfurt/Main 1677

Contents

Part IV Assessing Progress in Supervision

Part V Phases in a Supervisor's Life

Part VI Supervision and Institutions

Contributors

James Astor is a training analyst at the Society of Analytical Psychology in London. He trained in Child and Adult analysis and worked in a Child and Family Department of a teaching hospital for a number of years but now is in full-time practice. He continues to teach and supervise for the S.A.P., and the British Association of Psychotherapists and is currently preparing a book on the work of Michael Fordham.

John Beebe, M.D., has been a control (supervising) analyst for candidates of the C.G. Jung Institute of San Francisco and Chairperson of the Institute's Certifying Board. The founding editor of *The San Francisco Jung Institute Library Journal* and the first U.S. Coeditor of *The Journal of Analytical Psychology*. He is the author of *Integrity in Depth.*

Crittenden E. Brookes M.D., Ph.D. is in the private practice of psychiatry and Jungian analysis in San Francisco. He is past Director of Curriculum and past member of the Board of Governors of the C.G. Jung Institute of San Francisco, and is also a member of the Inter-Regional Society of Jungian Analysts. A fellow and past member of the Board of Trustees of the American Academy of Psychoanalysis as well as a Fellow of the American Psychiatric Association. Dr. Brookes also holds a degree of Black Belt in Aikido.

Jean Carr trained first as a social worker, and worked in a variety of settings, including the Adult Psychiatry Department at Guys Hospital, London. She then trained as a Jungian Psychotherapist with the British Association of Psychotherapists. She now works as a senior manager in Oxfordshire Social Services Department and in private practice. Her interest in supervision arises from working and supervising in an organisational context, and the influence of the wider system on the supervisory pair.

Lionel Corbett, M.D., graduated from the Medical School at the University of Manchester, England in 1966. Following his psychiatric training, he moved to the USA in 1972. On the faculty of various medical schools, he spent several years as a researcher in psychopharmacology. For 12 years at Rush Medical College and Presbyterian St. Lukes Hospital in Chicago, he served as clinical director of both the psychogeriatric and general psychiatry units. He is a graduate of the C.G. Jung Institute of Chicago and has been instrumental in the development of the new analytic training program in Santa Fe, New Mexico, his home since 1989.

Gustav Dreifuss, Ph.D., Diploma C.G. Jung Institute, Zurich, 1959. Training Analyst and former President, Israel Association of Analytical Psychology. Former lecturer and Supervisor, Psychotherapy Section, University Tel Aviv and Psychotherapy section, Medical School, Psychiatric Department, Rambam Hospital, Haifa. Author of many papers since 1965. Currently he is in practice in Haifa.

Michael Fordham, M.D., is a training analyst in the Society of Analytical Psychology. He is also coeditor of the *Collected Works of C.G. Jung* and was the first editor of *The Journal of Analytical Psychology*. He has written numerous papers in scientific journals and several books, three more recent ones being *Jungian Psychotherapy* and *Explorations into the Self,* and an autobiography: *The Making of an Analyst.*

Joseph Henderson, M.D., is an analytical psychologist in private practice in San Francisco, a founding member of the C.G. Jung Institute in San Francisco and former Vice-President of the IAAP. He is author of *Threshold of Initiation*, a coauthor of Jung's *Man and His Symbols, The Wisdom of the Serpent* (with Maud Oakes), *Cultural Attitudes in Psychological Perspective* and *Shadow and Self.*

Judith Hubback, M.A. (Cantab.), is a training analyst of the Society of Analytical Psychology, London. She does individual and small group supervision. She was Editor of the *Journal of Analytical Psychology* from 1977 to 1986, and Consultative Editor from 1986 to 1994. Many of her papers were published under the title *People who do Things to Each Other*, Chiron 1988.

Elie Humbert, Ph.D., was personally trained as a psychoanalyst by Jung. An internationally renowned lecturer, he taught at the University of Paris in the Department of Psychoanalysis. Co-founder of the French Society of Analytical Psychology and past President of the French Jung Society, he served as chief editor of *Cahiers de Psychologie Jungienne.* He is author of *C.G. Jung* (Chiron) and numerous other works in French.

Mario Jacoby, Ph. D., is a training analyst, lecturer, and member of the Curatorium (Board of Directors) of the C.G. Jung Institute in Zurich. Analyst and psychotherapist in private practice. For ten years before becoming an analyst he was a concert violinist. He has lectured throughout Europe, the United States, and the Pacific Rim and is the author of numerous articles and books on analytical psychology. Available in English are his books *Longing for Paradise* (Sigo Press), *The Analytic Encounter* (Inner City Books 1984), *Individuation and Narcissism* (Routledge 1989), *Shame and the Origins of Self-esteem.* (1994, Routledge).

Donald Kalsched, Ph.D., is a clinical psychologist and Jungian analyst in private practice in New York City and Katonah, NY. He is a member of the teaching and supervisory faculty of the C.G. Jung Institute in New York and the Inter-Regional Society of Jungian Analysts. Currently he is working on a book on the "Inner World of Trauma" from a Jungian standpoint (Routledge).

Paul Kugler, Ph.D., Diploma C.G. Jung Institute, Zurich, 1979, is former Director of Training and current President of the Inter-Regional Society of Jungian Analysts. He has taught at the State University of New York and is the author of numerous articles ranging from contemporary psychoanalysis (Lacan, Kohut, Langs, etc.) and childhood seduction to experimental theater and postmodernism. His books include *The Alchemy of Discourse* and the forthcoming *Clinical Psychopathology.*

Mary Ann Mattoon, Ph.D., is a Jungian analyst in private practice in Minneapolis, Minnesota. She received her Diploma from the C.G. Jung Institute of Zurich in 1956 and her Ph.D. in psychology from the University of Minnesota in 1970. Currently she is a Clinical Professor of Psychology at the University of Minnesota and a Senior

Training Analyst with the Inter-Regional Society of Jungian Analysts. She is author of three books – *Understanding Dreams, Jungian Psychology in Perspective, Jungian Psychology after Jung* – and is Editor of the *Proceedings of the International Association for Jungian Psychology: 1986, 1989, 1992.*

Norah Moore is a training analyst and supervisor of the Society of Analytical Psychology, London. She is the author of a number of papers on clinical aspects and the transference, as well as on archetypal themes, and is particularly interested in integrating these two approaches. She is a former Director of Training of the S.A.P. and has a special interest in matters of training and supervision. Her practice is in London and in Surrey, England.

Alfred Plaut, M.D., was born in Düsseldorf, Germany. In 1913 he emigrated to South Africa and in 1933 completed his medical studies. After serving as a medical officer during W.W. II, he specialized in general psychiatry, child psychiatry and trained as an analytical psychologist. He is a Fellow of the Royal College of Psychiatrists and a former editor of *The Journal of Analytical Psychology*. He has authored numerous publications, the most recent being *Analysis Analyzed* (Routledge, 1993). In 1986 he returned to Berlin where now is in private practice.

Joan Reggiori first trained as a Psychiatric Social Worker before training as an Analytical Psychologist with the Jungian section of the British Association of Psychotherapists. As a B.A.P. Training Therapist and Training Supervisor she teaches and supervises its qualifying course. She also supervises the qualifying course of the Institute of Group Analysis and is a psychotherapist at St. Bartolomews Hospital. She has a private practice and has written on "Psychotherapy in the National Health Service."

Marga Speicher, M.S.W., Ph.D., faculty member and former President of the C.G. Jung Institute of New York. Active in professional organizations with an interdisciplinary and multi-theoretical perspective, she is a Founding Member and President of the International Federation for Psychoanalytic Education (IFPE) and often represents the Jungian point of view at interdisciplinary conferences. She has lectured and written on symbolic understanding in folklore and literature and on aspects of the educational process in the analytic field.

Ann B. Ulanov, M.Div., Ph.D., L.H.D., is the Christiane Brooks Johnson Professor of Psychiatry and Religion at Union Theological Seminary, a psychoanalyst in private practice, and a supervising analyst and faculty member of the C.G. Jung Institute, NYC. With her husband, Barry Ulanov, she is the author of *Religion and the Unconscious, Primary Speech: A Psychology of Prayer, Cinderella and Her Sisters: The Envied and the Envying*; by herself she is the author of *The Feminine in Christian Theology and in Jungian Psychology, Receiving Woman, Picturing God, The Wisdom of the Psyche, The Functioning Transcendent,* and *The Wizards' Gate.*

Joseph Wakefield, M.D., studied medicine at Stanford Medical School and completed his analytic training at the C.G. Jung Institute, San Francisco. Among his interests are the psychological aspects of supervision and ethics. His recent publications are: "The Supervisor," in *Closeness in Personal and Professional Relationships*, ed. Harry Wilmer, Shambhala, 1992 and "Am I My Brother's Keeper? Impairment in the Healing Profession," in *Cast the First Stone: Ethics in Analytic Therapy*," ed Lena B. Ross, Chiron Publications, in press.

Hans-Joachim Wilke, M.D., is a member of the German Society of Analytical Psychology, training analyst and lecturer at the Institute of Psychotherapy, Berlin. Executive editor of *Zeitschrift für Analytische Psychologie*. In private practice since 1967.

Louis Zinkin, M.D., who died suddenly in March 1993, was a Jungian analyst in private practice in London. He was a Fellow of the Royal College of Psychiatrists, a Training Analyst of the Society of Analytical Psychology and also of the Institute of Group Analysis, and Honorary Consultant Psychotherapist and Senior Lecturer at St. George's Hospital, London, where he had worked for ten years before his retirement in 1989. As well as working with individuals, Dr. Zinkin practiced group and marital therapy. He was the author of many papers and coeditor with Dr. Dennis Brown of The Psyche and the Social World, published by Routledge, London, 1994.

Acknowledgments

I am particularly grateful to the following persons for their support at various phases in the development of the book and the preparation of the manuscript: Joan Buresch, Patricia Cox, Harry Hunt, Thomas Kapacinskas, Richard Mennen, David Miller, Andrew Samuels, John Talley, Barbara and Dennis Tedlock, Joe Wakefield and especially the members of The Inter-Regional Society of Jungian Analysts for their support over the years of my efforts to organize continuing education programs related to issues of training. A special thanks goes to my personal supervisors, David Hart, Marie-Louise von Franz and Adolf Guggenbühl-Craig for providing me with deeply meaningful experiences of supervision. Robert Hinshaw, an old friend and talented publisher, is due a particular thanks, for without him this book would never have been possible. A note of appreciation goes to all the authors for their hard work and patience throughout the editing process. And a special thanks is due to Marga Speicher for her generous financial support for this project.

I would also like to acknowledge my indebtedness to *The Journal of Analytical Psychology* and the authors for their generous permission to allow me to reprint the following essays: "Suggestions Towards a Theory of Supervision," Michael Fordham (1961, 16); "Michael Fordham's Theory and Practice of Supervision," Norah Moore (1986, 31); "A Symposium: How Do I Assess Progress in Supervision?", Alfred Plaut, Gustav Dreifuss, Michael Fordham, Joseph L. Henderson, Elie Humbert, Mario Jacoby, Ann B. Ulanov (her essay appears in a revised form), Hans-Joachim Wilke *(1982, 27);* "Supervision, Training, and The Institution as an Internal Pressure," James Astor (1975, 22). A particular acknowledgment is in order for the work done by the various past editors of *The Journal of Analytical Psychology* on these essays: Michael Fordham, Fred Plaut, Judith Hubback, and Rosemary Gordon.

The following essays are reprinted from *The IAAP 1993 Yearbook* with the permission of the authors: "Supervision and the Interactive Field," Mario Jacoby; "Styles of Supervision," Judith Hubback; "The Transition From Training Candidate to Supervising Analyst," (in a revised form) Paul Kugler.

I am grateful to the following authors for permission to reprint their essays: "The Impossible Profession," Louis Zinkin; "Some Thoughts on the Clinical Process," Joan Reggiori; and "A Model of Clinical Supervision," Jean Carr. Louis Zinkin's essay, "The Impossible Profession," appears in this book in a considerably revised form. These essays were originally published by the British Association of Psychotherapists in a monograph entitled "Clinical Supervision: Issues and Techniques," 1989.

And finally, a warm thanks goes to Karen Wolff, my wife, for her endless patience and gentle support of the project.

Notes on Conventions

Gender Reference

In recent years we have developed a greater understanding of the problem of gender reference in the use of personal pronouns. There is no longer a specific convention governing the use of pronouns in published works. Some writers still exclusively use the male pronoun, others use the pronoun specific to the gender of the author, while still others use "she/he" or, even, randomly mix the use of pronouns between the male and female gender. This lack of a single convention, coupled with the personal nature of such decisions, has led the editor not to seek a uniform position on this point in the volume, but instead to let the authors speak in their own voices, reflecting their own preferences.

A Note on Spelling

A number of the essays reprinted here were originally published in England and adopted the English spelling of particular words. To establish a certain consistency with respect to spelling, we have opted to use American spelling as the standard through out the volume.

Part I

Background

[1]

Introduction

In recent years the role of supervision in the training of psychologists, psychiatrists, social workers and psychoanalysts has taken on increasing importance. While the various training programs for psychotherapists range from behaviorism to depth psychology, and differ as to whether or not the therapist-in-training needs to undergo personal analysis, all programs require some form of supervision. Even though supervision has long been an essential part of the training of psychotherapists, remarkably little had been written on the subject until ten years ago. Our understanding of the supervisory process has had a slow evolution and, even today, there is limited formal training available for the would-be-supervisor.

The conception for this book developed out of several programs on supervision I organized while a member of the Training Committee for the Inter-Regional Society of Jungian Analysts. As we worked to develop continuing education programs for supervisors and training analysts, it became increasingly apparent that Jungians had published very little on supervision. This volume answers the need in Jungian psychology for more open discussion of the various facets of supervision in clinical practice, the training of analytic candidates and related fields. My primary objective in editing this book has been to provide a forum for discussion of the various practical and theoretical aspects of supervision. The papers included consist of nearly all the previously published material on supervision in the Jungian literature, supplemented by many new essays commissioned specifically for this book to provide a broad *multi-theoretical perspective*. The topics discussed will be of particular value to professionals using a Jungian-oriented approach to the supervision of analysis and psychotherapy in the fields of clinical psychology, psychiatry, social work, psychiatric nursing, religious counseling and spiritual direction.

Supervision involves a variety of important aspects which attempt to enhance the supervisee's work, elaborating technique, elucidating transference and countertransference issues, proposing direction and focus to the clinical inquiry, suggesting dynamic and archetypal formulations about the analytic process, and exploring repeated patterns of behavior, thought, and fantasy.

Some Questions of Supervision

Where the analyst needs the skills of an analyst, a supervisor needs the skills of both analyst and teacher. But what is supervision and how do we become supervising analysts? The distinguished American philosopher and educator, John Dewey, once noted that a question properly formulated is a question half answered. So, to begin this book on supervision, I would like to formulate a series of questions concerning the subject:

1. In supervision how do we approach supervisees just beginning to work analytically? How do we help them structure their understanding of the analytic process, delineate it, pace and work with the flow of psychic material, cultivate empathy, teach how to analytically inquire, to visualize what is being told by the analysand and to ask more reflective questions when a complex is constellated or when what is being discussed is not clear?

2. What are the different styles of supervision? There is, for example, the holding and confirming supervisor who sits in silence saying almost nothing, the pedagogical supervisor who teaches theory and technique, and who amplifies through mythological images and cross cultural parallels, the metatherapeutic supervisor who approaches supervision largely as an extension of the candidate's analysis, the Zen supervisor who continuously creates an atmosphere of creative disorganization, constantly calling into question the candidates unconscious assumptions and fantasies. And, there are, of course, many half breeds of these, as well as many other styles of supervision. How do we become more aware of our own unique approach to supervision and remain conscious of its shadow aspects?

3. How does typology influence the supervisor? Does a feeling type focus more on empathy, while a thinking type emphasizes insight and consciousness? Does the intuitive supervisor look to the capacity for imagination, while the sensation type values more engagement with reality? And how does the typology of the candidate impact on supervision?

4. What is it we are supervising? Is it the actual analysis of another person (the patient)? Is it the supervisee's behavior as therapist? Is it the fantasy image of the patient as separately imagined by supervisor and supervisee? How do we keep conscious of the limitations on what we can actually know of the "analysand" as we enter the complicated hall of mirrors known as supervision.

5. To what extent does the requirement that supervisors write evaluations affect the candidate's choice of supervisor and limit openness in the supervisory process? In what way might the institutional need for evaluations conflict with the candidate's need to be honest, open and exposed?

6. What role does countertransference play in supervision? How important is it for the supervisor to differentiate those reactions resulting from complexes in the candidate from reactions resulting from complexes in the patient or supervisor? Does the supervisor work with all three types of reactions or refer the therapist-induced reactions back to the personal analysis?

7. How does depth psychological supervision differ from other forms of therapeutic supervision?

8. Who has the ultimate responsibility for the case? Supervisee or supervisor?

These introductory questions are intended simply to begin the process of opening up for discussion some of the complicated issues associated with depth psychological supervision.

An Overview of the Book

The volume is divided into six sections: (1) Background, (2) Individual Supervision, (3) The Case Colloquium, (4) Assessing Progress in Supervision, (5) Phases in a Supervisor's Life, and (6) Supervision and Institutions.

Part One, "Background," consists of an "Introduction" by myself and "Historical Notes" by Mary Ann Mattoon. Presenting an account of the history of supervision in Jungian psychology, Mattoon interweaves her personal experience of training in Zurich with the larger history of the discipline. The evolution of supervision in analytical psychology is traced from Jung's early seminars and case discussions to the more formal requirements of "control analysis" as adopted at the various training institutes, providing the reader with a valuable genealogy and setting the historical context for the present volume.

Part II, "Individual Supervision," contains seven papers ranging from a model of supervision, to an analysis of the archetypal structures underpinning the supervisory dyad, to the clinical management of interpersonal dynamics and transference projections. Michael Fordham starts off the section with his classic essay, "Suggestions Toward a Theory of Supervision," in which he carefully differentiates the role and function of the supervisor in relation to supervisee and personal analyst. When a training candidate in analysis begins supervision several problematic consequences may develop, extending from a premature dilution of the analytic transference to an idealized transference onto the supervisor. Calling for a humanization of the relationship, Fordham recommends that from the very start the supervisor treat the supervisee as a junior colleague, not a patient. The supervisor is encouraged to limit discussion of the supervisee's countertransference to client-induced reactions, avoiding analytic interpretations of personal material except under exceptional conditions.

Norah Moore's chapter, "Michael Fordham's Theory and Practice of Supervision," provides the reader with a valuable and poignant reminiscence of her personal supervision with Fordham. Intermixing theory and clinical experience, Moore concisely summarizes many of Fordham's most salient contributions to supervision. The chapter succeeds in unpacking some of the practical implications of Fordham's thirty plus years of clinical writing and teaching.

In his chapter, "Supervision and the Mentor Archetype," Lionel Corbett presents an analysis of various archetypal structures underlying the process and cogently argues for developing a specifically Jungian approach focused on discerning the workings of the Self and its archetypal constituents in the supervisory process. Particularly sensitive to the importance of being conscious of the theoretical bias of both supervisor and supervisee, Corbett provides practical illustrations of how he works to develop an appreciation of the supervisee's theoretical approach in such a way as not to set up an antagonism with his own. To effectively do this, supervisors must be sensitive to the clinical effects of their own theoretical bias, as well as their "personal equation."

Jacoby's contribution, "Supervision and the Interactive Field," extends the more traditional Jungian approach to include the various dynamics of the interactive field. The classical focus on symbolic "contents" of the unconscious is expanded to include unconscious interpersonal dynamics as expressed in the therapeutic space. Subtleties of the interactive field, such as voice inflection, body language and other nonverbal communications are touched on, as well as the importance of monitoring the therapists' countertransference reactions to their patients' feelings of love, aggression, devaluation, ambivalence, and so on.

The focus on transference and countertransference dynamics is continued in Wakefield's thought-provoking paper, "Transference Projections in Supervision." The chapter explores various unconscious perceptions and expectations which may develop between supervisor and supervisee, providing useful insight into the management of these dynamics. The reader will find the review of current clinical literature on syntonic and therapist-induced countertransference reactions particularly useful. The various projections constellated between supervisor and supervisee are analyzed from the perspectives of analytical psychology, drive theory, object relations theory and self psychology.

"Styles of Supervision," by Judith Hubback, differentiates the various types of supervision ranging from the permissive to the didactic. Enabling the development of the analytic identity of supervisees involves empowering them to explore their own unique style and analytic abilities. Facilitation of this process may be improved through efforts to reduce anxiety in supervision and develop a colleague-type discussion.

The section on Individual Supervision closes with John Beebe's provocative chapter on "Sustaining the Potential Analyst's Morale."

The essay is a further exploration of the supervisor's role in developing the analytic identity of the supervisee, but this time from the perspective of providing a therapeutic space to meaningfully contain and work through disappointments in their personal analysis. The supervisor is in a unique position to constructively work with and help metabolize analytic wounding which may have occurred in the supervisee's personal therapy. The author persuasively argues that perhaps the most important function the supervisor can perform is to facilitate the working through of necessary wounds to the naive *idealization of analysis.*

Part III, "The Case Colloquium," includes three chapters devoted to the study of supervision in clinical case seminars. This section opens with Donald Kalsched's exploration of the "Ecstasies and Agonies of Case Seminar Supervision," a moving personal account of the emotional rewards and pitfalls encountered in a case colloquium. Emphasizing the importance of the seminar as a working group, not a process group, the author sketches out the two primary tasks of the seminar: first, to develop a deeper understanding of the presenting therapist's patient and, secondarily, to gain insight into the interaction between patient and therapist. To accomplish these goals a "safe enough" atmosphere, free of judgment and evaluation, must be provided for an inquiry into the unconscious communication of patient and therapist. The shadow side of group dynamics is analyzed: splitting, acting out, sibling rivalry, envy, scapegoatism, triangulated collusive alliances, co-dependency and so on. The chapter provides a valuable antidote to the potentially toxic dynamics encountered in case seminars.

Crittenden Brookes' essay, "On Supervision in Jungian Continuous Case Seminars," examines how the extraverted dimension of the psyche may be constructively mobilized in the case colloquium to deepen the participants understanding of the therapeutic transaction. The seminar has the potential of bringing a variety of perspectives and emotional responses to bear on the clinical material presented, each opening up different and important aspects of the analytic process. To best realize this potential the group leader must work to cultivate a mutually supportive and open-ended environment, free of hierarchies and judgment.

In the final chapter of this section, "Some Thoughts on the Clinical Process," Joan Reggiori examines the differences between individual and group supervision in a variety of professional settings ranging from mental health organizations to training institutes. Various group dynamics encountered in case colloquium are discussed and practical techniques for managing them presented. Common to both individual and group supervision is the need for creating a space in which the supervisee can safely play, experiment with ideas, explore possible approaches, and become more conscious of what is already known, as well as what is as yet unknown. The chapter ends with a section summarizing three seminars on supervision conducted by Reggiori as a follow-up to her original public presentation of this material. The section provides valuable insight into the possibility of peer-group work on supervision as a means for further developing professional skills.

Part III consists of eight essays by training analysts, each grappling with formulating a personal response to the thorny issue of "Assessing Progress in Supervision." Alfred Plaut initiates the discussion by putting his criteria in the form of three questions: (1) "Can the trainee make use of supervision?", (2) "What are the obstacles which prevent the trainee from making full use of me?" and (3) "How, in practice, do I know – or believe to know – that the requisite progress has been made so that I can recommend the trainee for associate membership?" In his response to these questions, the author provides many valuable insights into dynamics encountered while evaluating the supervisee.

Assessing progress in supervision is approached from the perspective of typology by Gustav Dreifuss. While there are certain objective criteria for assessing a supervisee, the relative importance of each is very much a function of the supervisor's personality. A feeling type might emphasize the importance of empathy in the supervisee, an intuitive type look for the capacity for imagination, a thinking type value insight (consciousness), while a sensation type may focus more on adaptation to reality. Practical clinical examples are given to illustrate each type.

Michael Fordham approaches the question in terms of supervising cases of child analysis. The formal setting and basic techniques used to maximize the interactional nature of the analytic process and, hopefully reduce the child's capacity to escape into acting out types of play, are presented. Two clinical situations are examined to demonstrate the subtlety needed to evaluate the supervisee's developing analytic attitude and clinical skills. The progress can best be assessed, Fordham suggests, from comparative experiences, rather than abstract standards.

Supervision as a *rite of passage* is examined by Joseph Henderson, who observes that analytic training programs tend to promote the archetype of initiation, beginning with a supervisor as master-of-initiation, and ending with an assessment of progress in accordance with the requirements of the larger peer group. An important aspect in the supervisor's role includes a sensitive discussion of the moral, ethical and psychological dimensions of the incest taboo.

A number of factors are considered by Elie Humbert in assessing progress: clinical ability, general cultural development, an understanding of the relation between supervisees' personal pathology and the choice and exercise of their profession, and the way in which their own unconscious makes use of the analysis of another person. The ability to recognize changes in the unconscious, as well as the flexibility to move from one epistemological position to another, are also important factors.

The capacity to overcome the preponderant concern with "What am I supposed to do?" is of particular significance to Mario Jacoby. Assumptions such as "one ought to like one's patient," or "ought to 'understand' his dreams," or "ought to know what Jung said about animus-possession," and so on are characteristic of the "good student" attitude and often impede progress and the development of a personal analytic style. Supervisors need to be aware of their own narcissistic tendency to form and evaluate the supervisee in their own image.

How supervisees' clinical skills have developed along with the deepening of personal identity and analytic style are important criteria for Ann Ulanov. The capacity to assimilate unconscious material and to relate interpersonally also are significant factors. Is there an increase of detailed perception of the analysand and how does the supervisee monitor and therapeutically use nonverbal responses, such as body posture, breathing rates, turn of the head and so on. Does the supervisee appear trainable and has the personal style moved from the persona into the person? Ulanov's erudite essay presents a wealth of insights, not only into the assessment of progress, but also into the very nature of supervision itself.

The section on assessment concludes with Wilke's stimulating discussion of supervision from various perspectives: supervision as assistance, supervision as seconding and the supervisor as adjunct. Beginning therapists need to be supervised in the following areas: (a) understanding the dynamics of the case, (b) use of therapeutic methods, and (c) coming to a valid estimate of their role and discerning how their own complexes are integrated into the analysis of the patient. The success of supervision can partially be assessed by the extent to which the supervisee is later successfully integrated into the larger professional group.

Part V, "Phases in a Supervisor's Life," focuses on various dimensions of the professional life, beginning with the early years as a student and their emphasis on developing clinical skills and an analytic identity, continuing with becoming a training analyst and supervisor, and finally, confronting the psychological and physical realities of the aging process. The period immediately following completion of analytic training through the assumption of the responsibilities of a supervising analyst is explored by myself in the initial chapter of this section. "The Transition from Training Candidate to Supervising Analyst" can be emotionally turbulent as the recent graduate works to build up an analytic practice, undergoes acculturation into the professional community, and begins to develop the necessary analytic, didactic, and clinical skills to function as a supervising analyst. Integration of the analytic identity during this period involves meeting not only the outer institutional requirements of the profession, but also those inherent to the psyche itself.

How does an analyst prepare to become a supervisor? This question is increasingly being raised in the professional community and forms the central focus for Marga Speicher's chapter, "The Education of the Supervisor." Following a review of the current practices and requirements of supervision in Jungian training programs, the author provides a thoughtful discussion of how a program of preparation for Jungian supervisors might be designed and implemented.

The final chapter of this section, "The Aging Supervisor," is a poignant presentation of the problems encountered in old age by the supervisor. Wilke notes that many of the abilities necessary for supervision are acquired later in life, and consequently, are more vulnerable to deterioration through the aging process. This essay provides a remarkably sensitive treatment of the psychological issues associated with supervisory responsibilities and the aging analyst.

Part VI, "Supervision and Institutions," addresses the dynamics and issues encountered in supervision as it is practiced in various settings ranging from professional training institutes to mental health organizations. James Astor contrasts supervision sought for professional development with supervision undertaken for the purpose of fulfilling a training requirement, in his chapter "Supervision, Training, and the Institution as an Internal Pressure." When supervision and training come together, candidates find themselves simultaneously confronted with the complexities of an organization, its institutional mentality, and their own psychic development. The author subtly articulates the difficulties encountered keeping faith with the analytic process within the context of institutional dynamics, concluding that supervision is a necessity for all of us to counteract the deadly effects of *inner institutionalization*.

Using a systems approach, Jean Carr explores the institutional framework within which the process takes place to develop "A Model of Clinical Supervision." The various components of the system (patient/client, supervisee, supervisor, and organization) are outlined and a particularly useful analysis is provided of the dy- and triadic relationships making up the total network. Each relationship contains its own set of complex dynamics: transferences and countertransference, ego and shadow, ritualized behaviors, as well as overt and covert needs and alliances.

In the book's concluding chapter, Louis Zinkin turns the tables on the profession and asks how do individuals and institutions assess a good supervisor. Struggling with this question, the author helps us to better understand the impossibility of our task as supervisors. What is it this impossible profession is supervising? Certainly the supervisor is supervising something, but that something is certainly not the patient's literal analysis. What we call "supervision," Zinkin suggests, is in reality a shared fantasy – the supervisee trying to imagine what the patient has been doing in analysis and the supervisor trying to do the same. And, "supervision works best if both remain aware that what they are jointly imagining is not true."

It is hoped that the papers presented here will contribute to the advancement of our understanding Jungian supervision. Few aspects of clinical practice provide the type of professional challenge encountered in supervision. The quality of this personal experience and its potential rewards are difficult to convey in language. Perhaps this volume will help the reader develop greater empathic understanding of the vitality of the supervisory process.

[2]

Historical Notes

Mary Ann Mattoon

Supervision (also known as "control") is now well-established in Jungian analytic training. It was not always so. I experienced some of the ramifications of this lack through my first Jungian analyst – a woman who practiced in New York and is long dead. She was analyzed in Zurich by Jung and in New York by one of the pioneer analysts there, Eleanor Bertine. When I began my analysis in the late 1950s (at the age of 32) my analyst, like most of the then-handful of New York analysts, worked the way Jung evidently did: focusing on dreams – especially archetypal ones – and discouraging discussion of highly emotional topics of waking life.

Her approach did not work well for me, partly – no doubt – because my typology was different from hers and I was 40 years younger. It may be, however, that her work could have benefited from supervision, to help her deal with a person who did not fit the pattern of introverted intuitive, middle-aged and older analysands who typically consulted her as well as Jung.

We cannot be sure that these early analysts, who studied with Jung in the 1920s and 1930s, had no supervision before they began to practice. They all had at least part of their analysis with Jung and, intertwined with it, there may have been some supervision, albeit in the context of Jung's stated depreciation of methods and techniques.

Training at that time consisted, evidently, of personal analysis and seminars conducted by Jung. At some point he apparently told each student that she or he was ready to practice as an analyst. But many of those students came from outside Switzerland – especially England and the United States – and some spent only a few months in

Zurich. Consequently, their training was limited – as compared to current practice.

The requirement that prospective analysts undergo personal analysis was a major contribution by Jung, as the first person known to make such a proposal, to the entire psychoanalytic movement. The Freudian school adopted the idea officially in 1918 (Fleming & Benedek, 1966). Since Jung evidently selected prospective analysts from among his analysands, personal analysis was integral to Jungian training from the beginning.

In 1925, the Freudian school formally added supervision to its training requirements. Jung did not use the term but had been providing a kind of supervision through his lecture and seminar courses.

The first such course was reported in the journal of Fanny Bowditch, an American who may have met Jung during his trip to the United States in 1909. According to William McGuire (1984) the course, "Einführung in die Psychoanalyse" (Introduction to Psychoanalysis) was given in 1912 and 1913 at the University of Zurich. In addition to theoretical material and the Association Experiment, the course included cases from Jung's analytic practice, which were transcribed and mimeographed for members of the class. In 1914, another such course was given privately by Jung. (He had resigned his University lectureship.)

McGuire's (1984) account continues: "After the war ended, Jung traveled again – to London for lectures to professional societies in 1919 and again in late 1920; to Algeria and Tunis in the spring of 1920; and, during the summer of 1920, to England, out to the tip of Cornwall, for his first seminar abroad" (pp. viii-ix). This seminar, arranged by Constance Long, included M. Esther Harding and H. Godwin Baynes. It was the only one of the 1919-20 seminars that is known to have dealt with case material. The subject was a book entitled *Authentic Dreams of Peter Blobbs and Certain of His Relatives.*

"The first *recorded* seminar," according to McGuire (1984) "convened also in Cornwall, at Polzeath, during July 1923. Baynes and Harding organized it; twenty-nine attended, including Emma Jung and Toni Wolff" (p. ix.). Longhand notes carry the title 'Human Relationships in Relation to the Process of Individuation" (Harding & Mann, n.d.).

Two years later still another seminar, organized by the British Jungians, was held at Swanage, Dorset, with about 100 participants. Dr. Harding's longhand notes survive, under the title "Dreams and Symbolism." It seems likely that both the 1923 and 1925 seminars included case material.

Earlier in 1925 Jung had presented a "Seminar in Analytical Psychology" in Zurich. It was the first of the series of Zurich seminars in English, held at the Psychological Club, that were to go on for 14 years. In it Jung described the development of some of his theories, and the cases on which they were based. This seminar comes close to case consultation but less so than do subsequent seminars.

The next seminar, on dream analysis, began in the fall of 1928. As McGuire (1984) reported, "In weekly meetings, broken by seasonal recesses of a month or more, the seminar met until late June 1930" (p. x). One of Jung's biographers, Barbara Hannah, arrived in Zurich in January 1929 and attended this seminar and subsequent seminars as long as they were given, through February 1939. About them Hannah (1976) stated: "Until the end of the summer of 1930 the subject of these seminars was a series of dreams by a man. From the autumn of 1930, until the end of the winter term in 1934, Jung dealt with a woman's long series of visions (active imagination)" (p. 191).

Of Jung's seminars (1930-41) at the Federal Institute of Technology, only those on "Children's Dreams" (1936-40) were close to case consultation/supervision.

Although Jung's primary interest was in the archetypal content of the dreams and visions, the seminars offered some clues regarding his approach to analysands' material and can be seen as a step toward case consultation, if not actual supervision.

By the time the Zurich Institute was established in 1948, the concept of supervision seems to have entered the picture. A printed "Report on the First Twelve Years: 1948-1960" included in its list of requirements for the analyst's diploma "Successful completion of at least 250 hours of control analyses under the supervision of a training analyst." The requirement specified only the number of hours the candidate was to spend with analysands; the number with the control analysts was not mentioned.

In 1962, when I began my control work in Zurich, it was usual to have a different control analyst for each case. Thus, a candidate was exposed to various points of view. Resolving any contradictions among them was part of the highly-valued development of one's own style. The control stage candidates had a weekly case colloquium, with rotating opportunity to present cases. In addition to getting feedback on one's own cases, there was great value in hearing about and discussing others' work. Writing up cases and having one's treatment of them critiqued in the diploma exams served as additional supervision.

Although transference was not emphasized conceptually, it was implicit in consultations with most of the control analysts and explicit with some. Consideration of countertransference sometimes presented a challenge to the Institute's policy of discouraging the mixing of control with personal analysis. Indeed, it was my experience and that of other candidates, that only the personal analyst could help at a deep level with the candidate's countertransference issues.

The most useful guideline to which I was exposed in relation to control work was my Zurich analyst's saying "It isn't what you do that counts; it's what you are." That was frightening to contemplate but kept the focus on my own psychological work – a sine qua non for an analyst – and opened the way to my developing my own style. Thus, the approach to control work manifested Jung's view that it is important to discover what supports one when one's usual supports fail.

The situation in Zurich – supervision becoming part of the training and increasing in quantity – was paralleled in other training centers. Alfred Plaut stated that he counted himself among the "first generation of trainees in the Society [of Analytical Psychology (SAP), London] to whom anything like a structured training program was presented, and remember very well when I became aware that none of the training analysts of those earlier days had had any proper training in the sense of what we were then about to receive" (Plaut et al., 1961, p. 98).

After the 1958 founding of the International Association for Analytical Psychology (IAAP), the situation internationally was reflected in successive changes in the IAAP requirements. The original

(1962) "Bye-Laws Concerning Membership" called for a candidate's spending one and one-half years in the Control Stage and 180 hours with clients; the requirement for the number of a candidate's hours with the supervisor was specified first in 1971: 50 hours. In 1983 it was increased to 100. Thus, as the profession of analyst became better defined other requirements increased (including personal analysis and academic degrees) in IAAP and its member societies, as did the supervision requirements.

Although I have been using the term "supervision," the traditional word for the process is "control," a transliteration of the German word "Kontrolle," meaning "examination" or "supervision" as well as what English-speakers call "control." (Freudians also use the term "control"; Freud, like Jung, was German-speaking.) Because of the connotation of control as a tight grip on power, my colleagues and I in Minnesota originally called the final stage of training "consultation." We adopted the Inter-Regional Society's term "control" when we joined that Society. In recent years, "supervision" has been used increasingly. Indeed, it was used by Plaut, and probably other Londoners, at least by 1961.

The Jungian publications on supervision are sparse enough to allow me to mention all the relevant works that I have found. The earliest such work available is found in a "Symposium on Training" (Plaut et al., 1961). Examining the Zurich and London SAP programs, both Alfred Plaut and Michael Fordham (in separate essays) focused – in relation to supervision – on the problems created by having a third person (the supervisor) complicate the relationship between personal analyst and analysand/candidate. (Fordham's article appears as chapter 3 in the present volume.) Although they do not discuss the teaching of technique as part of supervision, Plaut and Fordham seem to assume such teaching.

In the same Symposium, Kathleen Newton identified supervision as one of the three "tools of training." Without elaborating that statement, she discussed other aspects of training.

A further contribution to the Symposium was made by Hillman (1962). As he described the training in the Zurich at that time, "Clear separation of training and analysis [did] not exist. This reflects the attitude that training *is* analysis and so cannot be separated from it"

(p. 8). At the same time, personal analytic sessions were not to be used extensively as control sessions.

Stating also his belief that Jungian therapy cannot be taught, Hillman said that it occurs "mainly through...the spontaneous activity of the unconscious ... [and] cannot be codified into repeatable techniques. ... Therefore, what is especially taught ... at the C.G. Jung Institute is knowledge about the manifestations of the unconscious, as related to the therapeutic situation." (p. 10)

Hillman explained that "It is more important [for the candidate] to develop a style out of one's nature and experience than to learn techniques. Technique is picked up in the control sessions, in the group colloquia, in the case material seminars, and of course from one's own training analyses. But only that which is picked up (integrated) is effective, not what is indoctrinated. Tight supervision might hinder the development of style, which could be ruinous if we take the practice of psychotherapy to be an art as well as a science. Too much control might only relieve immediate insecurity, preventing more profound constellations. Often, therefore, the candidate relieves the insecurity in his personal analysis. But this too belongs, because his case work is a most important part of his life problems at the moment, and so will appear naturally in his personal analysis" (p. 14).

Minimizing of technique continues in Hillman's further statement that "The main aim is to leave the responsibility as much as possible to the ... candidate and to step in and correct only where danger or damage seems to begin. Thus, the problem of intervention on the part of the control analyst is nicely managed" (p. 15).

The next published work on supervision, to my knowledge, was a Symposium, "How Do I Assess Progress in Supervision?" (Plaut et al., 1982) A few years later Norah Moore's (1986) "Michael Fordham's Theory and Practice of Supervision" appeared. Both of these works are included in this volume.

Most recent in the Jungian literature is James Astor's (1991) article "Supervision, Training, and the Institution as an Internal Pressure." He mentioned the earlier work on supervision and responded especially to Fordham's 1961 article. Astor pointed out that "Never far away during training is the internal pressure arising from the evaluative presence of the training committee. Present too is the compatibility or incompatibility between the way the supervisee was analyzed and the way the supervisor is showing ... how to analyze. ... [Moreover,] writing down what the supervisor is saying...can be a process of taking over the supervisor's knowledge without thinking about it." (p. 183) Astor concluded that the trainee should be treated as a junior colleague and that "Supervision becomes a chewing over, reflecting on, and scrutinizing of the interactions in the session with the opportunity of having the material listened to by another analyst as if it was [his or her] own." (p. 189)

A few works on supervision by Jungians have appeared in non-Jungian publications. Three of these are were presented to the International Federation for Psychoanalytic Education and appeared in its Newsletter. A revised version of John Beebe's presentation (1991) appears in this volume. Marga Speicher (1991) pointed out that the task in supervision is to focus on the candidate's work, and not to engage in pseudo-analysis. Moreover, both supervisor and candidate must be aware of the evaluative function of the supervisor as well as the mentoring function. Susan Bostrom-Wong (1991) discussed supervision from the point of view of the candidate. She emphasized the impact of the supervisor on the candidate's psyche and that the evaluative function of the supervisor can be a help to the candidate in facing the less-familiar evaluating committees of the institute.

From the early years of supervision, as is evident from my Zurich experience, group supervision has been used along with individual supervision, at least in some training centers. In Zurich now, a given candidate may participate in more than one such "case colloquium" each week. As it happens, my own experience in acting as supervisor has been more group than individual. This situation originally was necessitated by the lack of certified analysts in my locality while the first candidates were preparing for certification as Individual Members of IAAP. We brought analysts from other localities for periodic individual supervision; the week-by-week supervision was done in a group which, perforce, I led. (The current Minnesota program includes both individual and group supervision.)

I hasten to add that I do not see group supervision as second best. Indeed, it is highly valuable in providing the richness of all the group members' points of view. A candidate may hear a variety of insights or difficult-to-accept perspectives.

Another concept that deserves more consideration is the continuing supervision of the certified analyst. Many analysts participate in such work, in groups or pairs. I feel that it is incumbent on every analyst to discuss cases with peers on a regular basis.

The training of prospective supervisors is perhaps the least-developed aspect of supervision. Such training has been given little consideration among Jungian analysts, indeed among mental health professionals in general. (There seems to be a small number of clinical psychology and social work programs in which clinicians are trained to be supervisors.) Clare Thompson, a San Francisco analyst and Professor of Clinical Psychology, was saying in the mid-1970s that Jungian institutes should provide training in supervision. (Dr. Thompson, now deceased, did much of the individual supervision in the Minnesota training program from 1974 to 1976.) Such training presumably would include supervision of the supervisor-in-training.

Training in supervision would require our abandoning the assumption that, if we know how to analyze, we know how to teach someone else to do it. Astor (1991) pointed out: "When the training is 'complete' no further systematic or supervised study is included in the progression through the gradations of the analytic hierarchy, from associate professional member to professional member to training analyst. Nowhere, therefore, is the ethos of the 'work group,' as a necessary part of individual development, fostered by the institution." (p. 181)

If we accept the premise of continuing supervision following training, we can expect that supervision is even more interminable than is analysis.

References

Astor, James (1991). Supervision, training, and the institution as an internal pressure. *Journal of Analytical Psychology, 36-2,* 177-191.

Beebe, John (1991). Sustaining the potential analyst's morale. *IFPE Newsletter, 1-*1, 16-17.

Bostrom-Wong, Susan (1991). (Untitled.) *IFPE Newsletter, 1-*1, 17-19.

Fleming, Joan. & Benedek, Therese. (1966). *Psychoanalytic Supervision: A Method of Clinical Teaching.* New York: Grune & Stratton.

Hannah, Barbara (1976). *Jung: His Life and Work.* New York: Putnam's.

Harding, M. Esther (n.d.). Unpublished typescript, 101 pp., in the Kristine Mann Library, Analytical Psychology Club of New York.

Harding, M. Esther & Mann, Kristine. Unpublished typescript, 38 pp., in the Kristine Mann Library, Analytical Psychology Club of New York.

Hillman, James (1962). *Journal of Analytical Psychology, 7-*1, 3-28.

McGuire, William (1984). Introduction to *Dream Analysis: Notes of the Seminar*

Notes of the Seminar Given in 1928-29 by C.G. Jung. Bollingen Series XCIX. Princeton, NJ: Princeton University Press.

Moore, Norah. (1986). "Michael Fordham's theory and practice of supervision." *Journal of Analytical Psychology, 31-*3, 267-273.

Plaut, Alfred.; Newton, Kathleen; Fordham, Michael (1961). "Symposium on training." *Journal of Analytical Psychology, 6-*2, 95-118.

Plaut, Alfred; Dreifuss, Gustav; Fordham, Michael; Henderson, Joseph; Humbert, Elie; Jacoby, Mario; Ulanov, Ann; Wilke, Hans-Joachim (1982). *Journal of Analytical Psychology, 27-*2 (April), 105-130.

Speicher, Marga (1991). (Untitled.) *IFPE Newsletter, 1-*1, 17.

Part II

Individual Supervision

[3]

Suggestions Towards a Theory of Supervision

Michael Fordham

When the Society of Analytical Psychology in London started to frame a program of training for candidates there were two issues on which agreement was soon reached, the first easily, the second after some hesitation. It was decided, first, that the training should be based on clinical studies, and with this end in view candidates were to take two control cases after two years of preliminary analysis. This was in line with Jung's repeated claim that his researches are based on clinical experience even though he has often chosen, for reasons which we need not go into here, to present his conclusions in terms of mythology.

The second decision, not so easily arrived at, specified that a training analyst was to supervise the candidate's management of his control cases and to teach on such matters as arose out of the material the candidate brought for discussion.

The doubts about the second decision arose from Jung's emphasis on the importance that the analyst's personality inevitably takes in any analysis. This essential feature of his ideas on analytic practice might have led the training analysts to decide that didactic teaching of theory and technique could best be done by the seminar method to trainees as a group, leaving the rest to the candidate's analyst alone. In this way, it might be assumed, the candidate's skills would be more certain to develop out of his personality and there would be less opportunity for him to separate the acquisition of them from his own personal development. The rejection of this policy was based on the belief that it would change the role of the analyst in important respects. He might well be tempted, or even feel under obligation, to act as teacher, in the didactic sense, as well as analyst, and so be unable to give his sole attention and interest to the inner development of the candidate. This was, I think, the main reason in the minds of some training analysts at least, and in my own in particular, for instituting a supervisor who was not the candidate's analyst.

As time has proved, these early reflections were a good example of how valuable it is to consider Jung's thinking with care; from time to time the issue has been raised again and, indeed, will make the basis for much of what will be said here. Another consideration that favored the institution of a supervisor was not so well founded but has none t he less been justified by subsequent experience. It was feared that if only the analyst knew the candidate well it would put too much responsibility on one person for estimating the candidate's suitability to conduct analyses. It was believed that the supervisor might be expected to act as a check on the analyst's identification with his candidate which might predispose him to support applications to the Society on inadequate grounds. At the present time there is uncertainty as to how often this consideration is justified.

An issue which needs to be raised here is this: in the beginning it was assumed that it was known in what analysis consisted; it has, however, appeared, over the years, that this was only true in a rather limited sense, indeed, critical examination of our practice has shown that what constitutes an analysis is very uncertain and that the term analysis itself was being used in a rather loose way. I have attempted to define it rather more closely elsewhere (cf. Fordham, 1957) and so need not develop the theme here. It is only necessary to note that analysis was and will here be regarded as essentially different from teaching, in that teaching does not involve handling the transference by means of interpretations.

In what follows it is intended to set down some of my own conclusions that have been arrived at on the basis of the early decisions of the training analysts, which have not been altered since training began. It will involve discussing aspects of the relation between the candidate and his patient, his analyst, and his supervisor, starting from two of the questions regarding supervision that were raised at the beginning and again in the course of years in a more developed form.

(i) Should supervision be in the nature of teaching?

(ii) Should it be regarded as a sort of extra analysis?

The answer to (i) has already been decided upon, but the whole subject of (ii) is not so easy and represents the recurrence of the question raised in the early years when regulations were being laid down. For purposes of this discussion (ii) will need formulating differently so as to avoid it being considered an alternative to (i); this it cannot be since (i) is desirable. (ii) implies the need for discussion of the role of the candidate's analyst when training starts, and this subject will provide a suitable jumping-off ground.

It will be assumed here, but only for the sake of brevity, that the essential features of ordinary analysis can be maintained within the framework of training, and so the analyst will not need to alter the essentials of his technique. Therefore it is necessary to consider only whether he is going to come upon special difficulties when training starts, and whether they are of the kind which warrant more analysis by a second analyst in the guise of the supervisor.

That changes occur in the transference relation between the candidate and his analyst when training starts is sufficiently evident, and the problems arising from them may be considered under the general heading of premature dilutions of the transference which are disintegrative; by this is meant that the candidate's transference is rendered less intense because of anxieties arising from the complex relationships set up as the result of an organized training.

1. The analyst may soon realize that a candidate comes to know more about him than before: the candidate will check his inferences about his analyst during analysis against the views of others and, further, will have accumulated more information about his analyst than may be desirable at any particular time. This is undesirable because the matching of projections against direct perception of the analyst's behavior (cf. Fordham, 1957, p. 79 f.) becomes more difficult since the candidate's judgment is interfered with by the opinions of other people.

2. The transference can be further diluted by projection into the control cases and then, as the result of the supervision situation, the development of a transference to the supervisor. It is clearly of the first importance how this is handled, as can easily be demonstrated by continuing analysis after supervision has stopped, a common feature of what may be termed post-training analysis. In this period

it becomes easier to analyze those aspects of the candidate which had been hidden in the supervision situation.

3. The seminar group will lead to the candidate working or acting out transference conflicts with other members of the group composed of other trainees.

There is only one suggestion I would like to make here towards management of these rather complex features of training: candidates need to be seen often enough for their analysts to circumvent too much defensive dilution of the transference, and it seems to me beneficial if they are seen on the same day after supervision has taken place or, at the latest, on the next day. Then if the supervisor hits on conflict situations in the candidate, he can feel more confident that they will be available for analysis and will not get covered over again.

Turning now to supervision. As already stated, it was originally instituted with a view to avoiding the analyst becoming a teacher and so obstructing the integration of unconscious contents. Only later did the question arise as to what the more detailed position of the supervisor might become.

Developing A. Plaut's formulation (*supra.* p. 100): the supervisor is the most important person in initiating the candidate into membership of the Society because he is mainly occupied in developing the conscious skills of the candidate, and functions as a check on the candidate's tendency to act out during regressions, arising either as part of his analysis or as the result of the stress of training. The complex social factors entering into supervision have been considered in some detail by Minna Emch (1955). There she convincingly shows the complex situation to which training gives rise. The possible combinations in a system involving seven elements, assuming one emotional valence, is 126. If emotional ambivalence is taken into account, the figure rises to 1183. The elements she considers are: a supervisor, a student, a control case, the training analyst, another past or present supervisor, the training committee, and a seminar leader. These figures compel us to reflect that the emotional stresses involved are so complex that they cannot be described, and they show the necessity to simplify by selecting the attitudes and roles that seem of more importance than others in any training program of an analytic kind; this simplification need not make us overlook the complexities, however, though it may appear to do violence to the subtle and often rapidly changing cross-currents continually met with during training.

As a starting-point, I wish to propose dogmatically that it is the supervisor's role, together with that of the seminar leaders, to treat the candidate actively as a junior colleague, and not as a patient, right from the beginning. By this is meant that the trainee has the free right to draw on all the supervisor's knowledge and experience as he wants it without respect to any deficiencies in the candidate's personality that may become apparent. In particular, there are the experiences he brings to supervision which will extend the supervisor's experience and so give him the opportunity to learn and to develop his theories and techniques.

Since the supervisor will be occupied in listening to the case-material presented by the candidate and will aim at discussing the cases as a colleague, he need not dilute the transference, and if he keeps this problem clearly in mind he can help the candidate's analysis in ways to be considered later. Discussion during supervision can be conceived as centering on questions of the general management of cases, and the supervisor suggests reading in so far as it is relevant to the technical and theoretical questions that arise out of his teaching on case-material. All this involves imparting technical skills such as the interpretation of all kinds of material brought by the control patient, particular attention being paid to the transference of the control case to the candidate. It will evoke a counter-transference from the candidate and so introduces the important but difficult question: is it desirable for the supervisor to show the candidate where his counter-transference lies and how it is either interfering with his relation to the control case or facilitating it? This question is of particular importance because it leads to the possibility of the initiating analysis of the candidate by the supervisor. In my view he should point out counter-transference manifestations but without analyzing the candidate, only confronting him with them. This is possible for the following reasons. The supervision time is mainly devoted to the presentation and discussion of material brought by the candidate. Since a candidate is asking for supervision, his time is mainly filled up and he will not want to give information about his own personal life. It is of particular importance that the supervisor *never* tries to elicit any. This procedure is supported by a further consideration. It is one of the unstated assumptions of candidates that supervisors will refrain from analyzing them, and the supervisor, realizing this, implicitly agrees. Unless both want consciously to alter the agreement it should be scrupulously kept.

This view of supervision would at first sight seem to exclude analysis from it altogether. Yet if both the analysis and the supervision are being well conducted, it still happens that a candidate occasionally gives clear indications that he wants bits of analysis from his supervisor. I consider that it is in order for the supervisor to give it because there are sufficient checks against it going far. By "clear indications" I mean that the candidate will state that he does not want supervision but wants to talk about himself, and even his transference to his analyst, for the next hour; at best he will ask openly for the supervisor's agreement. The theory of transference as a social phenomenon makes it easy to understand why this happens. When training starts it is manifest that each candidate will need to project the archetypal forms related to supervision into the Society, the committees, the lecturers, and also the supervisor, who will consequently become not only a real person but an ambivalent figure. If it be borne in mind that the supervisor aims to relate and build on the energies available to the candidate's ego, then it can be realized that in doing so he is fulfilling the archetypal role of initiator. As such he will not draw attention to and indeed will resist discussion of the transference processes involved and will, rather, aim at fulfilling the role that may be expected to match the candidate's deliberate aim of acquiring knowledge and skills in contrast to his unconscious ambivalent needs. Inasmuch as it is not possible to do this with complete success all the time, the candidate and also the supervisor may spend sessions in clarifying the affective situation that has arisen between them. This need not go far so long as the supervisor refrains, as I think he can usually do, from interpreting the unconscious motives of the candidate. Clearly, transference interpretations need to be avoided if the policy I am proposing is to be pursued.

Only when the supervisor is led to act so much as an analyst that his role of supervisor is interfered with for long, will he need to inquire what has happened. There are two possibilities:

1. Suppose the supervision has been correctly conducted along the lines so far defined, then the candidate's transference to his analyst must have run into difficulties; either it is not being taken up by the analyst because the candidate is not being seen sufficiently often by him to allow this, or else the candidate has run into a very strong resistance and needs to use supervision as part of his defense system. In these circumstances I do not believe that the supervisor need do anything but continue supervising as much as possible. It can, however, happen, in spite of the supervisor's efforts, that this state of affairs develops so that a candidate wants analysis from supervisor in place of his first analyst; by "wanting a change" is meant that he will ask for it from his supervisor after going into the matter with his analyst. Then the change can be openly made. Such a change need not reflect on the candidate so long as the clear need for it comes from him and he gets it recognized as desirable by his analyst as well as his supervisor.

2. The second possible cause for supervision breaking down is that it has been so conducted as to induce a transference neurosis to the supervisor in contrast to the archetypal transference held to be inevitable, and the trainee can then want a change of analyst on neurotic grounds. This will happen when the supervisor's counter-transference to the trainee is not recognized. The change will not take place if his analysis is being well conducted, but angry conflicts between supervisor and analyst can result and the candidate will justifiably want to change his supervisor. If the supervisor has induced a neurotic transference, the desire for a change can appear as a neurotic manifestation. This has occurred in the London Society, but it was understood that a change needed to be made, and the candidate went on to become a member of the Society.

The most frequent source for the difficulties just enumerated lies in that part of supervision which consists in showing the candidate where his counter-transference to his control case lies. In the process of doing so the candidate's failings inevitably become particularly apparent to the supervisor whose aim, indeed, is to highlight them. But the candidate can then begin to show neurotic phenomena so that the supervisor may get presented, almost on a plate, with the candidate's whole residual neurosis; this is one situation in which the supervisor, who may after all have induced this state, can wrongly believe that the analyst is at fault. It is worth underlining that the manifestations will not lead the candidate to asking for analysis from the supervisor because he will want to take them back to the analyst if all is going well; this formulation holds only when the supervisor neither denies nor manipulates the situation but only sustains it (by sustaining is meant realizing it without doing anything). In this connection, I believe that if the supervisor tells the candidate to disclose to his analyst what has been found in supervision this needs to be classed as a manipulation which interferes with and does not facilitate the candidate's analysis and, if done clumsily, endangers the supervision relationship.

In my opinion the following criterion for giving interpretations holds in supervision: they should not be given unless the candidate offers sufficient personal information to make it quite clear that he wants the interpretation to be given. It is because of the nature of good supervision, whereby information of this kind will not be available most of the time, that only bits of analysis can take place.

To summarize: a supervisor may point out and discuss the candidate's counter-transference to his control case and confront him with it, but will avoid making analytic observations or interpretations except under exceptional conditions.

In all this the question of the relation between analyst and supervisor is implied. It seems to me that the analytic methods pursued by each should be reasonably close, at least in the first year of training. When they are considerably different, it can be serious; and the seriousness of it tends to get rationalized and so glossed over.

If the supervisor disagrees too widely with the analyst or if he is convinced the analyst's analyses are not adequate, he will be under considerable strain. He cannot supervise without showing the candidate how to conduct the analysis of his control case according to his own view, but in doing so he knows that the candidate will inevitably compare what he is taught with how his own analysis has been conducted. The risk of seriously diluting the transference is then considerable. This became a very difficult problem for me at one time when I was developing ideas about the transference not held by some other training analysts; also supervision of candidates in analysis with me obstructed their analysis because the supervisor exploited the candidate's bit of transference to him by using a combination of analytic and manipulative techniques. I gained the quite clear impression through the candidate that the supervisor thought my analysis grossly defective and that he tried to complement it. This, however, only led to a preponderantly negative transference to the supervisor and fixed the projections made by the candidate on to him; they could be defined but not reduced. As the candidate continued analysis after supervision, it became clear how damaging the experience had been to the candidate's training, even though he became reasonably clear about what was happening at the time. During this period of conflict over the meaning of analysis within the Society, my supervision increased a candidate's wish for analysis of the kind I was showing him how to conduct. I believe it was because I had been conducting supervision in the way here described that the change of analysts was brought about with the conscious agreement of all parties.

The point that has interested me, as an analyst in contrast to being a supervisor, has been that supervisors only take up or try to analyze points that have already come into the candidate's analysis, but were not ready to be resolved. This is of interest because the supervisor could be under the impression that this was not the case.

Bearing these considerations in mind, and also that supervisors often think analysts are not analyzing properly when they discover the candidate's residual neurosis, it is manifestly advisable that analyst and supervisor should be selected from amongst analysts who can communicate and map out their points of agreement and their differences, which should not be too great. I do not think it is necessary for the two to meet for discussion of the candidate, but it can be valuable for them to discuss their ideas about analytic practice. I have with few exceptions refrained from discussions with analysts when supervising, and vice versa, and it has worked out well enough in the end as far as I know. I do not think that discussions benefited the candidate, though they have been quite illuminating in terms of the triangular situation which is manifestly at work and is important; the most prominent feature in this appears to be the tendency for rivalry to develop between analyst and supervisor. In view of this eventuality, it follows that when this situation is well handled it leads to a good training, but if it is not then the candidate can be made the instrument of a conflict of two contending parental figures, to his detriment. Whereas some candidates can survive this, others with a less favorable background are liable to become casualties. As in families, this is particularly damaging if the conflict is unconscious.

There is one further function of the supervisor not so far mentioned. It is the function of the supervisor, and not the analyst, to exert control over the trainee's application for membership to the Society. It is of advantage if he makes clear to the candidate his opinion of the candidate's suitability to analyze patients. This grows inevitably out of his aim of treating the candidate as a colleague.

In conclusion, it will be evident that in all training we need to remember this: candidates are put under greater stress than is any trained analyst and so we need to find out how to diminish it. One way to do this is for analyst and supervisor to be clear about what they are doing as part of the training setup.

References

Emch, M. (1955). "The Social Context of Supervision," *Int. J. Psychoanal.*, 36, 4 and 5.

Fordham, M. (1957). *New Developments in Analytical Psychology*. London, Routledge & Kegan Paul.

[4]

Michael Fordham's Theory and Practice of Supervision

Norah Moore

We owe a great debt to Michael Fordham for his contribution to supervision over a period of thirty or more years. He has always seen supervision as an initiating, integrative journey, during which the supervisor fulfills the archetypal role of initiator; he neither analyses it nor interprets other unconscious processes, but builds on the energies available to a student's ego; for supervision is separate and different from training analysis in Fordham's view. This distinction has become more necessary as transference has taken on major importance, since the transference that belongs to the training analysis on one hand, and that which belongs to teaching on the other, can only have due care if they are kept separate. It follows that analysts should not teach their analysands nor supervisors analyze (Fordham 1, 2).

The separation of supervision raises problems about handling the trainee's countertransference (which Fordham points out but does not analyze), and teaching him to use it in his work (Fordham 2). In 1969 Fordham reviewed Racker's book on countertransference (Fordham 5). Racker had said: 'the danger of exaggerated faith in the messages of one's own unconscious is less than the danger of repressing them and denying them any objective value.' (Racker 15)

Fordham had been thinking similarly and commented: 'In supervision the importance of showing up the countertransference gets renewed importance from Racker's book and a way of approaching it in a positive light is opened up. Countertransference is first a matter for the candidate's own analysis, but once conscious its use can be worked out in supervision.' (Fordham 4)

This led to a description of the trainee's illusory countertransference, in which he stressed the importance of integrating the trainee's own experience in analysis with his work with patients (Fordham 6). An account of the trainee's syntonic countertransference as a source of information followed (Fordham 8). There he suggests teaching trainees an open system approach, with full use of their countertransference, and their complete involvement with their patients (Fordham 8). Engagement between analyst and patient is thus vital.

A theoretical model is also decisively important in integrating a patient's material; but it must be one that relates to the analyst's own personal experience either in life, in his personal training analysis, or in his experience with patients. He also needs to understand what he reads and is taught in the light of his personal experience in analysis, so as to integrate the theory with himself, and he needs to learn to keep sessions open and allow their full development without imposing a model (Fordham 10).

The Relation of Supervisor to Training Analysis

Analysis is always the center of training for Fordham. He considers that it is deepened and made more transforming during training, not threatened. Supervision is essentially different, although a candidate's affective response comes into it, but he does not tackle these countertransference reactions (leaving that to analysis). He assumes that 'a trainee can confront, elucidate, interpret and work through conflicts aroused by the case and pointed out in supervision.' (Fordham 10)

Analyst and supervisor should see eye to eye, especially for the first case. Too much difference causes strain both to trainee and supervisor, especially if the two parent figures are contentious or rivalrous. It is important that the trainee analyst pair trust other persons involved in training. Fordham thinks that although talks between training analyst and supervisor on analytic practice are desirable, argument about or discussion of the trainee are not. With supervision a very complex social situation arises since trainees need to project archetypal forms and other infantile components on to society, training group, seminar leaders and directors of training; and this may come into supervision and be clarified there (Fordham 2, 4).

A supervisor may find it hard to avoid indoctrination or intrusion into the analysis. This is the more so if the training analyst's methods are too different from his own, and splitting of transference may then occur. When supervisor and analyst are opposed over scientific conflicts, if: 'the trainee makes recurrent blunders or departs from analytic standards, or behaves with recurrent inadequacy, the supervisor becomes critical of the analyst and the trainee may become aware of it.' (Fordham 4, 11)

Once when Fordham was supervising during a time of dispute over transference in the society, he came to think that the training analyst did not understand its relevance, and although he could trust him in general, he could not agree with him on this question. Later the trainee became angry because Fordham did not change from being his supervisor to starting an analysis with but had thought that unethical. Another supervisor thought Fordham's analysis was defective and tried to complement it, the result being that the trainee developed a negative transference to the supervisor. On another occasion a trainee brought evidence suggesting his supervisor was not as satisfactory as he thought his analyst would be. (It is unclear here if Fordham spoke as analyst or as supervisor.) The analyst might feel rivalry in a case like this and be tempted to agree, especially if he knew the supervisor was less competent in some area (Fordham 2, 10).

Uses and Problems of Countertransference

Countertransference is not only inevitable but necessary and valuable; when a trainee affectively engages with a patient he needs to understand its nature and importance as a source both of error and of information, and training must take this fully into account (Fordham 10).

When countertransference is noticed by the supervisor, Fordham considers that he should not analyze it (since he does not know the candidate well enough), nor should he ever elicit personal information, nor manipulate the trainee into disclosing this countertransference to his analyst. Illusion is inevitable in Fordham's view. Analytic ideas are formulated in relation to the trainee's transference to analyst and supervisor, and these enter into his countertransference to the patient, causing anxiety that may interfere with a smooth working process; or a trainee may behave as a patient, or experience patients as parents (Fordham 9, 10).

A supervisor should aim at showing a trainee his wrong or inadequate interpretations, and his illusion (unless it is unconscious and so inaccessible to supervision). Since illusion helps a trainee to change and develop, it is important to make his liability to it plain, and to encourage him to find its fruitfulness in himself through his analysis and self analysis. Training is the time when countertransference is being discovered as a living thing by the training. Jung said:

> The treatment is the product of mutual influence, in which the whole being of the doctor as well as that of his patient plays a part. There is an encounter between two irrational factors, between two persons who are not fixed and determinable quantities but who bring with them, besides their clearly defined fields of consciousness an indefinitely extended sphere of non consciousness. For two personalities to meet is like mixing two [different] chemical substances: if there is any combination at all, both are transformed. You can exert no influence if you are not susceptible to influence. (Jung 14, p. 71)

When a trainee tries to use what he has learnt in his own analysis he may become disillusioned about himself, but as a result, if analysis has made him flexible, he can learn to mobilize interest when he loses heart, find what he can and cannot do, and develop his own style; he finds regular features in what he does and grows to understand his technique (related to personal experience), such integration as an individual being an unique discovery (Fordham 10).

> The analyst will know that every single statement he makes is an account of the state of his psyche, whether it be a fragment of understanding, an emotion, or an intellectual insight; all techniques and all learning how to analyze are built on this principle. It is thus part of the analyst's training experience to realize that he is going to learn, sometimes more, sometimes less, from each patient, and that in consequence he himself is going to change. (Fordham 7)

The Place of a Theoretical Model and the Open System View

Hillman has asked if the essential interaction of therapist and patient could be taught without it disastrously interfering with the alchemical process (Hillman 13). Fordham holds that skills are wanted and should be acquired, theory being essential, but that it comes from seminars, not from supervision. He does not give trainees a theoretical framework into which their observations may be fitted, but tries to convey his experience and encourages their own gifts, so avoiding the danger of indoctrination and making possible an empirical, not doctrinal, encounter.

A trainee's identification with analyst and supervisor is the basis of this style. In defining this style, Fordham listens to the different detailed accounts that students bring, discusses, advises on general management and reading, and elucidates questions arising from the material. He creates a situation to apply what has already been learnt of analytical procedure, teaching how to listen, how and when to intervene by confronting a patient with his situation, how to detect transference and countertransference, how to interpret, and how to avoid using technique to interfere; helping him to define where improvement in analytic skills might be made (Fordham 2, 4, 12).

Supervision concerns a student's work with his case, not with his inner world. But the technique of relating to patients is of little use to anybody unless he succeeds in integrating what he learns intellectually with his personal experience, and discovers in himself the equivalent of what he is taught:

> Psychopathology cannot be taught, and rather needs to be discovered in the candidate's own analytical experience ... I lean towards this position because it is dynamic, and avoids a static, even formal idea of psychopathology. ... What is learnt out of books, lectures, clinical observations, mental hospital experience, and outpatient departments will be of little help until the candidate has experienced and worked through his own pathology. Unless he has done so, intellectual knowledge will become a positive obstruction, in that all he has learnt will be used to bolster up defenses, making them rigid when they might have been flexible. (Fordham 10)

An open system view, in which therapist is engaged totally with patient, is taught by Fordham:

> This open system view, when applied to interpretations, means that their timing takes the analyst as well as patient into account in any interchange. This makes for complexity. (Fordham 9)

An open system implies being unsystematic by intention, with total reaction to the patient, countertransference then becoming a source of information and a therapeutic influence on the patient. (Fordham 8, 10)

Such a view may mean the trainee must allow himself not to know what is going on, and to start each session as if he knew nothing of the patient:

In almost any interview, the analyst may experience hesitations, doubts, gropings in the dark and false clues that, in the end, lead to a favorable outcome expressed, in each interview, in one or more interpretations that the patient could use. (Fordham 11)

Assessment and Self-assessment of Progress

A supervisor should avoid evaluation during the work together, in Fordham's view, not only to help available gifts and personal style to develop, but also to judge how improvement can take place. He prefers comparative experience with trainees to abstract standards in judging candidates. For instance, he describes one student who was good at seeing surface defenses but poor at containing, and another who was the reverse. When he has to assess for the application for membership Fordham tells the trainee his opinion and tries to lessen stress, for, as supervisor, he controls application but not its acceptance or rejection. His aim is to guide self-judgment ??an?? integrative process central to the concept of self, which percolates to all spheres of the trainee's life. Trainers may be overanxious about revealing supposed faults, or on the other hand, may comply, thus appearing spuriously competent (Fordham 2, 10).

A Personal Reminiscence as Fordham's Supervisee

I vividly remember how Fordham started where I was, not where he thought I should be, and built on that. He made me feel our work was one of discovery, setting up and testing hypotheses unique to the patient and to me: he was as interested and excited about it as I was, and made me feel valued. He was certainly at pains not to interfere with my analysis. I do not remember him pointing out my counter-transference: he was usually more subtle, complimenting me for not falling into recurrent faults, or alluding to difficulties of his own that

I then applied to myself. I never knew if he made these up for my benefit or not (perhaps he did, for he said he made up dreams for his analyst when certain topics were not being discussed). He attended to practicalities, the room, pictures, double-glazing, finances, to making oneself comfortable and allowing for one's weaknesses. He made few comments and let me analyze. Sometimes I was angry with him and sometimes acted out, but he always made me understand it was something we shared responsibility for.

He discouraged me from listening too assiduously to the patient or making too many interpretations by showing me that it did not work when I did so, allowing me instead to find and to listen to my countertransference (as I had not dared to do). What he taught me about illusory and syntonic countertransference was right at the front of current developments. Some, he said, considered it all the same, as bad, and wanted to get rid of it. But, he said, we all make projections all the time (some being projectors, some introjectors), and if one examines the countertransference one finds it constantly at an infantile level: one may either be caught in it, or see it, stand back and distinguish one's own from that of the patient. Sometimes, he said, one becomes relatively aware of something going on and can wait for it to clarify, tolerating uncertainty, not making warding off interpretations. A patient may need the analysts unconscious projection to go on (Fordham 3).

The setting of supervision with Fordham was almost analytic, boundaries being strict in many ways. Although not analysis, being about patients' material, it had some correlates, each session starting with a not-knowing attitude and with something like an open system view in reportage and discussion, using unconscious as well as conscious information.

58 Norah Moore

References

1. Fordham, M. (1958). 'A suggested center for analytical psychology.' In *The Objective Psyche*. London. Routledge & Kegan Paul.
2. – (1961). 'Suggestions towards a theory of supervision.' *J. analyt. Psychol*, 6, 2.
3. – (1966). (Personal communication.)
4. – (1969). 'Technique and countertransference.' *J. analyt. Psychol.*, 14, 2.
5. – (1969). Review of Racker's *Transference and countertransference. J. analyt. Psychol.*, 14, 2.
6. – (1970). 'Reflections on training analysis.' *J. analyt. Psychol.*, 15, 1.
7. – (1970). 'Notes on the transference.' In *New Developments in Analytical Psychology*. London. Routledge & Kegan Paul.
8. – (1972). 'The interrelation between patient and therapist.' *J. analyt. Psychol.*, 17, 2.
9. – (1975). 'On interpretation.' *Zeitschrift für analytische Psychologie* 6, 2.
10. – (1978). *Jungian Psychotherapy, a Study in Analytical Psychology*. Chichester. John Wiley.
11. – (1978). 'Some idiosyncratic behaviour of therapists.' *J. analyt. Psychol.*, 23, 2.
12. – (1982). 'How do I assess progress in supervision.' *J. analyt. Psychol.*, 27, 2.
13. Hillman, J. (1962). 'Training and the C.G. Jung Institute, Zurich.' *J. analyt. Psychol.*, 7, 1.
14. Jung, C. G (1931). 'Problems of modern psychotherapy.' *Coll. Wks.* 16.
15. Racker, H. (1968). *Transference and Countertransference*. London. Hogarth.

[5]

Supervision and the Mentor Archetype

Lionel Corbett

Introduction

In spite of the crucial importance of supervision, the subject has received scant attention in the Jungian literature. This strange indifference is consonant with the classical Jungian tendency to neglect the process of psychotherapy in favor of the analysis of content, so that the particulars of intrapsychic material were traditionally valued more than interpersonal dynamics. The danger this created in the past was that Jungian training programs focused almost exclusively on Jungian psychology and rather little on the practice of psychotherapy. With our present day sensibility, this situation is no longer tenable; both are important aspects of training and supervision. But this new focus on process rather than only content has brought with it a new difficulty, found much more within Jungian programs than in the rest of the psychoanalytic world, where training institutes tend to be relatively homogeneous. In our institutes, although we all share a core philosophical adherence to Jungian thought, at the personalistic level there are Hillmanian, Kleinian, Freudian, Kohutian and Langsian Jungians, to mention only some species. This fact complicates the training processes, and needs special attention. It raises difficulties especially for candidates within institutes where the analysts are of different theoretical persuasions, so that there is a choice of supervisor and of theory. The positive aspect of this situation is the opportunity for enrichment it offers the candidate, but the negative side is seen in the resulting political consequences, not to mention the constellation of shadow problems of splitting and envy. This little-dealt with situation adds to the already considerable responsibility of the supervisor, which is the result of several factors which are worth repeating:

1) Supervision has a pyramid effect; via our influence on one candidate, for good or ill we indirectly influence the therapy of many of the people he or she will treat throughout his or her career.

2) Although supervision is not synonymous with therapy, they have some elements in common. Supervision can have a therapeutic or an anti-therapeutic effect on the candidate. Because of unanalyzed identification with, or transference to, the supervisor, or because of a need to defend against the traumatic aspects of the situation, the process can both benefit or consolidate the candidate's personal health or pathology, as well as that of his patient, and can help to reinforce or dissolve certain of the candidate's therapeutic habits.

3) Just as the therapist must be conscious of his own difficulties, so must the supervisor be conscious enough not to hurt the candidate by the imposition of an unsuitable theoretical position, based on the supervisor's own needs. If the candidate is forced to adopt or adapt to a theory which is wrong for his temperament and abilities, it may take years to outgrow the damage.

The Need for a Conscious Choice of a Training Model

While acknowledging the value of the psychoanalytic literature on supervision, it is time for us to characterize a specifically Jungian approach to training, which requires that we discern the workings of the Self and its archetypal constituents in this process. Because of the wide range of possibilities that this endeavor opens up, I intend to focus only on those factors in supervision which either enhance or interfere with such a process. In particular, I have chosen a particular archetypal form which I feel is most appropriate to supervision and training in general – that of mentorship – in order to contrast it with other pedagogical possibilities.

Obviously it is possible to train within different archetypal attitudes. I hope that the model of the mentor will stand in useful contrast to those attitudes found in some analytic institutes, which consciously or unconsciously promote a parental attitude to trainees which is either one of Apollonian remoteness or narcissistic parenting. It is my belief that an unnecessary infantilizing of trainees occurs when their teachers utilize inappropriate pedagogic models. It is not sufficient to insist, as I often hear, that the transference to the supervisor or institute is inevitably a parental one; the nature of the relationship may actually be imposed on the trainee. To insist that the trainee's transference is solely the result of the trainee's endogenous fantasies, with no contribution from the environment, is no longer tenable, in view of the advances made in understanding the intersubjective foundations of psychic life (Stolorow and Atwood, 1992). The attitude of blaming the trainee for everything that he or she experiences is an extension of the traditional analytic attitude that attributes the entire content of the analysis to the analysand's personal material, as if the analyst, or reality, contributes nothing. In fact, the student is profoundly affected by the tenor of the training institute and the approach of his supervisors. When the atmosphere of the institute is destructive, it opposes the maturational needs of the candidate. The candidate's persecutory and depressive anxieties are then not necessarily the result of the projection of fantasies – the institute, or a committee, may actually be persecutory. If the supervisor is unable to allow a relationship of trust to develop, the development of a 'learning alliance' will be prevented. Condemnation, unhelpful criticism or contempt of the candidate tend to prevent him from presenting material that cause him shame, and condition him to present and train in ways which deny or distort his real potential in the service of the needs of the supervisor.

Even in more benign situations, presupposing a parent-child model of training itself tends to constellate, or overemphasize, this particular archetype within the supervisory relationship. The unconscious of both participants responds accordingly, and the transference is so colored. Deliberate choice of a mentor model similarly affects the tenor of the process. Therefore I suggest that the adoption of any particular training model should be a conscious choice on the part of the institute and the supervisor, and not left to chance. For those interested in feminist theories of psychotherapy, I suggest that the mentor model solves some of the problems of hierarchies, which are so problematic to those who wish to work in a relational mode. Of course it will be argued that there is a need for some kind of authority in the training situation. I believe that the most applicable form of authority is that which Paterson (1966) terms 'sapiential,' which is the right to be heard by reason of wisdom and expertise. This authority resides in the person, and is not simply held by virtue of one's structural position in a hierarchy. Sapiential authority allows one to advise, teach and direct but not order another.

The Mentor Model of Training

Etymologically, according to the Oxford English Dictionary, the word 'mentor' means an advisor, from the root *men*, meaning to remember, think or counsel. Mythically, the name belonged to an Ithacan noble, a friend of Ulysses. Athena assumed the form of Mentor when she wished to guide and advise Ulysses' young son, Telemachus, during his search for his father. In this mythologem can be seen many of the archetypal elements of mentorship. The search for the qualities of father among the young is facilitated by an older figure, father-like but not exactly father, who is able to embody wisdom, specifically Athena-like qualities. Although Athena is especially a protector and advisor of heroic men, the mentor-mentee relationship is of course found among women, and also between women and men, either one of whom may assume the mentor role.

Burton (1979, pp. 507-517) has clarified the importance of the mentor aspects of psychotherapy, highlighting the mutual effects of the therapist and patient *aside from* those of the transference/countertransference. For Burton the mentor is: "a charismatic person who can help with difficult life transitions in a manner different from the average…a powerful person who has transformed himself or herself and now has social visibility as a considerable achiever. "The mentor is a personality model "that can stand in a special creative relationship to us – not as father, mother, friend or lover … but as peer and self-possibility." Among several such creative relationships, Burton quotes those of Freud and Lou Andreas-Salome, and Jung and Toni Wolff. Perhaps the most detailed description of mentoring is that provided by Levinson (1978), in his description of the mid-life transition. In his usage, a mentor is a teacher, advisor and sponsor, a host and guide to the world his or her protegee wishes to enter, an exemplar who provides counsel and moral support. Most important, the mentor facilitates the younger person's realization of his or her youthful dream, or vision, of the kind of life they would like to live.

The mentor is an analog of the 'good enough parent'; he or she fosters development by believing in the mentee and blessing his or her dream. But, importantly, the mentor is not a parent, but rather a transitional figure, allowing the mentee to shift from immaturity to becoming a peer with other adults. The mentor is therefore a mixture of both parent and peer, for: "If he is entirely a peer, he cannot represent the advanced level toward which the young man is striving. If he is very parental, it is difficult for both of them to move toward the peer relationship that is the ultimate (though never fully realized) goal of the relationship. The actual parents can serve certain mentoring functions, but they are too closely tied to their offspring's pre-adult development (in both his mind and theirs) to be primary mentor figures." (ibid., p. 99). The mentor relationship feels like an apprenticeship to a 'more advanced, expert and authoritative' person. As time goes on, the mentee gains a 'fuller sense of his own authority and his capability for autonomous, responsible action.' The relationship gradually becomes more mutual, with a balance of giving and receiving. This enables the mentee to transcend the parent-child division. Levinson cautions that it is difficult to end this relationship reasonably. It may end in friendship or with bad feelings and disappointment, but the internalization process it produces is of critical developmental importance. Here two additional comments are necessary. First, that the trainee's relationship with the supervisor, which results in the internalization of technical knowledge and a philosophy of treatment, must be used to build up the professional aptitudes of the trainee in his own unique way, so that he becomes his own type of therapist, without gross identification with the supervisor. Second, a certain degree of manageable disappointment in the supervisor-mentor is essential for the growth of the trainee. As long as the degree of such failure is optimal, it will allow the trainee to take over for himself those functions of the supervisor which he previously relied on his mentor to provide. The mentor must allow this disappointment to occur, based on his or her inevitable shortcomings, without suffering narcissistic injury, realizing its importance for the trainee's development. Indeed, the supervisor's weaknesses can become springboards for the trainee's further knowledge, if the supervisor encourages him to pursue these areas.

It is of course obvious that infantile transference elements must enter into such a relationship, as they do in all important relationships. Indeed it is important to note that some of the candidate's behavior towards the patient is actually a function of his transference to his supervisor and is not simply determined by the candidate's countertransference to the patient. Idealizing, mirroring and twinship strands, as determined by the mutual self-object needs of the participants, are clearly necessary for supervision to be successful; parent-child aspects cannot be entirely avoided, although they can be largely outgrown with the help of the supervisor. Erotic components, both homo – and heterosexual, may also play a part. However, the mentor-mentee relationship is too rich and complicated to be dismissed as entirely a confluence of transference phenomena. It seems to be an irreducible archetypal form in its own right. Levinson regards it as essentially a love relationship, which is why it has such a proclivity to go wrong, but I believe that, based on the mythic imagery described above, it is more accurate to characterize the purpose of mentorship as the transmission of wisdom, and that this is its irreducible archetypal meaning. If the supervisor is working within this model, he will certainly notice transference elements between himself and the trainee, but only needs to spend time on them in specific situations. These are: 1) when the transference to him is decidedly negative. When this situation causes real difficulty it can be tactfully pointed out and referred for detailed work within the trainee's personal therapy, as long as the supervisor is also honest about possible ways in which his own behavior is contributing to the candidate's feelings. 2) In the case of parallel processes between supervision and the case being supervised, attention to the details of the supervisory transference is very valuable. If the supervisory transference is unobjectionable or helpful it can be ignored.

Resistance to the Adoption of the Mentor Model

The outstanding feature of the mentor model which can cause difficulty is that it encourages the trainee to develop his or her own style of practice, and become the therapist he or she was destined to become, based on that theory of therapy which is best-suited temperamentally and spiritually to the individual. Ideally, the mentor will support this choice if it is reasonable, without insisting on the trainee's adoption of the supervisor's own treatment model. This is the educational analog of the hope that, after successful psychotherapy, the patient will not be a clone of the therapist, as a result of gross identification, but will use the therapeutic relationship to develop his or her own self-structures. I realize that viable alternative models of supervision exist, for example that which says: "take it or leave it, this is what we teach in this institute." Here I am not concerned with valid theoretical or technical objections to the mentor model, as much as to identify sources of resistance to it based on the defensive needs of the supervisor. I have noticed various sources of such resistance, usually based on the problems which arise when the trainee is not prepared to completely adopt, or yield to, the supervisor's treatment philosophy.

It must be said that, just as parents can use children to meet their own narcissistic needs, so the unconscious supervisor may expect that the trainee will automatically idealize him and respectfully adopt the supervisor's personal model of therapy, rather than finding his own. Naturally this presupposition is more likely to occur if the supervisor is using his particular model of therapy defensively. This is so for instance when the supervisor himself was treated and supervised in a way which was inadequate or unhelpful. In such situations, the supervisor may turn to a particular theory itself, and the community of like-minded true believers, as self-objects which reassure him and help him maintain his self-esteem and professional position. In the worst case, when the supervisor was actually abused or retraumatized during his own therapy, he may identify with the aggressor and treat his own analysands and supervisees in the way he was treated. For the trainee not to work in the same way as the supervisor then threatens the supervisor's defensive structures and becomes a source of narcissistic injury. It is important that the supervisor not use the candidate for the purposes of dealing with his or her own self-esteem problem by either training disciples or by being omniscient. The supervisor, like the analyst, must have his or her own emotional needs reasonably in check. For instance, an intense need for sameness, that is to be surrounded by "people who are like me," among the senior analysts of an institute means that the candidate has to distort herself in order to meet the requirements of her teachers. They can blame the candidate for not being theoretically (read politically) correct, while ignoring the candidate's need to be true to her own self. This re-traumatizes her in the service of protecting the trainer's theoretical commitments, which the candidate may understand perfectly well but simply not agree with.

A potentially difficult situation also arises when the trainee utilizes a model of therapy in which he is trained, but which the supervisor simply does not understand, or worse still thinks he understands but in fact does not. Ideally the supervisor can then learn from the trainee, which is a part of the mutuality of the mentor model, especially when working with advanced candidates. But the supervisor's emotional investment in his or her own way of working, or the narcissistic demands of being a training analyst, may preclude this outcome. Again the risk is that the supervisor projects onto the candidate his or her model of the 'ideal analyst,' based on the supervisor's own strengths and weaknesses, and the education the supervisor wishes he or she had received. We are then in the position of parents who insist that their children live out the parents' own unlived life, regardless of its suitability for the child. The institute then repeats the traumatic need to develop a therapeutic false self by insisting that the candidate develops in only one way, not allowing his or her real therapeutic self to emerge.

I would now like to outline some of the applications of the mentor model in supervisory practice, under various headings.

Selection of Material to be Attended to in Supervision

Many possible elements of therapy can be selected for special attention in supervision, but of necessity we can only deal with a part of the trainee's work, so that selection of his material is necessary. This is a most revealing process. Just as in therapy we select certain aspects of the interaction to attend to and ignore others, based on what we really think is important, so it is in supervision. The supervisor or the trainee may wish to focus on dreams, the archetypal or symbolic dimension, the transference/countertransference, the frame, and so on. Something, usually something important and unconscious, is thereby ignored. In both therapy and supervision, elements we attend to are a function of several factors which inevitably cause a bias in particular directions. Some of these bias-inducing factors are: areas of theory and practice that we really understand, areas that we know enough about to know that we are relatively ignorant of them, areas that we do not know that we do not know, our own emotional needs, personal material that we successfully defend against, and personal material that we must avoid altogether. The latter two situations of defense prevent the trainee from bringing certain material into the supervision, and they operate in the supervisor when he subtly inhibits the trainee from presenting certain material, or projects the problem onto the trainee or his patient.

The supervisor may like to think that the selection of material for supervision is guided by material brought in by the trainee, but the trainee's perception of the supervisor's likes and dislikes, and what he knows will advance him in the institute, soon mold and influence the content of this material. The nature of these selection processes, and the supervisor's attitude to what the trainee himself thinks is important, are good indicators of the model of supervision being utilized. There is a tendency in certain "father (or mother) knows best" schools of training to assume that the supervisor is automatically correct in his approach to the trainee. In such a case, which in effect deliberately imposes a particular model of therapy, the supervisor decides on the content of what is brought into the supervision, and tells the trainee what to ignore, what to listen for and how to interpret it. For example, the trainee may be exhorted to ask for dreams, bring process notes, listen for derivatives, attend especially to the negative transference, frustrate the patient to encourage the expression of rage, attend to disturbances in the frame, watch for disruptions in the self-object tie, etc., etc. As a result, instead of behaving naturally, so that the situation in the treatment he is presenting emerges organically, the trainee consciously or unconsciously elicits, or at least presents his material, according to the supervisor's prescription. Often this leads to his either distorting the real nature of what actually happens in the therapy, or his treatment of the patient suffers from the awkwardness of the tacit presence of the supervisor. Absolute rules of practice imposed on the candidate, like rigidly maintained therapeutic frames, certainly lead to the candidate meeting his own infantile rage and pain because of frustration and shame, which may provide fruitful grist for the trainee's own therapy. But such absolutism also leads to infantile, regressive compliance or persona solutions with unspoken resentment, that look like adherence to the rules but which actually ignore the candidate's real training needs and betray his authentic selfhood. These pseudoresolutions to conflict with the institute or with individual supervisors are difficult to detect in trainees who are experienced survivors of difficult families. Candidates who are made of sterner stuff, who refuse to submit to what is accurately perceived as a repeat of childhood trauma, may leave training altogether, in certain cases greatly to the loss of the analytic community.

Within the mentor model of supervision, we allow the trainee to present his case without telling him what to select, or how to present, just as we do not tell patients what to talk about. It is axiomatic that what is not reported is probably important. But such omissions are tactfully noted and inquired about at the correct moment. Supervision uses the same principles that govern the timing of interpretations in psychotherapy with the work proceeding in gradually deepening stages. The goal of supervision is to understand what is actually happening between therapist and patient, because it is assumed that real understanding will lead to correct therapeutic behavior. It is inevitable that the formulation of this understanding can take many forms, based on particular theories. The supervisor will point out his personal belief about what is happening, but he must be well enough educated to be able to cast the dynamics of the therapy in other ways, would this be necessary for the professional development of the trainee. It is assumed that the therapist actually knows a great deal about the patient which he does not yet know how to articulate; the supervisor helps him to find words and a suitable framework for what is happening, and explains that this understanding can be cast according to different theoretical outlooks. Supervisor interference in the trainee's work as a therapist, and the imposition of the supervisor's theoretical stance, although inevitable to some degree, are thereby minimized. This is also achieved when the supervisor acknowledged his biases, giving his reasons for them as necessary.

The mentor-supervisor will remember that his personal style in supervision, and what he feels is important, is not universally applicable. It is influenced by what he thinks is important in therapy, by what happened to him in his own therapy and supervision, and by his personal hates and passions. To be of value to the trainee, the supervisor will distinguish his own needs in these areas from those of the trainee, and will try to discern who the trainee is, or is trying to become. Some skills are important for all therapists, while others are a matter personal style. For example, in the former category it is always important to stress the training of the therapist's attention to the patient; attention itself can lead to amazing changes without the application of any other therapeutic device. Attention can take the form of a close tracking of the patient's material, and his affective state, as well as attention to the therapist's own imagery and somatic reactions. When the beginner asks what he should be doing, I recommend the 'obstetric' approach to therapy, which is simply to try to deliver the presenting part – that is, to stay very close to what the patient is saying at the moment, rather than going after something else. In the personal style category, it is useful to remember that certain therapists are temperamentally 'hunters,' who like to be relatively active and somewhat pursue the patient, while others prefer 'trapping,' a more patient, waiting style. Each of these has advantages and drawbacks. My point here is that the mentor tries to discern how this particular candidate works best, and not try to force-fit him into a system of thought. To this end, the supervisor must be sensitive to the effects of his or her theoretical as well as personal bias. Here I offer my personal attitude to this problem.

The Theoretical Bias of the Supervisor and the Candidate

Where I am conscious of my theoretical bias, I declare it to the candidate, on those occasions in which I realize that there are different ways of conceptualizing the particular clinical situation which is presented to me, if I feel that the candidate will not be too burdened by hearing it. When I discern the candidate's theoretical bias, I point it out to him, non-judgmentally, by simply indicating that what he said reveals a Kohutian or Kleinian or whatever underlying attitude. Many candidates do not realize that what they have just said to a patient represents a theoretical commitment, and may not realize the underpinnings of the theory out of which they have spoken. Here I am interested in trying to bridge the eternal gap between theory and practice as much as possible; sometimes the candidate is horrified to hear what is implied by what he has said, while sometimes he agrees with it, but I believe he should know its implications. If the therapist does not know the ramifications of his approach, he is just painting by numbers.

When different approaches are possible in a given clinical situation, if the candidate is interested in this exploration and is sufficiently advanced to grasp the possibilities, I might say something like: "Here Freud would say this, Klein would say that, Kohut would say such and such, the intersubjectivists would point out this aspect, the Jungian view is this, here is how I see it, and this is the position you seem to espouse." In each case I try to clarify the underlying assumptions, so that the candidate can choose what seems right to him. As long as he does so consciously and not out of ignorance, I can support his choice. My experience is that it is often a relief to hear options. I present them because I believe that the candidate needs to be exposed to a reasonable range of choices of how to work, so that he can decide what fits him best. These choices are based on the fact that all therapists are dealing with a set of fundamental questions. He must decide what he thinks are the source of human motivation, what are the major factors in human development, what is the place of relationships in the development of a self, what is the source of healing in therapy, how does the patient 'use' the therapist in the treatment process, what is the place of the transpersonal Self in therapy, and so on. Their own answers to these questions will influence their work, and I believe that these should at least be conscious, if still unsolved, problems for all practitioners. Here I am against eclecticism, partly because I believe that some therapeutic choices are mutually exclusive, and partly because constant changes of attitude on the part of the therapist are confusing and disorienting to the patient.

Let me outline some of the typical decision points in therapy which are controversial, which I think make a major difference to practice, and above all which should not be presented to candidates as if they were settled issues for all practitioners, even if they are settled in the mind of the supervisor. I point these issues out as they arise contextually, not didactically.

1) We can view the drives as primary motivators, or as disintegration products of a fragmented self; these attitudes result in radically

different interpretations of the patient's sexuality and rage, and are grounded in different theories of human nature.

2) We can view therapy as a two-reality situation, in which the patient's transference is a distortion of the 'real' nature of the interaction, which of course the therapist alone is privy to, or we can stop to consider how our behavior interacts with and influences the patient's valid view of things. (Sometimes the patient's negative view of the therapist is not a transference, but exists because the therapist has been hurtful).

3) The candidate needs to know that there are theories that blame the child or the patient ("excess innate aggression"), theories that blame the parent or the therapist (empathic failure), and approaches which consider the fit between the two.

4) The candidate needs to know that for some content-oriented analysts, only intrapsychic material is important. For them, the 'therapeutic alliance' is simply the helpful medium within which to work with dreams and fantasies. For others, the relationship itself represents the critically important self-object field, created by both participants. Rather than being taken for granted, this field constitutes the holding power of the Self, and within this relationship constituents of the Self unfold in order to be met in the form of self-object needs.

There are other major controversial issues, such as: The question of gratification and frustration, the actual value of insight or of making the unconscious, the various ways of understanding of the Oedipal phase, the real nature of what is called projective identification, use of the couch, challenges to the concept of unconscious fantasy, and so on and on. At the present state of knowledge, all of these are debatable; I believe that our training responsibility to candidates is at least to be aware that none of these sacred cows can be taken for granted.

Faced with this welter of possibilities, a choice now arises. At such junctures in supervision, we can either try to help the candidate with the resulting confusion, or leave him somewhat confused, dealing with a Zen-like *koan;* something to the effect of: "how do you work when you realize that you don't realize what you are doing?" The hope here, as in Zen, is that a breakthrough in consciousness will occur which is beyond the everyday mind; this is sometimes called creativity. But obviously the caveat is that we have to take into account the candidate's level of experience, his anxiety level, his narcissistic vulnerability, and so on. However, for advanced candidates, the confusion of models of therapy to which they are exposed within some institutes is usually helpful, if it results in a clarification of personal preferences. But as teachers we must be aware that we are open to, and can create, a problem of splitting, since the candidate knows which of his teachers adheres to which theory.

But all of this potential confusion is better than having a supervisor who is merely a brain-washer, or one who is so invested in his pet theory that he cannot see whether it is usable by the candidate. We must be aware that both the candidate's training and his treatment of patients will decay if he suddenly starts trying to apply an approach which does not suit him. On the other hand, the technical aspects of therapy must be taught, for instance because a great deal of what passes for "countertransference" is actually the result of simple ignorance of the therapeutic process. A mature candidate, who is not too daunted by authority or possessed by a father-complex, can feel a gut-level of recognition or repugnance when he hears the articulation of a theoretical position, and when I suggest approaches I listen for this resonance or the lack thereof in the attitude of the candidate. Of course it is futile and hypocritical for the supervisor to pretend to be neutral about the candidate's choices, but sincere differences, held with conviction at an intellectual and feeling level are mutually growth enhancing.

A major potential problem arises when there are intractable differences of opinion between the candidate's personal analyst and his supervisor. In this situation, good will is needed between them, together with a fair understanding of each other's approach. It is potentially harmful to challenge the candidates necessary identifications or therapeutic alliance, or in any way to undermine the work he is doing with the other analyst, by subtle allusions to its weaknesses ("someday you will have to get a real analysis"). It is also crucial to recognize that to insist on the position that what *I* do is analysis proper but what Dr. X does is not, is merely a political statement. There is no place for polemics here. Differences of approach to problems such as primitive destructiveness are based on different theoretical substrates, and as far as we know may be dealt with effectively in more than one way.

Parenthetically, in the context of the connection between therapy and supervision, it is worth recalling the long-standing debate between Balint, in Budapest, and Bibring in Vienna about this relationship. In the 1930 s, the Budapest group believed that supervision was an extension of personal analysis, and should be carried out by the personal analyst. They stressed transference in analysis and countertransference in supervision, The Viennese insisted on the separation of the two, saying that supervision is didactic and the countertransference, once identified, should be brought to personal analysis. The Viennese won the debate, but I believe that this distinction is sometimes held too rigidly. I find that analysands can usefully bring in problems with their patients to their own therapy, and the personal analyst can help with the elucidation of the transference/countertransference difficulty because of his knowledge of the candidate. Similarly, it is obvious to me that some supervisees use their supervisor to meet certain self-object needs which are not fully met in their analysis, and can even be tactfully encouraged by the supervisor to face their transference to their personal analyst, especially when this is similar to their patient's transference to them.

The Problem of the Supervisor's Ignorance

One of the supervisor's worst difficulties is his area of ignorance, which burdens candidates most when it is denied or unconscious. This problem manifests itself in lofty attitudes of: "my analysis and training were so good that I have all the answers, and now I'm just passing on the doctrine." It is much more preferable to value one's own doubts. I used to bemoan the fact that my own analysis and training were incomplete, but now I see this fact as an essential part of my individuation. This incompleteness has forced me to constant inquiry, instead of allowing intellectual laziness, and I know that my own analysands receive better treatment than I did. If the idea of being inadequately analyzed and trained is intolerable, one is then forced into an omniscient, defensive position which requires that we hold onto theory to make up for what we did not receive in our analysis and training. Adherence to theory is used to buttress self-esteem and stifle doubt, in ourselves and our candidates. Such a supervisor deals with the candidate, and his colleagues, authoritatively, instead of with an attitude of mutual exploration. As T.S. Elliot puts it, if we want to discover something, we must approach it by way of not knowing, not by way of already knowing. Defensive or narcissistically motivated adherence to a theory is a gross disservice to both analysands and trainees. Rather, we should face the fact that much of what is taught as gospel proves to be inadequate in practice. All experienced practitioners discover that the application of what they were laboriously required to learn occasionally has as much effect as writing on water. The resulting disillusionment may force us into blaming the patient, or into therapeutic nihilism, or make us take refuge in dogma. None of these mechanisms are useful as our own creativity, and the sooner the trainee is helped through some similar crisis by the steady hand of the mentor, the better.

It is important to realize that the supervisor's technical strengths and weaknesses may or may not coincide with what the candidate knows, needs to know or is afraid of. Therefore in order for a useful interface to occur, the supervisor's self-knowledge and clinical judgment are as important in supervision as they are in therapy. And, because of the contrasts between supervisor and candidate, supervision, like the practice of therapy, can become an important source of further knowledge for the supervisor.

A Jungian Contribution

In view of the large psychoanalytic literature on supervision, can anything specifically Jungian be added? The answer is a definite yes; Jungian theory is useful in emphasizing specific contributions, such as the importance of the constellation of the Self in therapy. This is a crucially important concept to convey to the candidate, which he will not find elsewhere. Instead of a focus exclusively on the personalistic aspects of the transference, we are also interested in its archetypal aspects, or in how the Self manifests itself in the therapeutic field. But we must also enable the patient to find his own relationship to the Self and the objective psyche; the Jungian attitude to therapy is unique in this respect. We must remember that the Self may be interested in training, if training is authentically a part of the individuation of the candidate and supervisor. This occurs for example synchronistically when the subject of a paper I read one night shows up in the material which a candidate brings to supervision the next day. Or, comments about training occur in dreams. Therefore it is as necessary to be as open to the operations of the Self in supervision as it is i n therapy.

It is important for us to teach all of the manifestations of the Self so that they can be recognized for what they are. Numinosity is the obvious criterion, but may not be recognized for what it is, just as the novice may not recognize the manifestations of the transference unless they are pointed out by the supervisor. An example of failure to recognize an archetypal manifestation, which is actually caused by supervisory or pedagogic failure, occurs when supervisors emphasize attention to image at the expense of tracking the patient's affect. It is not always sufficiently recognized or emphasized that the presence of affect, via the complex, is the effect of the archetype just as much as image. Jung conceives of the archetype as a spectrum ranging from a somatic end to an intrapsychic or spiritual end. To 'stick to the image' in the psyche and ignore the affect in the body is to pretend that only half the archetype is present. When the patient or the trainee is gripped by intense affect, the Self is present as surely as it is in the presence of awesome dream imagery. This affect may be positive or negative; the important quality is its autonomy from the point of view of consciousness. Just as we teach subtle manifestations of the transference/countertransference, so we must point out subtleties of the effects of the archetype. There is a tendency for them to be ignored in practice, as though they are forgotten after the propaedeuticum examination. When the candidate grasps their transpersonal nature, or experiences the Self within the transference via the *coniunctio*, he will remember that he alone is not responsible for the patient's improvement or individuation. (He has probably forgotten all about the *coniunctio* since he struggled with volume 16 during a long-forgotten course.) The candidate may need to be reminded of the possibility of this essentially religious approach to therapy if it suits him temperamentally. Just how the Self is best constellated is a matter of opinion; my personal belief is that the establishment of a self-object transference actually means that elements of the Self have entered the therapy, and are operating to build the personal self, but there are other approaches to this question. What matters is the supervisor's ability to convey the importance of the autonomous psyche; exactly how the individual trainee arrives at the experience of the Self in his own therapeutic work is a matter for his own development.

I have alluded to the importance of synchronistic events in supervision. In all the deeply therapeutic encounters I have a part of, the complexes of the two participants are connected in this way. Here I take seriously Jung's idea that who we are happens to us, or that the unconscious presents itself to us from the outside, as the events of our lives. Thus it is that the people who find their way to our office bring us aspects of ourselves. I believe that it is important for the Jungian candidate to experience this fact. He will then realize that the self, and of course the Self, does not end at the skin, but includes others to whom we are destined to relate. This makes the supervision complicated; the patient is a psychological aspect of the candidate, who is in turn not psychologically separate from the supervisor. This reminder is not a recommendation for some kind psychotic merger; rather it is an attempt to deepen the therapeutic relationship by acknowledging its complexity. It also does wonders for any hubris we may have. To be fair to the candidate of whom this level of awareness is requested, the supervisor has to ask himself why this candidate is in his office with this patient, now.

Choice of an Archetypal Model of Supervision

In therapy, we have very little choice about which archetype manifests itself, and how it does so. We are respectful, participant observers. But in supervision I believe that we can have some conscious influence on which archetypal manifestations between supervisor and candidate is emphasized or even constellated in the first place. This choice is a function of our attitude to the candidate, and the philosophy of the institute. Of course a transference to the supervisor may exist before they meet, based on a father complex or the like. But unlike the situation in therapy, where we have to pay attention to everything that occurs between us, in supervision we can consciously reinforce or extinguish different aspects of the situation by selective attention, according to how we wish to structure the relationship. We can be paternal or maternal or even avuncular, but my suggestion is that the candidate is best approached as an apprentice to whom we are mentor. The candidate is there to learn, and this archetype, which is inevitably present to some degree, should most influence our attitude.

Our biggest problem may be that many supervisors do not actually practice what they teach. Traditionally, it has been common for senior analysts to teach the kind of orthodoxy that is expected which essentially repeats the party line. They have been reluctant or unable to really articulate what they actually do in practice. Many of our most gifted clinicians are successful because of the way they actually work, not for the reasons that they declare in pedagogic situations, which tend to be politically toned. Our most gifted supervisors are those who are able to help the candidate have the courage to put all theory aside when necessary, and be able to report what actually happened.

References

Burton, A. (1979). *The Psychoanalytic Review*, Vol. 66, no. 4, pp. 507-517.
Levinson, D.J. (1978). *The Seasons of a Man's Life*, Ballantine, NY.
Paterson, T.T. (1966). *Management Theory*, Business Publications, London, England.
Stolorow, R.D. & Atwood, G.E. (1992) *Contexts of Being: The Intersubjective Foundations of Psychological Life*. Analytic Press, Hillsdale, NJ.

[6]

Supervision and the Interactive Field

Mario Jacoby

Supervision is considered by all schools of depth-psychology to be an integral part to the training of candidates who want to perform the art of analysis or analytical psychotherapy. The trainees are required to reveal their experience with analysands and their analytic procedure to a designated supervisor. What a trainee may "learn" from such an encounter depends a great deal on the attitude and the ideas of the supervisor as to what analysis is all about. In the classical Jungian tradition one shared Jung's own skepticism about any kind of "technique." It is not what the analyst "says" that is important, but what he or she lives and emanates as a personality. The main emphasis is therefore placed on the personality of the analyst and his or her maturation in terms of the individuation process. There is something else Jung was adamant about: Analysts must, to the best of their ability, learn to understand the language of the unconscious. For this reason it is required that they study the symbolism in wide areas of our history and culture and that they train their ability to use a symbolic approach towards the unconscious material of the analysand. Foremost importance in training was therefore given to the personal analysis of the analysts and also to the studies of amplification. Supervision was regarded as being necessary indeed, but as a matter of fact, it seemed less important. The task of the supervisors most often consisted in adding their interpretations of the dreams of the candidate's analysands, perhaps adding some advice on how to relate these ideas to their conscious situations. The question of how often a candidate needed to see the supervisor was left to the trainee's own judgment.

Today the number of hours are prescribed and the process of training is regulated by the quantity of sessions. "The more hours the better." There still is discussion going on as to whether this great number of supervision hours furthers the quality of training or not. Some colleagues argue that trainees may rely on their supervisors for too long, or that candidates may just come to get the required number of hours, and this is sterile. One hears the opinion that they should only come to supervision when they feel stuck in the process.

I, personally, am in favor of an increased number of sessions. Yet, in order to change quantity into quality, it is necessary to reflect on how to use this number of hours productively. For all those analytical schools which require an analytic technique, a detailed discussion of the different moves and interactions is obviously needed. But also in the schools of analytical psychology, which allow much freedom and individual openness, encounters with a good supervisor serve an essential purpose.

This is especially so, since, for many analysts, there has been a shift in emphasis. The focus on the so-called "contents" of the unconscious has been enlarged to also include a more sensitive awareness of the unconscious dynamics as they express themselves in the here and now of the "therapeutic space" – or of "the interactive field," as Nathan Schwartz aptly puts it. I personally do not think that there is an "either/or": either focus on dream content or transference/counter-transference, either symbolical or clinical approach. It is well known that the effectiveness of dream-interpretation depends as much on the person who interprets as on what the content of the interpretation is. On the other hand, interpreting everything in terms of the transference may not do justice to certain contents coming up from the unconscious. Yet, although Jung was the first to discover the mutual influence in the analytic encounter (the relationship founded on mutual unconsciousness), this whole area remained quite neglected and undifferentiated for a long time – with the exceptions of some training centers such as the "London School."

As soon as the subtleties of the interactive field between patient and candidate are included in the supervision-sessions, things become much more complex. The focus will also be put on questions like: How perceptive are the trainees in terms of the nonverbal communications of the analysand, his or her body-language, voice inflections, undertones, etc.? And, how differentiated is a candidates awareness of what the patient's presence is evoking inside him or herself in any given moment? How do they react to the patient's love, aggression, devaluation, ambivalence, etc.? Do they have to take those affects too personally and retaliate in an unconscious and subtle way? Or are they rather unaware, repressing their feeling reactions? And once they are open to what happens inside themselves, can they effectively differentiate their own unconscious projections on the patient from their perceptions of what may come from the patient's unconscious? In other words, is there the capacity to discriminate between what M. Fordham called "illusory" versus "syntonic" counter-transference? I think those distinctions are sometimes extremely difficult to make. The most difficult task is also to differentiate the ability to stay in touch with oneself while at the same time taking distance from oneself, and, also trying to see oneself through the eyes of the patient – by way of empathy. Can trainees understand those subtle issues at all when the supervisor tries to point them out? And once they have become sensitively aware, can they develop enough therapeutic flair and instinct to follow through with what their insight may be to verbalize parts of it for the benefit of the analysand in an effective enough way? Can they to some extent integrate enough their knowledge of the symbolic approach and of whatever theories they cherish, to be able to use it according to the necessities of the individual situation? Those are all important questions to be dealt with in the course of supervision.

So far I have focused on the ability of candidates to be perceptive enough regarding their place and their differing roles in the dynamics of the interactive field. In my experience as a supervisor I must admit that some trainees seem very unaware in this respect. They also seem confused or resistant when confronted with questions of that nature. As a consequence, I may feel frustrated about their lack of any "feel" for the art of analysis. I may doubt their giftedness for this profession and also doubt that they will ever be able to learn it. Of course, I may also begin questioning myself about my ability to evoke their potential. Sometimes I may notice that they are in the grip of a complex during a supervision session. In any case disturbances in the mutuality of our dialogue may arise. Yet with other trainees, the sessions may bring a lively give and take, a mutual inspiration for new insights.

In one instance I also experienced that a candidate, with whom it never seemed to click, later turned out to be one of the finest analysts. Years afterwards, when we were colleagues and friends, we could talk about his earlier defensiveness which had been constellated by a heavy father-authority complex activated between us. This incidence has taught me that it may at times be necessary to focus on the transference issues going on between candidate and supervisor, even if it is a piece of personal analysis. As much as it is important to keep analysis and supervision separate, this cannot be an inflexible rule because an interactive field between trainee and supervisor obviously gets constellated. The supervisor must always take into account that most everything candidates share with him or her, may also be influenced by what is going on in the interactive field between them.

How is the supervisor then able to grasp what really is taking place in the sessions of candidates with their analysands? The best thing in this respect would be to employ/use videotapes. Yet taking tapes in a session may hinder the free flow as the "observing eye" of the camera does have its influence. So, usually the supervisor has to rely on the candidate's account. I personally obviously listen to what candidates are *telling* me regarding what has been going on in their sessions. At the same time I try to become aware of how I am affected by their *presence as a personality*, which partly reveals itself by the intonation of their voice, the expression of their face, their body-language, their kind of vitality, harshness, softness, warmth or lack of emotion or whatever. Sometimes there are facets of their way of being with me which puzzle me, and it may happen that the patient they talk about hardly appears before my "inner-eye." They themselves then stay in the foreground of my attention. But hopefully the patient they are talking about may become alive for me in his or her particular individuality. It happens, for fleeting moments, that in phantasy I may get into the shoes of a described patient and may even get a glimpse of how he or she may feeling the presence of the respective candidate. This is all very well as long as I take into account that I may project the feelings I experience myself while sitting with that candidate on this unknown patient. But it may also be that in this way I perceive something which is essential to their interactions.

It is not easy for candidates to transplant, so to speak, their patient/analyst field to the interactive field with the supervisor. Some can do it more successfully than others for various reasons. Telling me the dreams of their patient and, more or less, the contents of their dialogue is relatively easy. But it is, for instance, more difficult to get a grasp of what is going on in relation to the subtleties of emotional interchange, or of what influence certain personality characteristics of the candidate may have on the interactions with his or her patient. Candidates may be quite unaware as to what those implications are about.

I often try to verbalize the issue according to the way I myself feel affected by the presence of the candidate. I may express – as I did in one case for instance – my sense of feeling invaded by the candidate's temperament and all the space he needs. I thus asked him in which way his invasive vitality may affect his clients and whether he has made any observations in this respect. He remarked that it was a matter of course to be much more passive with clients that when he is with me. I actually had my doubts as to what degree he could restrain himself when being with patients, but the two clients he supervised with me were doing quite well. It may be that they could incorporate some of his surplus-energy.

In general I tend to express to candidates the way I feel in their presence. Thus I try to sensitize their awareness as to how their personality-features and their manner or responses may shape the interaction with certain patients. I think this is an important part of supervision. And yet this may also be counterproductive as it may touch sore spots which are so vulnerable that they cause a depressive insecurity and may even harm the treatment of the case. Furthermore some candidates may be too defensive or may not have an antenna to grasp what I try to talk about.

An essential aim of analysis or analytical psychotherapy is to further consciousness and understanding of self and world. How does a candidate learn to acquire a more differentiated understanding of psychological interconnections and an ability to convey these to his or her patient? Is this at all possible without theoretical concepts and without any methods – not to mention techniques – of how to implement these? I think it is an illusion to conceive of oneself as working without theories, concepts or methods, because our mind cannot function without them. On the contrary, we have to study many different theoretical ideas in order to be more or less conscious of which ones we wish to apply. Only by being aware can we handle such ideas flexibly and individually enough to get a sense of those models which suit our way of proceeding. I therefore feel that discussion of theories and methods in addition to eventual recommendations for further reading, are part and parcel of supervision.

Analyst have, by necessity, their own ideas of what analysis is all about. I remember seeing a woman for supervision, quite a strong personality, who firmly seemed to know what she wanted. She handled the issues of her analysands in a very directive way, gave much advice and took a lot of initiative. She felt sure that this was the right way to act and she could always tell me of some progress her clients had made. I was terribly frustrated about her insensitivity in analytic matters − -but what could I say in view of her clients' progress? Of course many roads lead to Rome. Some patients may need a more directive approach, it does not really matter to me whether we call this analysis or not. What was so frustrating in this particular case was my impression that this woman was too well defended against her unconscious power issues and that there was no flexibility, and not even an antenna to grasp what I wanted to convey to her.

Another trainee was just the opposite. She tried her best by reflecting on her procedures in terms of Jung, Kohut, Winnicott etc. Yet it seemed all too theoretical and was not related to the spontaneity of her "true" feelings. I also suspect that she did this to fulfill what she phantasized as my expectations. But it became obvious that she tended to be absorbed by theories in the situation with analysands as well. This basically had to do with lack of trust in her own subjective reactions, identifying instead with the teachings of an authority figure.

I sometimes wonder whether we are not asking too much of our candidates. Such processes of finding oneself, of trusting one's subjective reactions and being critical at the same time, of getting personally involved yet remaining simultaneously a figure of the patient's phantasy − all this takes time and much experience. Yet I am often amazed when some gifted trainees can use the slightest hints they get from supervision to develop their own ways of proceeding. They develop their flair for symbolic understanding in addition to their skill in verbalizing and their feeling for the right timing and even the right tone for certain interventions. Of course there may be phases when they tend to identify with the person of the supervisor or introject his or her way of proceeding. I feel it is therefore advisable for trainees to work with more than just one supervisor.

I personally enjoy being a supervisor as long as productive cooperation is possible. As analysis is basically an art, it is difficulty to teach. As supervisors we are often limited to lending support and helping towards the differentiation of natural talent. And last but not least, I feel that supervisors, by being part of the learning process of the trainee, may also learn something themselves. It gives us the necessary opportunity to reflect with another person on the subtleties of our work. There is also a healthy narcissistic gratification if one can share one's ideas. I must also confess that trainees may sometimes handle certain difficult situations in an astonishingly effective way, often better than I probably could have done. Thinking of the truth of Jung's statement that also the analyst is in analysis, I feel it appropriate to say that the supervisor, by doing his job, may also at times experience a good piece of supervision.

[7]

Transference Projections in Supervision

Joseph Wakefield

This chapter has evolved from work done on supervision within the Interregional Society of Jungian Analysts. In 1989 the Inter-Regional Society held a conference in Salado, Texas on the theme of closeness in personal and professional relationships. Since that time the Society has continued to explore the ethical and psychological aspects of closeness through various lectures, small group and panel discussions.

Closeness between a supervising analyst and a candidate in training can be a stimulus to learning, yet it also can become problematic when it interferes with supervision (Wakefield, 1992). When the supervisor and the supervisee have other types of relating in addition to supervision they can be said to have dual role relationships. Dual role relationships can create a conflict of interest between the goals of supervision and other goals the participants may have. Ethical and organizational constraints, "rules," develop to protect the participants and the integrity of supervision. The situation is not difficult to understand when supervisor and candidate are conscious of what they are doing, but what happens when they are unconscious? This chapter focuses upon the unconscious perceptions and expectations, i.e. transference projections, which can develop between supervising analyst and candidate.

In preparation for this presentation I reviewed a variety of essays by analytical psychologists and psychoanalysts on the supervision of training candidates. Regardless of the theoretical position, several themes were repeated:

One theme is the question of management of transference when it develops from the candidate towards the supervising analyst. Should

the candidate complete his or her personal analysis prior to beginning supervision to avoid "splitting" the transference between the
personal analyst and the supervisor? Or should the candidate be in
personal analysis so that the supervisor can suggest the candidate
take his or her personal issues back into analysis? Frijling-Schreuder
(1970) emphasizes that supervision is not analysis because it does
not stimulate regression. It remains a consultation between colleagues rather than a therapist-patient relationship.

Another theme is the question of the management of countertransference. Several authors use different terms to refer to this problem.
When a candidate's countertransference arises from unresolved personal issues, it is suggested that the supervisor not explore the
reactions, but instead refer the issues back to personal analysis.
When the countertransference is a reaction to what the patient has
presented, (projective or syntonic countertransference) then it is
suggested that the supervisor work with the candidate on the material. Grinberg (1970) examines a variety of issues in the supervisor/
candidate relationship. He explores such questions as to whether the
supervisor should focus on the therapist or his patient, whether the
supervisor and candidate should share the same theoretical standpoint, whether to record sessions, and whether the candidate should
be in personal analysis. He also discusses the choice of cases and
problems which arise from different personality patterns in both the
candidate and the supervisor. I agree with Grinberg when he stresses
that supervision should be an educating situation rather than a therapeutic experience. The candidate should be in personal analysis
separate from supervision. Supervision should avoid encouraging a
type of splitting which converts the supervisor into an idealized
analyst and projects the persecutory image on to the training analyst,
or vice versa. "The candidate should be treated as a colleague and not
as a patient" (p. 375).

In another paper Grinberg (1963) describes problems derived
from a breach of the supervisory setting:

> "The analyst's work forces him to be isolated in his consulting-room
> most of the day and therefore he has very few possibilities of communi-
> cation with the outside world. Furthermore, the regression that takes
> place during the analytical situation affects not only the patient but also
> a certain extent the analyst himself. Moreover, he has to restrict himself

to interpreting only the material contributed by the patient. In this way, isolation, regression and a deficient communication with the outside world will occasionally give rise to a strong longing for stimulus coming from outside. This may account for a particular reaction supervisors may experience towards candidates under supervision, as they are a sort of escape valve which provides the supervisor with a longed for so contact and free dialogue. It is then important to bear risk in mind so that the supervisor's open and friendly attitude may not exceed reasonable limits which might endanger the supervisory setting." (p. 376)

Grinberg presents in a clear way some basic guidelines for the supervisor. Unfortunately, transference projections at first are not conscious and neither the candidate nor the analyst may recognize them as present. Transference projections from both supervisor and candidate are built into the supervisory situation. The task is to understand and become conscious so that unconscious projections will not get in the way of the legitimate work of supervision.

Supervision includes training, assessment and being a role model with apprenticeship. At times various aspects of the supervisory work may be in conflict. To train, the supervisor encourages the candidate to be open about his or her errors, yet the candidate knows the supervisor is judging the performance. In such circumstances I question the usefulness of pathologizing the candidate's reaction with terms such as "paranoid," "narcissistic preoccupation with how he/she appears," etc.

It is difficult enough for supervisor and candidate to achieve openness and cooperation when judgment is involved. The encounter is even more difficult when it becomes entangled with unconscious projections. Supervision contains many of the same factors which generate transference in analysis, such as personal contact over a prolonged time and the revealing of important personal matters including countertransference reactions with patients. The supervisor is a power figure whom the candidate may wish to please plus the supervisor may experience a certain personal closeness in the encounter. In contrast to analysis, the supervisor may reveal more of his own feelings and doubts as a therapist. Analysis is a lonely profession, and the supervisor may experience the candidate as a colleague with whom he may confide "what it is like." The result can be a mutual entanglement of transference and countertransference reactions.

What sort of projections may occur between supervisor and candidate? It would be possible to describe such projections in the terms of analytical psychology, such as projection of "a negative mother complex" or of "the wise old man" etc. One of my concerns is our discipline's tendency to become too isolated, insular and unable to translate itself into the language and concepts of other disciplines. (For an effort to overcome this barrier, see Redfearn, 1983). In order to provide a mirror from outside of analytical psychology, my examples will be expressed within three main currents of contemporary psychoanalytic metapsychology: drive theory, object relations theory, and the self psychology of Heinz Kohut. (Greenberg & Mitchell, 1983).

Drives

The so-called primary instincts are Eros and Thanatos, sex and power. Within the context of drive theory, either supervisor or candidate may experience the other as a source of gratification of instinctual desire. The world is filled with potential sources of gratification, so why select precisely the one that is forbidden? Sex becomes power and power becomes sex. A supervisor engaged in a sexual relationship with a candidate might not dare give a negative judgment, and a candidate wanting to complete training might not dare to turn down a sexual overture from a supervisor. The problem with "dual role relationships" is the imbalance of power. The supervisor has power over the candidate's advancement, and so the candidate cannot without risk reject overtures from the supervisor. If the supervisor and candidate do enter into a sexual liaison, other candidates may become fearful either that the "special" candidate may receive special treatment, or become fearful that they also may be asked to become available for such a relationship. The result can be secrets, hidden liaisons, splitting and distrust within the training society. These results are destructive to the process of training.

Dual role relationships can develop in an unconscious way, in spite of the best intentions. It had been customary for my wife and I to invite candidates in my training seminar to join us for a social evening. My conscious thought was that such contact made the training more personal, less rigid, and assisted apprenticeship. Several of the candidates, more conscious than myself, pointed out the problems my social overtures created for them. The candidates were not free to decline the social overture of a required seminar. While attending the "social event" they feared their conduct might be graded. Though not my intention, I had nevertheless created a dual role relationship interfering with their training.

Power may express itself also in nonsexual forms. Suppose the supervisor wishes to dominate or control the candidate, insisting that the candidate adopt the supervisor's theoretical point of view. If so, the candidate may feel that he or she must submit in order to graduate, either in case supervision, writing a thesis, or oral exams. In a subtle, corrupt way the candidate may select a power-driven analyst as supervisor precisely to neutralize that analyst through flattery. The candidate may well be conscious of the analyst's unconscious needs, but feel that he or she dare not say anything for fear of retribution.

A subtle form of dual role relationship may occur when the supervisor also serves as an officer within the Society, especially when the supervisor serves upon training and evaluation committees. When I served on the Interregional Society's Evaluation and Review Committee there was a notable increase in the number of candidates seeking supervision with candidates who sought me dropped to less than half the number before. So the question arises: Were my services sought for the supervision I could provide, or to obtain my vote in a Committee decision? The question is complicated because officers are more visible than regular members and therefore more likely to be thought of by the candidates for supervision. I doubt that the candidates who worked with me consciously intended to influence committee decisions. I do think that protection of the integrity of the supervision process is subtle, complicated, and requires efforts at consciousness by both supervisor and candidate.

Object Relations

In object relations the focus shifts from instinctual gratification to the importance of relationships in early stages of development. The question is not discharge of sexual or aggressive drives, but rather the quality of relatedness. Various psychoanalytic theorists have developed their own colorful vocabularies to describe such relatedness. In the terms of analytical psychology, we enter the world of complexes, including parental complexes and sibling relationships. These early life patterns of relatedness may become transference projections between supervisor and candidate. For candidates, the supervisor may represent the caring, guiding parent they never had, or the cruel, withholding parent, or even the possibility of achieving Oedipal triumph at last by becoming the favorite child, intensely if secretly loved. For supervisors, the candidate may represent the child they lost, or the child they never had, or the child in themselves to be nourished the way they wish they had been nourished.

The most difficult complexes to recognize are those which are socially reinforced. If a man has a neurotic need to commit ax murders, society will soon point out to him that what he does is a problem. If a man has a neurotic need to sacrifice himself for the poor, society may laud him as a saint and not encourage him to reflect upon his complexes. Some of the transference projections between supervisor and candidate are condemned and some are socially reinforced. The examples given before of sexual liaisons, or of power manipulations for money or prestige, usually are condemned when recognized. In contrast, object relations transferences between supervisor and candidate may be reinforced by society. Suppose a supervisor takes special interest in encouraging a candidate's progress, for example by providing extra reading, sharing his personal experiences as an analyst with the candidate, or intervenes with the training committee to assist them in understanding the candidate. Suppose a candidate attaches special importance to being part of the supervisor's group of colleagues, or works especially hard at tasks the supervisor assigns. My examples are not necessarily of wrong or unethical conduct. Such examples might represent a positive teaching relationship. Such examples might also represent unconscious projections of parent-child transferences. The unconscious nature of the projections could hinder the participant's judgment and interfere with supervision.

Self Psychology

In recent years, the symptomatology of the narcissistic wound and its effect on transference and countertransference has come more into focus. Heinz Kohut has developed his own vocabulary in exploring this clinical phenomenon. In the supervisory setting Kohut's description of three types of narcissistic transference is particularly useful.

In the idealizing transference, the person projects ideals onto the other and expects the other to live up to the projection. In terms of analytical psychology, we could say some aspect of the Self has been projected, perhaps as the Hero or the Wise Old Man or Woman. (See Corbett & Kugler, 19.) If the other fails to live up to the projection (as eventually happens, all of us being human, "all too human"), the idealization quickly turns into denigration and rage. Either the supervisor or the candidate may project an idealizing transference onto the other. Since it feels good to be viewed as wise, good, and heroic, the recipient of the projection may question nothing. Idealizing transferences may lead to the candidate's overvaluing the supervisor, loss of the ability to see weaknesses and shortcomings, and a type of enslavement in which the candidate blindly follows his or her ideal while attacking analysts who have different points of view. I suspect that it is from such unanalyzed transferences that psychoanalytic "schools" based upon the Great Founder surrounded by devoted disciples have evolved. If the supervisor idealizes the candidate (perhaps as an embodiment of youthful energy, creative possibility, or some other ideal the supervisor longs to encounter), then the supervisor may be unable to see and correct flaws in the candidate's development.

In the mirror transference (or self-object transference), the projector expects the recipient of the projection to mirror back what the projector wants to see of himself or herself. The projector wants to be idealized and may become enraged if this is not done. Either supervisor or candidate may project such a transference upon the other. The supervisor may expect the candidate to be a mute witness of the supervisors brilliance and skill. Conversely, the candidate may expect the supervisor to say nothing while listening in silent awe to the superb presentations of the candidate. As you may expect, efforts to correct shortcomings may be met with resentment. An issue often discussed among supervisors is the problem of the candidate who "just won't listen," who will not take in the observations and advice of the supervisor. Though less often the focus of discussion, I believe a similar problem is the inverse phenomenon: The supervisor who "just won't listen," who is so involved in being admired that he or she fails to pay attention to the reality of the candidate. I think the mirror transference described above helps explain how these problems come into being.

In the twinship transference (or alter ego transference), the projector wishes the other to be a double of himself or herself. Consider the supervisor who acts as if "we are all equal," as if no power differential or gatekeeper function exists. Such a supervisor might view a candidate as a peer, friend or confidant. A candidate might treat the supervisor similarly. While it is true on a level of basic humanity that we are all equal, it is illusory to have such a belief about the relation between supervisor and candidate. Built into the very role is an inequality, a difference. To ignore such differences is to become blind to the reality of what each is required to do for the other. While the blurring of boundaries in the twinship transference might appear as a generous act of sharing oneself, the effect can be frightening for the candidate. After all, the candidate sought the relationship for supervision not friendship. If the supervisor insists on being a peer, friend or confidant, then the supervision relationship is distorted, often to the candidate's detriment.

While transference projections exist and remain unconscious between supervisor and candidate, closeness is problematic. With such projections intimacy is illusory. The projector may feel love, rage, desire or awe toward the recipient of the projection. Sadly, the actual other person is not known. As Elie Humbert describes it, the projector is "in pursuit of his own desire." With such projections intact, empathy toward the actual other cannot occur, and the other is known as an extension of the projector's needs rather than as a separate unique person.

When transference projections arise in analysis they become a focus for the work of analysis. The analyst's job is to help the analysand become conscious and work through the emotional meaning of the projections. The analyst is obligated also to monitor his or her own countertransference, alone or with consultation with a colleague. What of transference projections which arise in supervision? Supervision is not analysis. No agreement exists for either the supervisor or the candidate to interpret the other's projections. I suggest that they should agree not to literally and concretely enact feelings that would cause them to depart from their roles of supervisor and supervisee. I suggest they try to make conscious the meaning of their feelings by discussing them with their personal analyst or with a colleague.

What sort of relatedness between supervisor and candidate permits supervision to occur? Such relatedness needs to avoid unconscious enactment of projections. Relatedness needs also to avoid the sterility of withholding one's authentic self. I have found useful ideas expressed by Douglas Ingram in a talk entitled "Legitimate Intimacy in Analytic Therapy" (Ingram, 1989). While Ingram's focus is on analytic therapy, much of his thought is applicable to the supervision relationship. Ingram understands intimacy within social role theory. Roles are described as goal-directed configurations of transactions between people within a social context. Roles mediate the interaction of oneself with the self of another. Just as roles have limits and boundaries, intimacy also has limits and boundaries defined within the role system. It is in appreciating the limits defined by the roles that intimacy itself is enhanced. The character of intimacy between persons changes as their role relationships change.

Pathology may occur when present relationships are burdened by attempts to overcome deficiencies in intimacy that occurred in earlier relationships. If one or both persons attempt to blur the social roles and overstep limits, there may be a loss of intimacy. Ingram describes this blurring of roles as familiarity. For example, in therapy an erotic transference may develop where the projector seeks fusion and merger in a closeness that "knows no bounds." If the projection is enacted, there is a blurring of the roles of therapist and patient. With this blurring of boundaries comes a loss of the intimacy that belongs to the therapist-patient roles.

Only in intimacy-valued relationships can empathy occur. Empathy involves the self of one person engaging the self of another. Such engagement can take place only where respect for the role structure allows intimacy to develop.

A "real" relationship between two "whole persons," which is intimate, develops when each relates to the other authentically, in a trustworthy manner, within the context of their social roles. For example, an analysand can experience his or her analyst as a whole authentic self as long as the vehicle, the analytic vessel, remains intact.

Consider the question of relatedness within supervision from Ingram's viewpoint. Some forms of closeness, such as familiarity, may actually destroy intimacy because they undermine the social roles required of supervisor and candidate. Other forms of closeness may enhance intimacy and therefore contribute to an authentic connection of self between the persons involved. When both supervisor and candidate perform their respective roles, over time and in a trustworthy manner, intimacy may develop between them. This intimacy is the expression of relatedness between the selves of each person involved.

Jung liked to quote the Gnostic gospel of Thomas, where Jesus was to have said, "if you know what you are doing you are blessed. If not, you are cursed." Power, sexual gratification, closeness and self-esteem all are legitimate human needs. Problems arise if the supervisor or the candidate attempts to gratify these needs in ways that interfere with training, assessment and apprenticeship.

Enactment of transference projections may interfere with supervision by blurring the roles of supervisor and candidate. To become conscious of the types of transference projections which may occur is to have some choice about whether or not to enact them. Within the respectful performance of the roles of supervisor and candidate, authentic relatedness can take place. The mutual exploration of these interpersonal dynamics is an essential part of work

A version of this chapter was read at a Inter-Regional Society of Jungian Analysts panel on the dynamics of supervision in Santa Fe, NM., April, 1992.

References

Frijling-Schreuder, E., "On individual supervision," *Int. J. Psycho-Anal.* (1970) 51, 363.

Greenberg, J. & Mitchell, S. *Object Relations in Psychoanalytic Theory,* (1983), Harvard Univ. Press.

Grinberg, L., "Relations between psychoanalysts." *Int. J. Psycho-Anal.* (1963) 44, 362-367.

Grinberg, L., "The problems of Supervision in Psychoanalytic Education," *Int. J. Psycho-Anal.* (1970) 51, 371-383.

Ingram, D., "Legitimate intimacy in analytic therapy." Panel discussion on erotic transference and counter-transference, the 33rd. annual meeting of the American Academy of Psychoanalysis, San Francisco, May 1989.

Kugler, P., "Essays on the supervision of training candidate." (1988) Unpublished.

Kugler, P., "Essays on the supervision of training candidates." (1992) Vol. 2, unpublished.

Redfearn, J., "Ego and Self: terminology." *J. Anal. Psychol.,* 28, 2, 91-118.

Wakefield, J., "The supervisor," in *Closeness in Personal & Professional Relationships,* edit. Wilmer, (1992) Shambhala, 216-238.

Wilmer, H., edit., *Closeness in Personal & Professional Relationships* (1992), Shambhala.

[8]

Styles of Supervision

Judith Hubback

I would like to begin with a brief comment about terminology. Personally, I do not like the term "control analyst" to designate the candidate's supervisor. It confuses the boundaries between analyst and supervisor. In the London Society for Analytical Psychology we use the term "supervisor," rather than "control analyst." Difficulties also come with the term "supervisor," but to a lesser degree. "Supervisor" can convey a picture of the senior analyst looking over the trainee's shoulder, possibly in a persecutory way. Nevertheless, the designation "supervisor" seems to convey more of the quality of helping, than controlling.

The trainee's capacity to present the clinical case has to be considered. Often it is difficult to discern what is going on in a patient's analysis as described by the trainee. Some trainees give a much clearer and more convincing account of the analytic process, the development of the patient's ability to symbolize, and the transference and counter-transference projections, than do other trainees. Transferences to the supervisor, as well as the genuine personal relationship, are also significant aspects of the work. While some trainees are difficult to relate to, others are very congenial. Thus, transference and counter-transference between supervisor and trainee are important factors to monitor.

The Spectrum of Styles

The spectrum of styles in supervision runs from the permissive to the didactic. Each supervisor has a unique style and this quality of individuality holds for the candidate as well. In addition to personal uniqueness, there are also cultural variations contributing to the different styles of supervision.

At the permissive end of the spectrum of styles, the supervisor comments very little and intervenes even less. This approach may be suitable for very gifted trainees, but it may also generate unwarranted anxiety. Candidates sometimes complain of wanting more guidance, or encouragement, or suggestions regarding other approaches. Yet, the supervisor may be well advised to let the trainee find his or her own pace, and to feel for the pace at which the patient can proceed. A trainee can benefit from the more experienced supervisor who may have something valuable to offer, but who is at the same time not insisting on being right. A senior colleague is offering the result of many years of professional experience to a junior colleague.

Then there is the didactic end of the spectrum of styles. In long-established Societies, the supervisor is an analyst with at least ten years of experience as a qualified member. The teaching aspect of supervision takes the form of enabling the trainee to learn. It is valid for the supervisor to convey that he or she has something to offer the trainee willing to accept the junior role, and to combine the teaching with a healthy amount of humility. Especially in the early days of working together, humility is necessary because the supervisor may not know the trainee well, and only gets to know the patient through the reporting of the trainee. Supervisor and trainee both may have been influenced by the assessment report of the medical doctor. To complicate the situation even more, the transference projections active in the patient's assessment interview may be very different from those which emerge either at once or gradually in the analysis and supervision. In the early stages, then, there are probably four psyches that the supervisor has to take into account: the assessor's, the trainee's, the patient's, and his or her own.

It is necessary, also, to remember that the trainee is almost certainly still very much under the influence of his or her own analyst's style, personality, model of the psyche and technique. The trainee's analysis must, obviously, be respected, and boundaries carefully maintained by the supervisor.

There can initially be friction with a trainee over the subject of asking the patient questions. In my personal analytic technique there is very little room for the analyst asking questions of the patient. I think questions are directive and not therapeutic. For example, I think it is more analytical to comment on the fact that the patient seems to be holding something back, or to say there is some difficulty in the way. This therapeutic comment draws the patient's attention to a block, or a defense, or a serious resistance, much more effectively than raising a question would do. This observational style of intervention focuses more on the interaction between the two people, while asking a question focuses more on content. But, I think it is also in order, and good quality supervision, to ask the trainee to explain why he or she made a certain intervention which did not work. The supervisor may probe to discover other factors which would have been more helpful to point out to the patient. This approach leads, usually, to a colleague-type discussion. Also, within supervision I may suggest papers the trainee might benefit from studying. The readings suggested do not necessarily conform closely to my personal views.

In Summary

Under the heading Style in Supervision, I think the key words are *enabling and facilitating*. As supervisors we need to remain in contact with our analytic identity as well as our unique individuality.

Enabling the trainee to become an analyst includes a certain amount of empowering, strengthening and getting the trainee to improve his or her individual analytic abilities.

Facilitating includes helping the trainee to find the work gradually a bit easier through the decrease in anxiety which comes with improved understanding of the art, the craft and the method of analysis. Those developments happen only gradually, and not automatically as a result of a set, or required, number of supervisory sessions.

[9]

Sustaining the Potential Analyst's Morale

John Beebe

Introduction

It is a commonplace of supervision that it should not be allowed
to become therapy, just as an individual analysis ought not to become
contaminated with any other binding relationship between analyst
and analysand. Within an analytic institute, however, the fact that the
analysand is being trained to do the job of the analyst introduces a
collegial reality and the burdensome prospect of legacy into the
analytic transference, and it is often left to the control analyst, the
analyst directly supervising the candidate's analytic work, to deal
with the implications of this problem. This inevitably involves the
control analyst hearing something about the candidate's personal
analysis. Often the control analyst, like other "second analysts," is in
the position of working through with the candidate the inevitable
disappointments of analysis, which become relevant to the task of
supervision since they are all the more potentially disillusioning to
someone poised to undertake a career in the very line of work that
has produced such disappointing results. The following notes outline
the psychological role of the training or control analyst who must
sort out this loaded transference situation.

Notes

1. a) The candidate in an analytic institute is in a state of induced
narcissistic vulnerability throughout the training period. This vulnerability is in fact a narcissistic transference to the whole discipline of

psychoanalysis, as well as to a particular training institution, its
members and candidates.

b) The control analyst enters the emotional field of this induced
transference as someone the candidate feels can take responsibility
for that transference, i.e. can accept and shape it into something that
helps and furthers the basic analytic selfhood of the candidate. In
Kohut's terms, the control analyst is a selfobject for the candidate,
one who can mirror, be idealized, and function as an alter ego while
the candidate goes through the process of shaping an analytic self.

2. a) The *telos* of this state of affairs, the purposiveness a Jungian
likes to find in any unconscious symptom, including a transference,
is that it gives the analytic institute, through the person of the control
analyst, a chance to demonstrate that analysis works.

b) Student analysts are often people who have lost their faith in
analysis or at least whose faith in the analytic process is at risk. This
demoralization is at bottom founded on their dawning recognition of
their own lack of skill in creating and making use of a truly analytic
container for psychotherapeutic work, but it is often underscored by
experiences that seem to belong to the expectable fate of anyone who
elects to become, not merely an analytic patient, but a future analyst.
Such experiences are those of unusually severe wounding in the
course of one or more analyses – often on the model of the first,
traumatic analyses of the founders of our field. One can expect that a
student analyst's analysis, like a shaman's initiation into healing
through disorienting illness, will have been characterized by particularly severe complications by the time the student enters the control
stage and begins to be taught directly how to be an analyst.

c) If at this point the control analyst can demonstrate to the student
that the analytic process helps in working through necessary wounds
to the naive *idealization of analysis*, and to the self-esteem of the
person engaged in pursuing analytic vocation, the student analyst
experiences a revitalization of morale.

d) This revitalization can only occur when the basic needs of the
embattled analytic self are met and when the control analyst is
experienced as a supportive self-object. But if the control analyst
demonstrates an understanding of what it means to be the candidate's
self-object, the candidate in gratitude will be willing to listen to the
objective information the control analyst has to impart.

e) The training proper can now occur, as the student is confronted with the deficiencies in the still immature analytic identity that has been presented to the control analyst. The immaturity of this identity is not hard to recognize; it usually shows up as specific deficiencies in the central analytic skills. Here, the control analyst's objectivity and honesty in pointing out these deficiencies are essential. The usual areas of difficulty are a lack of attention to the patient's need for containment; an inadequate grasp of the importance of interpretation (accompanied, often, by technical limitations in either the timing or the content of interpretations, or both); and an incapacity to get past a concrete interventive style of "doctoring" to the symbolic, holding attitude with which an analysis must be conducted.

3. a) The willingness of the student analyst to really metabolize, in Winnicott's sense, what the control analyst has to offer by way of corrective feedback is a function of the degree to which the student analyst feels his or her self-experience to be meaningfully contained and interpreted. The experience of having one's suffering metabolized even after the naive expectations of analysis have been severely disappointed is an extraordinary one, and it is how the student analyst comes to believe in the analytic process as a permanently available healing reality.

b) The candidate may at this point be more able to talk directly about past disappointments in personal analysis and supervision, as well as past mistakes that have contributed to the demoralization of the young analytic identity. Or, resistances to the analytic model may be acted out in such an unmistakable way that they can easily be identified as material for further work. Even if these resistances seem daunting in their degree, it is relatively easy to work them through within the supervision if the control analyst has won the candidate's trust. The presentation of such resistances should be recognized as tests of the control analyst's ability to work analytically with such material, rather than dismissing it with moralistic or doctrinal condemnation.

c) As the resistances to becoming an analyst are worked through, it becomes apparent to both candidate and control analyst that the central training modality has been the control analyst's capacity to assimilate the candidate's suffering in an analytic way and thereby to

102   *John Beebe*

sustain belief in the student analyst's capacity to survive in the analytic field.

Comment

Behind the viewpoint that is outlined in this chapter is a conception of the analyst's training period as difficult. But what might be the purposiveness of the passion that the student analyst suffers? It is not enough to assert that a bad experience in personal analysis gives the control analyst a chance to demonstrate directly to the student analyst that analysis can work. For even the control analyst may fail the student, and yet the latter can still succeed in becoming analyst. There is a bit more to the pain that propels analytic training than I state here.

It is my conviction that a student analyst's experiences of wounding at the hands of his or her personal analysts are not just unfortunate events but necessary traumas. Such woundings belong to the journey of becoming an analyst. Their purpose is to initiate the student into a more or less permanent sense of vulnerability in relation to the analytic process. The analyst's vulnerability has to be greater even than the vulnerability any other patient has to learn to accept. It is a good thing for an analyst to learn early that every patient suffers from the analytic process, but the vulnerability that the analyst must learn to accept goes beyond the humility that every physician must find toward the mystery of wounding and healing. The analyst's specific discovery, beyond her or his initiation as patient and physician, is of a certain helplessness in the face of the unconscious.

Only a period of helplessness at the hands of the unconscious can promote openness to the unconscious's own solutions that is the analyst's stock in trade. Such radical openness is never achieved through a graded series of gentle shocks. Rather, it is almost always the effect of at least one sudden, unexpected wounding, what James Hillman has called "betrayal." And, as Hillman points out in that justly celebrated essay,[1] development of the radical receptivity that he calls "anima development" and that I am calling "openness to the unconscious" is not the only possible outcome to the reality of betrayal. Just as frequent as the emergence of faith in the unconscious is the development of cynicism, a closing down on the part of the student analyst. The control analyst's job is to see that openness to the unconscious, and not cynicism, is the outcome of the student analyst's shock at being wounded by analysis itself. But the control analyst must work within the unwritten law of analytic training that suffering uncontained unconscious material is the precondition to the later motivation to learn how to contain and metabolize such material. An analytic identity consolidated by a student analyst in his or her apprentice phase, if I am correct, begins with a posttraumatic reaction to a bad analytic experience. This is what Freud learned from Fliess, and what Jung learned from Freud, and that all of us have been learning ever since from our own wounding healers.

What exactly is the wounding that a future analyst may be expected to endure? Analysis is a species of healing, and the more we learn about the archetype of healing, the more it becomes clear that some variant of the trickster archetype is involved. Jungians who accept the analogy of alchemy to analysis, understand this through the figure of Mercurius, the wily god who presides over the alchemical work. Those who need to find an affective experience to flesh out their understanding of this archetypal image need only reflect on their own training experiences. These experiences will reveal with specific force the general rule that to enter a healing identity is to be placed in a double bind, and double binds are the hallmark of the trickster archetype.[2]

Let us rehearse the double bind that obtains in the student analyst's personal analysis. A double bind, according to communication experts[3] involves two or more persons, repeated experience, and then (1) a primary negative injunction, (2) a secondary injunction conflicting with the first at a more abstract level, and like the first enforced by punishments or signals which threaten survival, and (3) a tertiary negative injunction prohibiting the victim from escaping the field. There is also the reality that all these ingredients are no longer needed when the victim has learned to perceive his universe in double bind patterns, for then any part of a double-blind sequence is sufficient to precipitate panic or rage (Bateson, 1968). If I am a student analyst learning to assume responsibility for my psyche in a personal analysis, knowing one day I will be an analyst, there will be (1), the primary negative injunction: I must let no harm befall my psyche, as it will one day be an instrument of healing. There will also be (2), a second injunction conflicting with the first at a more abstract level: I must not fail to let the failures of my analyst have their way with me, because these very woundings, through the transference neurosis they provoke, are my process of self discovery and the way to know the complexes my own analysands will elicit in me and that they will have to endure in the countertransference. And there will be (3), a firm injunction against leaving this contradictory emotional "field": I cannot abandon analysis without subverting my goal of being an analyst. It should go without saying that this bind operates at the very least in the two-person relationship of me and my analyst and I will experience the bind over a period of time. Given the induced narcissistic vulnerability of the person undergoing training, it doesn't take much, once the bind pattern has been perceived, to provoke panic or rage in the student "victim" of this ongoing situation.

The control analyst has an opportunity to reverse the terms of this double bind in such a way as to release the student from the most destructive aspects of its grip. The control analyst is in a position to affirm (1) that it is okay for the psyche of the student analyst to have been wounded, (2) that an analytic experience can be one of healing, rather than merely wounding, the self into recognition of its complexes, and (3) that a bad analytic experience can indeed be abandoned and mourned. The control analyst can demonstrate that analytic woundings may be metabolized. But any true healing must proceed on the basis of a tragic sense of the reality that the student's training has put him in an impossible position. Perhaps the most crucial function the control analyst can perform is to welcome the fellow casualty of the impossible training, recognizing a colleague who will one day understand that there really is no other way to become an analyst.

References

1. James Hillman (1965). "Betrayal." *Spring 1965.*
2. John Beebe (1981). "The Trickster in the Arts," *The San Francisco Jung Institute Library Journal*, Winter, 1981.
3. Gregory Bateson, Don. D. Jackson, Jay Haley, and John H. Weakland. "Toward a Theory of Schizophrenia," in Don D. Jackson, ed. *Communication, Family and Marriage* (Human Communication Vol. 1) Palo Alto, California, Science and Behavior Books, 1968, pp. 31-54.

Part III

The Case Colloquium

[10]

Ecstasies and Agonies of Case Seminar Supervision

Donald Kalsched

Autobiographical Remarks

Case seminar supervision has been a regular part of my professional life for almost 25 years, the first third of that time as a supervisee, the latter two thirds as a supervisor. In 1968, with no outpatient psychotherapy experience whatsoever, (but a lot of therapeutic enthusiasm) I saw my first patient at a small private clinic in Manhattan. I still remember that case – a young woman my own age with psychological difficulties very similar to those that had brought me into analysis a few years earlier. Even more than my psychotherapeutic work with this woman, I remember the anxiety I felt presenting her material for supervision in case seminar. I vividly recall how difficult it was to adequately describe this patient and my experience with her, in language that communicated to my colleagues what I thought was really going on. I recall how vulnerable I felt in this situation, and how frustrating it was to have people in the seminar interpret the patient's material prematurely, reducing it to abstract formulas which violated the complexity and nuance of her life. (I also recall how much fun it was to offer these interpretations when someone else was presenting!) And so I learned something about how, in the clinical situation, *a too rapid need for meaning can serve as a defense against meaning's emergence.* One of the things that always startled me was the "feeding frenzy" of interpretations that would occur when dream or fantasy material was presented, and how wise we all were with someone else's unconscious material. I remember my fear of the groups' disapproval or of negative judgment by the leader and the general anxieties of not knowing, of getting it wrong and possibly (I thought) thereby doing the patient harm.

Fortunately, the leader of that first group experience was herself both a skilled clinician and a skilled group leader. So despite my anxieties and insecurities, group supervision of that first patient and others that followed, was a rich learning experience. Looking back, there were several important elements in this learning that I'd like to try and articulate.

First, I learned about theory by witnessing how each colleague in the seminar had a way of formulating his or her work with patients – a linguistic idiom in which this work was described and which provided a framework of meaning for that particular colleague. These individual "theories" were not coherent systems, but represented the "personal equation" of the therapist – a way of formulating what was seen, a lens through which otherwise chaotic information came into focus for him or her. Some of my early colleagues' theories seemed to encompass the patient's experience better than others – or so I thought – and this led to a nascent understanding of theories as heuristic devices, not objective truths. Someone once said very wisely that we should rent our theories, not buy them.

Secondly, I learned about TRANSFERENCE by witnessing my colleagues' struggles, seeing where they were stuck with a case – not by being told in my own presentations where I was stuck. Usually unable to see my own blind-spots I could nonetheless see those of my colleagues and could IDENTIFY with their struggles. This gave me a face-saving way of *learning by observing someone else in a learning situation*. Gradually as the seminar became safer, and, by realizing that we were all in this group situation together, I could risk a certain amount of disillusionment with myself, which is what countertransference work is all about. But for this to happen, an unusually "safe" environment must be created by the leader and this is not always the case in training situations.

Finally I learned about SUPERVISION, i.e., what worked and what didn't – what could be "heard" vs. what could only be "listened to" by a presenting therapist. Case seminar is unique in this respect. *It is the only place in our training where candidates are invited to comment on their colleague's work.* The way this unfolds, the atmosphere of the group, and the way the colleague is able to accept or reject these comments, is part of learning how to supervise. Certainly candidates "learn" supervision by watching and internalizing their individual supervisors. But it is only in case seminar supervision that they actually get to practice on their colleagues and get feedback on the effect of their efforts. It is very rewarding for example, when a case-seminar participant realizes that through his/her sincere participation, a colleague's work with a patient was deepened.

So case seminar has always been my favorite place to learn the art and science of psychotherapy. Since those early experiences, my commitment to this form of learning has grown and now it is also my favorite way of "teaching" psychotherapy. Of all the clinical practice, teaching, and administrative work that I do, case seminar is still the favorite part of my week's activities. However, having thus sung its praises as a learning situation, I would like to also emphasize that case seminar supervision is simultaneously one of the most dangerous, potentially destructive, learning environments in our training. Some of these dangers will be the focus of my remarks in what follows later.

Optimal Psychological Atmosphere of the Case Seminar

Before I outline some of the darker aspects of case seminar, let me say that whether this particular form of learning is an ecstasy or an agony depends on whether the seminar is working AS A GROUP or not. Like any group, case seminar involves both task and maintenance functions but it is primarily a *work group, not a process group*. The group reflects on its own process (and the internal process of its members) when things are stuck or the task is impeded or sometimes when "parallel process" issues are being considered. This happens often enough and the leader must facilitate these moments with sensitivity. However, I am not one who believes the small supervision group is a substitute for group therapy, or confession, or individual analysis.

The primary task of case seminar is clear – namely, to understand what is going on with the presenting therapist's patient. A secondary task which serves the primary task, is to understand as much as possible of what is going on between that patient and his/her therapist. These ostensibly simple tasks prove to be very difficult, because the presented patient is a mystery to him/herself and also a mystery to the therapist presenting him/her. To complicate matters, the presenting therapist is also – more or less – a mystery to *him/herself.* When these two enigmas meet in the transitional space of "relationship" we have a third "unknown" to be explored, and these combined "mysteries" mean that much of the discourse in case seminar is *fantasy.* This fact is too often forgotten in supervision, even though we call ourselves "depth psychologists" and believe in the unconscious. A conviction about the importance of the unconscious carries implications for the way we train. Optimally there ought to be room for the unconscious of the trainees involved in the process of learning depth psychology. This means an atmosphere relatively free of judgment and evaluation – *a safe enough* atmosphere – to borrow an idea from Winnicott who reassured us that all the developing child needs to grow psychologically is a *good enough* mother. Naturally if there is no "room" provided for the unconscious in training, it will come in anyway, for example as splitting and acting out.

To facilitate a safe enough atmosphere I encourage a spirit of inquiry in the case seminar. Inquiry into what? Inquiry into the unconscious communication of the patient and his therapist. Honoring this level of the unconscious means there are no right or wrong interpretations of the patient's material and the presenting therapist's interventions. Of course, there are exceptions to this, as in the case of gross malpractice. The patient communicates to his therapist in words that have *known* meaning, but also in coded words with unknown meaning, gesture, acting out behavior, dreams, transference and the so-called "induced" countertransference.

The case seminar leader must encourage an atmosphere of open exploration, hunch and intuition, play and hypothetical speculation. If this is done well, *the group has a better chance of understanding the patient's unconscious communication, than any individual in it, including the supervisor.* The many facets of the group-members' perceptions and contributions are far more likely to pick up and formulate dissociated material in the patient and in the presenting therapist than any one participant. Moreover, with the group functioning in this way, *group-participants have an experience of a psychological culture instead of a political one.* Power dynamics are minimized and the democracy of the psyche is actualized as a lived experience. The picture that emerges of the presented patient/therapist dyad being discussed by the group, is a deep picture, enriched by the pooled experience of many voices. A wholeness greater than the sum of the parts is actualized resulting in a vivid experience of what Jung meant by the Self. At the end of such a group there is almost always consensus about a network of connections in the patient's material. This does not resolve the mystery of the patient's unconscious communication, but rather gives it deeper meaning and dimension. A group training-experience like this can be truly inspirational, leaving training candidates more open to the mystery of their own work and their own unconscious.

The Dark Side of Case Seminar: Dysfunctional Groups

Now for the agonies of case seminar. We all know that groups are breeding grounds for unconscious processes, including projection, splitting, acting out, to say nothing of dysfunctional family dynamics such as sibling rivalry, envy, scapegoating triangulated collusive alliances, codependency etc. W.R. Bion has gone so far as to suggest that every group is really two groups. The first is a work group, and the second, a basic assumption group (the Ba-group), characterized by primitive unconscious fantasy dynamics, high levels of anxiety, and paranoid/schizoid splitting defenses. Jung's suspicions about groups was directed to this second aspect. He thought the threshold of ego-consciousness was inevitably lowered in any collective (group) situation; individuality therefore compromised, and the stage set for the primitive mentality of "the crowd." Whether we agree with these "inevitable" conclusions or not (and I do not), there are nevertheless many factors in our training programs that contribute to regressive behavior in candidates. And case seminar is often a place where these "complexes" show up.[1] I would like to illustrate some of these training dynamics and their corresponding group complexes by means of a diagram.

This diagram is an adaptation of a model of clinical supervision presented by Jean Carr at a public conference on supervision organized by the Jungian training Committee of the British Association of Psychotherapists in 1988 and reprinted in chapter twenty-five of this book.[2]

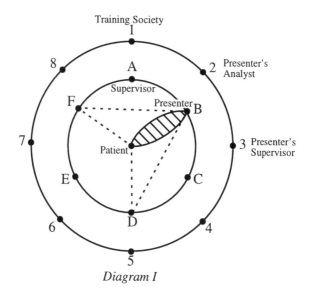

Diagram I

The Inner Circle in the diagram represents the case seminar itself and letters ABCDEF designate individual seminar participants, including in this case, the supervisor or group leader (A) and the "presenter" for the week (B) etc. A group of five candidates and one supervisor is chosen because each candidate has an opportunity to present every five weeks as the wheel turns one at a time. Notice that the patient is represented as present – if only imaginally – and is placed at the center of the circle to emphasize that the central concern of the group is to understand what is going on with the patient. I always ask each therapist to present the same patient to the seminar at least three or four times. In this way, over the course of a year's work, the participants get to know this particular patient/therapist dyad in more depth and have a chance to see how their colleague and his or her patient is taking in the supervisory input.

The elliptical "field" in our diagram between presenting therapist and patient is the main axis of relationship along which the group members' attention oscillates during the presentation of the patient – if the group is working well. The focus within this field for any one participant usually oscillates back and forth between the patient's material and the presenting therapist's experience, including countertransference reactions This shifting focus is represented by the dotted triangles for participants "F" and "D."

The Outer Circle (1-8) represents the individual analysts making up the training society within which the case seminar functions – the professional analytic "culture" if you will, within which the "family" of the small supervisory group lives. This includes all the analysts and supervisors involved in the presenting therapist's personal analysis, evaluation and review. These individuals (numbered 1-8) are also represented as "present," albeit indirectly, in the background of the group's interaction but affecting the group members in palpable ways. Prominent influences in this powerful group are the presenter's analyst ("2") and the presenter's private or control supervisor ("3").

Here is often where group complexes get constellated. Diagrammatically these complexes are represented as competing triangles which intrude from the outer circle, intersect and confound the main work of the group which is to understand the patient (as in diagrams 2 and 3 below). There are many of these triangles and they are present all the time under the surface. They need not be disruptive. I will give a couple of examples where they become very disruptive.

Example One

Here, the presenting therapist is in trouble with the training organization (represented as "1" in diagram II) and is having his/her candidacy questioned. Suppose, also that the case seminar leader is not so sure this is a fair judgment against the candidate on the part of the evaluation committee. Then we have a competing triangle formed in our diagram between the training society (#1 outer circle), the presenting therapist ("B") and the supervisor ("A") in diagram II below.

The stage is set for the supervisee to present his/her case only to the supervisor-not to his/her colleagues in the group – in hopes of establishing a collusive alliance. This puts the supervisor under stress. If the supervisor has his/her own conflicts with the training society, they will be exacerbated in this new situation and the result will be his/her inability to listen openly to the case being presented and to focus his/her attention on the elliptical field between the

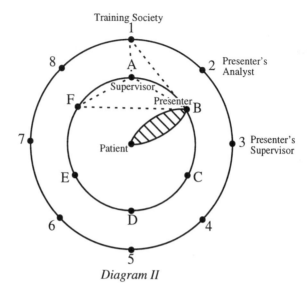

Diagram II

presenter and his/her patient Also the other participants in the seminar are consciously or unconsciously aware of these dynamics. They
resent or envy their apple-polishing sibling for currying favor with
the group "parent." Their otherwise conflict-free attention is drawn
away from the patient-therapist axis into an intense Oedipal rivalry
between the presenting trainee and the supervisor (triangle FAB). In
this situation the patient, while ostensibly at the center of the group s
task, is made incidental to the competing triangular alliances. Dysfunctional groups are breeding grounds for this kind of triangulation.

One of the worst situations I encountered in this regard occurred
in a training institute full of paranoid/schizoid dynamics attributable
to the fact that several advanced candidates had recently been
"washed out" of the program after failed evaluations. The case was
that of a marginal candidate who had eked through the training
requirements into an advanced seminar with otherwise "secure" and
generally "competent" trainees. The situation was like having an
adopted orphan in the family. Because of the paranoid atmosphere in
the training program, no-one could talk about it. Group behavior was
characterized by splitting and projective identification. Candidates
exchanged "knowing glances" when this trainee presented material.
They talked to their analysts about the ugly duckling in their nest of

swans, colluded against the rejected candidate socially, and by year's end, despite a relatively positive evaluation, the candidate in question had also been asked to leave the training program. The seminar was completely dysfunctional. The inner group was not free to function as a working group.

Of course there is a great deal more that could be said about this individual situation. It is an extreme case of the "toxic" dynamics that occur in training programs where success is keyed to arbitrary evaluations by a powerful few. From experiences like this I have concluded that training organizations should admit only candidates in whom they have a reasonably high degree of confidence and then endeavor to provide a "good enough" environment for those candidates' growth and development. We cannot eliminate evaluation from training, but we can minimize its destructive impact through careful selection.

Example Two

The second competing triangular relationship I'd like to look at is the potentially adversarial role of the personal analyst or individual supervisor of a candidate vis-a-vis the work of case seminar. Let us consider a situation where the presenter has described his/her case and the consensus of the seminar is that the supervisee is somehow over-identified with the patient's victimized and is therefore not sufficiently confronting. This impression is conveyed in various supportive ways by different individuals in the group. The presenting therapist listens to the feedback politely, perhaps even expresses gratitude for the seminars feedback. However, the next week the candidate returns with the announcement that he/she reviewed the group's criticisms with his/her personal analyst and individual supervisor both of whom affirmed that he/she was on the right track with the patient. Here we have a triangle in diagram 3 between the presenting therapist as a member of the inner circle, and points "2" and "3" on the outer ring (see diagram III below).

When this happened, it led to a great deal of irritation among group members who viewed the presenting therapist as setting up a collusive alliance outside the group to deny the validity of their perceptions. As supervisor, I also was triangulated, wondering if the

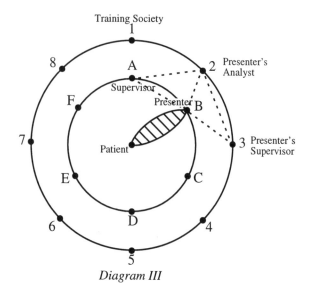

Diagram III

ostensible disagreement of analyst and supervisor was directed at me as head of the group (A-2-3). Other seminar members were triangulated between their anger at the presenting therapist and their need to have their leader deal with this dysfunctional situation (A-B-E & A-B-C etc.). Under these conditions, it was my job as supervisor to process the group irritation, helping the presenting candidate at the same time to reveal the source of his/her anxiety in the perceived criticism of the previous seminar. This led to a review of the prior week's group process where the seeds of the current dysfunction had been planted. Eventually, group members were able to admit how antagonistic they had felt the prior week and how hostile their criticism had in fact been. This opened a field for the acting-out candidate to admit how vulnerable he/she felt when presenting work to colleagues in group supervision. Once the source of anxiety could be discussed, the acting out behavior could be acknowledged and the group's attention refocused on the task at hand.

Danger of the Supervisor's Inflation

There is one final factor among those destructive to case seminar's effectiveness which I would like to mention and this seems to represent a shadow-side of supervision itself. Ed Levenson of the White Institute in New York discusses this as the temptation to infallibility in supervision.[3] I have found this an especially destructive dynamic in group supervision. Levenson acknowledges that he spends most of his time as an analyst in a total fog, searching for an understanding of his patient's material, usually confused, lost and at sea. But whenever a training candidate brings in a clinical problem with one of his/her cases, it takes him only about 20 minutes to be absolutely clear what is wrong. This is, says Levenson, because supervision is conducted on an entirely different level of abstraction than psychotherapy. In supervision we are never really discussing a specific patient, but a general category of patients for whom this patient is an example. Our apparent clarity is a consequence of this step up in level of abstraction level.

As Jungian analysts, I think we are especially vulnerable to this because we love abstraction. We frequently think in terms of types – even *arche*-types. I think this inclines us sometimes to move away from the particularities of the data to the "common elements of the class." It is easy for subjective prejudices and projections to slip in here, especially if people are under pressure to sound intelligent or get it "right." Pretty soon the central mystery at the core of the group's task (understanding the patient) has slipped away and "formulas" fill the vacuum. Unless a psychological attitude is cultivated by the case seminar leader, the presenting therapist can very easily feel overwhelmed by a "Roshomon" of multiple projections onto his/ her patient and his/her work. The presenting candidate may feel that the patient is being violated by the group and lost to him/her in a barrage of questions, comments and projections by colleagues. It is *one of the main jobs of the group leader to quiet the "feeding frenzy" of interpretations that flood into the seminar's space of unknowing.* This space must be kept open as long as possible so that the mystery at the core of the patient/therapist dyad that is trying to communicate itself can unfold in its own idiom. It is this central mystery – the mystery of unconscious communication – that the case seminar serves.

Louis Zinkin makes essentially the same point from a Jungian angle and I will close these remarks with his important observation. Supervision, he says, is really a shared fantasy of what is actually going on – it is the result of a "trainee trying to imagine what he and his patient have been doing together and the supervisor (plus case seminar participants) trying to imagine it too." Supervision works best, he says, "if all parties remain aware that what they are jointly imagining is not true."[4]

Notes

1. Otto Kernberg has drawn attention to the idealizing and paranoid/persecutory atmosphere in many of our training programs and sees this as resulting from the fact that small group seminars exist in training organizations that are "structurally out of tune with their own aims." See Kernberg, Otto, "Institutional Problems of Psychoanalytic Education," *Journal of American Psychoanalytic Association*, Dec. 1986, pp. 799-834.
2. Carr, Jean. "A Model of Clinical Supervision" in *Clinical Supervision: Issue and Techniques*. Special printing by J.C. Press, London, 1988.
3. Levenson, Edgar A. "Follow the Fox: An Inquiry into the Vicissitudes of Psychoanalytic Supervision," in *Clinical Perspectives on the Supervision of Psychoanalysis and Psychotherapy*, Edited by Caligor, Brombert, Meltzer, Plenum Press, New York, 1984, p. 153 ff.
4. Zinkin, Louis, "Supervision: The Impossible Profession," in *Clinical Supervision: Issues and Techniques*, Special printing by J.C. Press, London, 1988, and reprinted in a modified form as chapter 17 of this book.

[11]

On Supervision in Jungian Continuous Case Seminars

Crittenden E. Brookes

The continuous case seminar, conference or colloquium is central to a thorough Jungian analytic training. Detailed reference to clinical process – the sequential events which transpire in the consulting room – was minimal or missing in Jung's writing. The focus of Jung's interest was in elucidating internal psychic events and experiences, but in doing so he left us with many gaps in our understanding of the application of Jungian concepts to the process of therapy and how it works. The continuous case seminar, together with one-on-one supervision of analytic work by trainees, functions to fill these gaps by deepening the training of new analysts, as they grow into and better understand analytic process.

An advantage can be gained from beginning such seminar experience as early as possible in the training process. Theoretical seminars and presentations, dealing with abstract and highly subjective phenomena of the psyche, are best complemented by ongoing attention to clinical material. It is only when therapeutic process is melded with theoretical constructs that the meaning and applicability of Jung's ideas, as well as other systems of the psyche, can be fully appreciated.

The clinical case conference fulfills a unique function in melding analytic process with theoretical construct. It provides an opportunity for the collective consciousness (i.e. the shared experience and evolving values) of professional colleagues to be applied to at least three aspects of individual clinical material: (1) the client's conscious and unconscious productions, (2) the therapist's conscious as well as countertransference-based interventions, and (3) the relational dynamics of the two parties. While undertaking this application, the case conference necessarily elaborates the dynamic of the conscious collective, a concept which remained undeveloped in Jung's writings.

It is important that cases be followed longitudinally for extended periods of time, to elucidate the various phases of the analytic process. But perhaps even more importantly, following individual cases over time enables candidates to put the dynamics of the psyche into the context of the life-span of an individual. These dynamics have a profound and far-reaching impact when assimilated into individual consciousness. When case material is followed over significant portions of the patient's life, members of the colloquium can begin to get a sense of the transformations of identity which occur in long-term analysis. On the other hand, it is important to remember that analysis is a highly subjective and personal phenomenon, and that no "objectification" of such a process, whether in case colloquia, written clinical case reports or elsewhere, can truly capture the experience. To honor this fact, case seminars should be open to as much subjectivity as possible.

The presence of highly subjective material puts a great deal of responsibility on the seminar leader. In any group process, the leader sets the tone or provides the container for the quality of the group experience. The case seminar leader must personify the very principles which are hopefully being elucidated. It is especially important for the leader to embody the "symbolic attitude," which allows for an unfolding of psychological awareness within the group. Such an open-ended atmosphere, when applied both to the discussion of clinical material and to the more subtle aspects of group process, produces a special quality of experience which is in marked contrast to the more traditional didactic seminars. In those settings, there is often an implied assumption that there are "correct answers" for everything. It may be further implied that such "correct answers" are already known to the seminar leader. This creates a situation in which seminar members are obliged to compete with each other in a contest to see who is most "correct." This can produce an underlying atmosphere of conflict and contention which is not conducive to good learning, and which obviates the very principles and dynamics which the seminar is supposed to teach.

Having argued for subjectivity and open-endedness and having issued a caution against objectivity, I will now proceed (in good paradoxical Jungian fashion) to permit myself a measure of the objectivity against which I have cautioned. Consequently it should be remembered that from a Jungian viewpoint, any statement about "the way things should be," including the statements to follow, should be seen as open-ended and open to revision under particular circumstances.

There are many definitions of "analysis" or of "analytic process." My own bias is that definitions based upon therapeutic format, technique, or even theoretical constructs are inappropriate and mis-leading. "Analysis" is a particular form of a more generic "psycho-therapy." From this perspective, analytic work is being done in a psychotherapy to the degree unconscious material is identified, elab-orated in consciousness, and translated into meaningful applications to the analysand's life-experience and behavior. An "analysis," con-sequently, is a relative matter, and both analytic work and more "mundane" process manifest themselves in varying degrees during the course of a particular psychotherapy.

Psychotherapy of a specific individual emerges from a willing-ness of both therapist and client to work initially within the context and framework of the present life-experience of the client – that is, within the pattern of values, attitudes, methods of problem solving and other mental operations which mark the client's consciousness at the outset of therapy. Such unique and idiosyncratic characteristics of the client's mental function may or may not include a recognition of those psychological phenomena which are a part of the awareness which the therapist brings to the consulting room. For example, the client may initially shy away from numinous experiences, although the therapist is aware of their potential significance and meaning. In this example, part of the early work of psychotherapy may be to find ways to help the client become comfortable with such experiences, so that they can be identified in consciousness rather than avoided, and tolerated with curiosity and with the intent to understand. Once identification, tolerance and curiosity of (in this example) the numi-nous quality of experience is obtained, the client may be on the verge of doing analytic work.

Most people come to a therapist because they are experiencing some form of pain and discomfort, and many of them need to be *taught* to confront the numinous and archetypal layers of their own psychological experience before they can begin to do the kind of analytic work which will both alleviate their symptoms and expand their awareness of self and others. In the continuous case seminar, it is possible for the members of the seminar to help each other correct the tendency to put theory before process when considering the unfolding of a particular case. Whether they do so or not will at least partly depend on the degree of receptivity to process manifested by the seminar leader.

Additionally, the *expectation* that analytic work is to be done sometimes makes the actual occurrence of such work less likely. This is why the psychotherapy of institute candidates is often the most difficult to translate into analytic process. Analysis occurs most fully when its process arises from the psychic demands of the individual who suffers and has come for help, rather than coming for "analysis" as a means to obtain analytic certification. At the least, such expectations can produce a resistance to analytic work. Institute candidates who have been selected as individuals who have first come to therapy out of personal need, and who have only secondarily discovered the possibility and significance of institute training, hopefully may be less likely to manifest such resistance.

The resistance of "expectation" can also easily arise during case colloquia in training institutions. If the expectation in the seminar is that archetypal material will be elucidated during the presentation, the complex psychological process by which such material actually arises and is integrated during psychotherapy may be missed. In my opinion, symptoms and psychological suffering are roadsigns pointing to the archetypal underpinnings of the complaints and conflicts presented by the patient or analysand. A properly conducted continuous case seminar elucidates the processes by which unconscious material manifests itself out of symptomatology. It also illustrates how the expectations of seminar members might interfere with the elucidation of such material. Group interaction has a great potential for bringing a number of different viewpoints and reactions to bear on the material presented. This potential can best be realized when a non-hierarchical, non-judgmental, open-ended and mutually supportive "culture" has been created in the seminar room.

What I have said does not imply that the seminar leader in the least abdicates his or her role as leader. Such a role is archetypally determined. Therefore, authoritarian behavior on the part of the leader, or correspondingly passive behavior on the part of seminar members, is not needed to either establish or maintain the leader's role. It will maintain itself, by virtue of the structure of the group-with-leader. In point of fact, a non-judgmental attitude on the leader's part will likely strengthen the intensity of whatever idealizing transferences will be engendered toward the leader in the group, as it will also engender whatever negative-competitive transferences already exist *in potentia* within the group membership as the group organizes itself for seminar work. The leader's job is to recognize such transferential material as it arises, and interpret it in non-judgmental fashion. Such interpretation should be directed only toward the manifestation of such material within the group process itself, and should not be expanded to include the lives of group members outside the group process. Psychological material involving group members must always be secondary to the purposes for which the group is meeting. The focus of the group is the elucidation of clinical material, and is not to be broadened to an analysis or therapy of the members themselves. Such a broadening would diffuse group focus, and in some cases could destroy the group as a viable tool for training.

However, since the seminar itself is a dynamic psychological situation, it should be both experienced and dealt with as such. In my own opinion, the movement toward wholeness which can occur in both analysis and psychotherapy, the healing which is the only excuse for analytic work in the first place, occurs and arises out of the framework of relationship between the principal parties. This point, I believe, holds also for case seminars: if the relational dynamic is not both recognized and honored, the essence of what happens in analysis itself will not be learned.

To reiterate, psychological dynamics of the group itself must certainly be recognized in order to facilitate learning within the group setting. But the recognition, interpretation and therapeutic manipulation of such processes must always be secondary to the educational goals of the group. An open and non-judgmental attitude on the part of the group leader is essential to facilitate these goals. In addition, it is usually helpful to refer any necessary interventions in regard to group process back to the group as a whole. The collective learning experience is the group's purpose for existence, and such experience can be diluted or destroyed by personalizing such interventions to individual group members.

A few especially important aspects of the continuous case seminar situation can now be amplified in greater detail:

The case colloquium allows an unusual opportunity for an ongoing examination and elucidation of the relationship between the "inner" and "outer" aspects of psychic reality. Symbolic and literal reality then become two aspects of one unitary reality. This avoids the traditional "Jungian bias" of overemphasis on the reality of the internally experienced psyche at the expense of the meaning and significance of external reality. At the same time it avoids the equally serious bias of overly-exclusive attention to the literal and behavioral aspects of the client's life, at the expense of the meaning and significance of the client's internal world.

Case seminars which utilize Jungian concepts have the potentiality to move from outer world to inner world, or conversely from inner world to outer world. One of the most meaningful seminars in which this author participated during his own training involved the exclusive utilization of sequential client dream material to reconstruct the client's external situation. Collective elaboration of dream and fantasy material is a much more powerful and comprehensive process than elaboration by one individual alone. Similarly, it should be possible (but probably more difficult) to move collectively from externally-derived data to speculation about the thematic content of dream and fantasy. The Jungian concept of compensation and balance in dream and fantasy process, together with many related concepts, comes alive with collective elaboration, a process which itself manifests and highlights many of the concepts being taught.

The case seminar leader needs to be familiar with aspects of group dynamics which are inevitably activated during the seminar experience. Transference and counter-transference phenomena which arise during group process can be handled in a positive and educative way by a leader who has some skill in the dynamics of groups, without pretending individual or group therapy in a situation which is not appropriate for therapeutic work. The point of reference should be the group itself in the present moment, rather than the individual histories and dynamics of group members. However, dynamic and interpersonal phenomena which arise in the group should be collectively recognized and acknowledged as an important part of the educative process. Typological factors may well need to be identified and taken into consideration when comparing and contrasting disparate reactions to the material being presented. Competition among group members, idealization of or negative feelings toward the leader, scapegoating, collective passivity and other difficult transferential material, may arise and should be made conscious by the leader (or ideally by members of the group) in a way that is helpful to the facilitation of good process. Positive and helpful dynamic factors, when acknowledged and underlined with appropriate timing, will help to reinforce a positive, learning-oriented and supportive group culture. Emphasis on the *mutuality* of dynamic factors in the group, as well as a focus on here-and-now as previously mentioned, will help to prevent the seminar from degrading into a pseudo-therapeutic experience. When such positive or negative phenomena are avoided or denied, the case seminar can easily become sterile, obstructive and unrewarding.

The overall value of the seminar will depend to a great degree on the skill and sensitivity of the leader in regard to making it safe for the group to acknowledge aspects of process which impinge on learning during seminar sessions. The leader must also set a tone which introduces habits of relating within the group which will in turn maintain a culture for learning.

In regard to the actual presentation of clinical material by the candidate, the rule of paradox holds again. A well-structured format is helpful for the elucidation of a broad range of material, but at the same time an allowance must be made for individual differences in recognizing and making use of psychological phenomena. Presenting symptoms, initial dreams and their interrelationship are of great importance, and their connection with historical events should be elaborated. The identification of archetypal material in either fantasy or behavior should be contrasted with the unique manifestation of such material as form and image in the life of the patient. In this way, the process of therapy can be brought to life as a dynamic involving the relationship between generalizable archetypal factors and their idiosyncratic constellation in personal life.

The Jungian viewpoint contributes a powerful idea which is not present in other dynamic formulations of the psyche except perhaps some of the existential schools of thought: the single individual (and the individual "neurosis" as well) is essentially undiagnosable and unrepeatable. The task of presenting and reinforcing this idea is the responsibility of every member of the seminar. Technical considerations such as the "analyzability" of the patient, the use of so-called "analytic technique" and so on, greatly increase the possibility that both the case material and the seminar members will be treated as objects, therefore subverting the entire process.

Summary

Jungian training can make particular use of the continuous case conference, colloquium or seminar, not only to acquaint trainees with the power of a collective examination of clinical material, but more specifically to compensate for the gaps left by Jung himself in picturing the relevant dynamics in the overall process of therapeutic analysis. Jung made no pretense of presenting the entire phenomenon of the therapeutic process. His interest was primarily focused on the events of the inner world. He left to others the task of filling out a more complete picture of the therapeutic process, including such topics as a careful description of the actual events which transpire during therapeutic analysis, as well as the detailed circumstances of the client's life. In addition, the literal or "real" as well as the transferential and countertransferential elements of therapy must be acknowledged as a part of the total picture of the therapeutic transaction.

The continuous case seminar brings together the dynamics of the inner and outer worlds. It can bring the power of collective consciousness to bear on the therapeutic transaction, and in so doing take functional advantage of the extraverted dimension of the psyche. It can bring theory and actual process together in a way in which each is revealed as a complementary aspect of the other, each contributing to a larger whole.

The group leader functions to encourage a process of melding disparate elements, as well as to embody the Jungian "symbolic attitude:" an open-ended position in regard to the outcome both of the case being presented, and of the in-the-moment consideration of case material by the seminar group. An honoring of the subjective approach to clinical material must complement objectivity as a vital aspect of the developing culture of the seminar group. Such an evolving culture includes a leader who embodies a non-judgmental attitude as well as a recognition of the relational dynamic within the group. This should be accomplished without replacing the educative focus of the group with an inappropriate and non-contracted therapy of individual group members, or for that matter of the group itself.

The power of collective elaboration of psychological material can be focused in the clinical case seminar on an examination of the relationship between inner and outer dimensions of the psyche. The group expectation that deeply analytic material will be forthcoming should not interfere with an understanding of the uniqueness and idiosyncratic nature of the client's psychological process. The analytic process appears not only in the "here and now" of the client's world, but also in the dynamics of the case seminar as the group "reexperiences" that world.

Finally, the continuous case seminar is a vital part of the training experience of Jungian candidates. Such a seminar can provide an important dimension within which candidates can learn and integrate a psychological attitude which is central to the "raison d'être" of a Jungian analyst. "Being with" a client in the consulting room is ultimately an exercise in synchronicity. Within such a synchronicity, both analyst and analysand experience a certain familiarity, not only with each other, but also with the material they are processing – as if it had been both separately and mutually experienced before, but now is being experienced again, in fuller awareness.

[12]

Some Thoughts on the Clinical Process

Joan Reggiori

This chapter will look at the practice of clinical supervision in a variety of settings. In trying to discern the essential factors in supervision across a variety of organizational situations, I shall touch on the differences between individual and group supervision; between supervision as part of in-service training and as part of a qualifying training; and on a few of the factors essential to a working alliance between supervisor and supervisee. This will not be an attempt to make us all better practitioners overnight, but to stimulate us into discussing further whatever aspects are relevant to our particular experiences.[1]

Individual and Group Supervision

First, there are two styles of supervision, namely individual and group supervision. Each can productively complement the other, but what they cannot do effectively is to replace one another. The intensity and depth of weekly individual supervision focusing on one particular case is reinforced by the intimacy and exclusivity of the ongoing one-to-one relationship between supervisor and supervisee. This reflects the earliest and most basic form of all human relationships. Aspects of what is happening between supervisor and patient can be reflected in this relationship and it is therefore a forum and a useful area for diagnostic exploration. However, the same exclusivity may also mean that an early prejudice continues unchecked without external observation and comment.

Group supervision, on the other hand, offers more extensive if less intensive experience. In this the supervisor or conductor may be quite active with a directive style of teaching, as may also happen in individual supervision, but at other times he or she will be more passively facilitating when the group members themselves are effectively overseeing or "supervising" the one who is presenting the case. This in itself can constitute another dimension to their training. In this situation a variety of thought and of attitude is brought to bear and to increase insight. Inevitably, however, there will not be enough time for weekly presentation and for the observed weekly following through of the case and its development as there is in weekly individual supervision.

Group dynamics, as in group therapy, will be activated. The presenter may feel that the patient he is talking about is being taken over by the group and lost to him when the image he had of this patient becomes distorted to an unrecognizable degree by the group discussion. His patient gradually becomes the recipient of projections when hitherto unconscious aspects of the case are exposed. This is a particularly sensitive area when the dynamics of the case coincide with the current dynamics in the group. The presenter may even feel robbed of the patient and feel helpless to rescue and restore within himself the familiar and identifiable image of the patient which he originally carried. I have heard the presenter protest that he and the group were not talking about the same patient. Eventually, however, his counter-transference becomes contaminated by the one which is coalescing in the group.

It is not only aspects of the case itself that become reenacted. It can be the conflicts stemming from relationships within the organization and within the group. The supervision group can also respond to aspects of the "shadow," i.e. unconscious and unacceptable parts, of the relationship between a supervisee and his individual supervisor. A presenter has been known to punctuate his presentation with "my supervisor says" as a defense against anticipated disturbing remarks from the group, which at the time were being experienced as a potential threat. The group responded at first with inhibition and later with irritation as they felt confronted with a separate subgrouping which had become split off and consequently was perceived by them in turn, as a threat to the cohesiveness of the group. There can also be sub-groupings, or pairing, if the span of experience and ability in the group is too wide, resulting in some members feeling frustrated and others feeling left behind.

A participant may receive group projections and identify with the role of, for example, the inferior and less-knowing one, the over intellectual one or the overanxious one whom the others use as a defense against accepting these same qualities within themselves. In other words, group projections can thrive and in so doing limit the growth of the individual who gets caught up in them. On the positive side I have known a group to miss the confrontational and challenging therapeutic stance of a particular member during his prolonged absence and eventually have to strive to find the positive aspects of that quality in themselves.

If the tension becomes obstructive the group supervisor is faced with the decision as to whether he should interpret what is going on in terms of group dynamics, or not. A supervisor needs to be especially sensitive to a member who may be internalizing the splits within the group and attempting to reconcile within himself on a personal level much of that which belongs to the collective. If the group supervisor does comment, he is crossing a boundary and raising into consciousness a process within the group which members are then left to deal with outside the session and without the presence of the supervisor. To my mind, however, it is always acceptable to make conscious the aspects of the case that are being reflected in the response of the group members. Feelings of anger, for example, if regarded diagnostically can be an excellent teaching aid.

In my experience the perfect size for such a group is about five members. A larger number, certainly for the discussion of individual therapy cases and especially during the early life of the group, can result in the presenter feeling that an intimate relationship to which he has sensitively contributed is being overexposed, and even violated, because the situation compels him to relate simultaneously to a greater number of persons than he can comfortably manage or contain. This is more likely to happen when verbal acting-out occurs in the group and responses are of a competitive nature, rather than a considered conurbation. This can result in an unconscious editing of aspects of the case by the presenter as he attempts to protect the analytic relationship.

I cannot leave this area without referring to a few of the very positive qualities of the group supervision situation. The potential for sharing and the consequent lessening of anxieties and the mutual active support which is engendered in a suitably sized group is immense. There is an impressive widening of perceptual horizons and an enriching pooling of ideas. How this process develops will depend on the personalities within the group; on how the supervisor stimulates the members into becoming a cohesive whole; on how much he can contain the splitting within the group and of course inevitably within himself. Ultimately the group supervisor is responsible for creating the boundaries. He needs to be experienced by the members as being an adequate container for the group as well as being someone who can respond to the needs of the individual.

Supervision within an Employing Organization and within a Training Body

In looking at the many ingredients that are common to supervision in a number of circumstances it has to be acknowledged that external factors, that is the setting, affect the content of supervision. An example of this is shown in the prospect of "losing" a patient. For a supervisor employed within an organization this is a valuable learning experience. For a supervisee on a qualifying course this same prospect, in addition to the experience, means that his training may be considerably extended, thus qualification is delayed and his expense is increased, because he is faced with the possibility of having to start again with another patient. This particular anxiety not infrequently invades the supervision of the latter and can distort the process if attempts to "keep" the patient take precedence over focusing on the analytic process as a whole.

As well the patient, supervisor and supervisee, another and influential factor is present in the form of the Employing Organization or the Training Body. The former will expect a certain standard of work from the supervisee, but there will be no ultimate qualifying moment of recognition and so at no fixed point will supervision formally and expectantly finish and thereby change the status of the supervisee and his view of his professional self. This implies that the Organization will always retain the final responsibility, and both supervisor

and supervisee through line management will be ultimately account-
able to them. This can bear on the vexed question of confidentiality,
a crucial ingredient in the therapeutic process. Management policy
will affect matters such as the frequency, intensity and period of the
therapy. This may well depend on the other commitments of the
supervisee, especially if he is employed primarily in a capacity other
than that of a therapist, for instance as a social worker with heavy
statutory responsibilities or as a psychologist with a lengthy caseload
of diagnostic testing. Quite a sophisticated level may be expected of
the psychotherapy, or it may be seen mainly as secondary to other
forms of help. The supervisee may be content with this predetermined policy or he may disagree. This conflict will then emerge in
supervision thus putting the supervisor in the difficult position of
trying to reconcile differing attitudes to the restraints imposed upon
the therapy, apart from discussing what would be best for the patient.
Supervision sessions can become focal points of many other conflicts within the organization and not infrequently these have an
oedipal quality.

The supervisor on a qualifying course is in a somewhat different
position. He carries with him the expected standard of the Training
Body with whom he is identified. He also carries the hopes of the
student from whom, let us not forget, he is directly receiving payment. Not only does he want to share some satisfaction and a sense
of accomplishment with the student at the end of their time together,
but he wants to see the student represent creditably the standard of
that particular body – and perhaps reflect positively his skills as a
supervisor of that particular body – and perhaps reflect positively his
skills as a supervisor too. He wants also to see the result as promoting the expertise of the psychotherapy profession as a whole. Let me
quote from Fred Plaut:

> How in practice do I know – or believe to know – that the requisite
> progress has been made so that I can recommend the trainee for associate
> membership? The answer is as subjective as it is brief, and the strength
> of my conviction depends on my being able to answer three questions in
> the affirmative. They are in ascending order: (a) Would I send him a
> patient? (b) Would I send him a patient whom I myself would take on for
> analysis? (c) Would I entrust myself to him or her for analysis? This last
> 'criterion' should not be taken to be more than a fleeting thought.[2]

I would add here that in my opinion some students blossom as therapists only after qualifying, that is after receiving formal affirmation as a therapist. An analogous situation can also arise over the selection of trainees.

The supervisor carries a manifold responsibility. This responsibility is to the patient, to the student, to the particular Training Body and to the analytical psychotherapy profession as a whole. The responsibilities of the supervisee are not that dissimilar for he is aiming at becoming a qualified member and thus a representative, and a carrier of the standards, of that same profession. Their respective positions are, however, different when it comes to the final decision about qualification to practice, for this is vested in the supervisor and not in the supervisee. The close relationship that can develop sometimes obscures this reality. However, it is essential that the final decision about qualifying is not taken by one or even by the two supervisors, vital as their reports will be, but by the Training Committee as a whole after other factors are taken into account. Without this process the supervisor would be in an impossibly dichotomous, if not incestuous, position in that he would be expected to be the final qualifying judge of the work of a student from whom he had been receiving payment for his part in that student's progress. A more objective decision is required based on a number of reports.

Process of Supervision

I see supervision not as a master-and-apprentice situation but as an evolutionary process. Here I am addressing myself more to the individual rather than the group supervisory process. To this relationship both participants bring the experience and insight that have brought them to this particular meeting place. The supervisee brings the personal experience of his analysis, including the stage he is at during any given time, the influence of his other supervisor or supervisors, and his life experiences. I do not want to omit here the influence of his earlier profession and training because this will inform his subsequent attitude as a therapist. The psychiatrist will be more sensitive to a psychiatric illness, the physician to a physical one, the social worker to a disturbance in the social or family environment, the priest to a spiritual dilemma, and so on. Similar forces operate in the supervisor. The supervisory process therefore becomes a vessel in which there is an amalgam of influences.

Nevertheless, to me the training for psychotherapy is like the training for the ballet. First one has to learn the classic steps, the basic disciplines and to know why the theory and structure are there and why they are imposed. Having assimilated these, only much later can an individual style be developed within the structure, using an inner authority, an inner informed response interlaced with theoretical knowledge. Some students have an innate therapeutic quality to their personalities while others have gifts in intuitive, theoretical or intellectual understanding. The fostering of these qualities in supervision contribute to an individual professional identity. Having said that, it must be added that there are situations when the supervisor may have to impose a firm line when the patient's well-being is at risk, such as a crisis situation involving an active suicidal component.

Students find their own method of presenting material. Some sessions are written up immediately and include a verbal accuracy that conveys the immediacy of contact. Others are written up later and so have a more integrated and reflective tone. Whatever the method, the patient is felt to be present in the room only when the student has been able to internalize the patient's image with sufficient clarity of consciousness to be able to project him or her into the session with an objectivity that includes empathy and separateness. Here I would comment that it is not only the supervisee's counter-transference but also that of the supervisor that needs to be explored. The counter-transference of the supervisor may be confirmatory – or the converse – of that of the supervisee, complementary or even prophetic. Whatever its quality it should be offered as an aid to understanding and not as definitive, for it is the supervisee's relationship with the patient that is the instrument of the therapeutic alliance and not that of the supervisor.

Within the supervisory process mutual projections and introjections take place. Thus, one person fashions something of the response of the other. The supervisee who is wanting a directive approach will stimulate something of that in the supervisor. But what is the student primarily seeking from the supervisor, given that each is reasonably well talented. Is the student hoping for a supervisor who will in the main stretch and challenge him or for someone who will for the most part be encouraging and supportive; for one who is intellectually stimulating or one who above all relates well and warmly? Is he or she chosen because of a well-conducted seminar, a well-delivered lecture or an impressively written book, or because another trainee has warmly recommended his own therapist as a supervisor because of a current positive transference? Maybe the student's own therapist has indicated a preference based on a compatible theoretical orientation – often an important consideration. No single supervisor can incorporate all these qualities in sufficient quantities for any one student. There is, mercifully, no ideal supervisor and for that matter no ideal supervisee or ideal patient either.

The Relationship Within Supervision

I have already referred to the respective merits of individual and of group supervision, and to the partially different expectations arising from supervision given as in-service training from that given in a qualifying training. But what is it in the process that is common to both circumstances? For me this is about creating a space in which the supervisee can play, can experiment with ideas, can explore possible approaches and can become more conscious of that which he already knows, as well as that which he needs to grow into knowing. Timing is important and if the supervisor, with mistaken zeal, hurries to inform, he will risk creating an anxiety in the student which can inhibit further development. I am reminded of Janet Mattinson's observations in her book *The Reflective Process*:

> If I and other supervisors overtaught a student, that student often tended to teach his client.[3]

The process is about creating a container in which he can feel safe enough to trust the supervisor with his anxieties and his mistakes and gradually and eventually take conscious and professional responsibility for his actions.

Ironically it is often the more experienced supervisee who is knowledgeable enough to perceive a difficulty and bring the crucial material. The student who has difficulty in integrating theory and the experience of his own analysis can be inappropriately and defensively self-confident. There is a misplaced confidence in his own abilities that the supervisor may not share. In these circumstances there may be a temptation to comment on what is perceived as omissions in the student's own analysis, thereby ignoring a boundary. This can promote divisive aspects of an oedipal situation. This Oedipal situation arises with the arrival in the training program of the first supervisor so that the previous twosome relationship becomes a threesome. Some other approach may have to be found – such as, for example, observing that the student continually avoids making a particular and obvious interpretation.

As in a therapy session, the most enabling insights are not necessarily those that come from one or the other of the two persons involved but from something that emerges or happens in the space between them. This space is where the patient too resides and has his being, and is ever present even in the midst of theoretical discussion. Ideally, for this created space to occur there has to be a certain mutual accessibility. On the supervisor's part this means resisting a temptation to be smart or clever. On the part of the supervisee this is dependent on the degree of the destructiveness in any envious feelings, often a denied ingredient in the relationship, being of manageable proportions. The effect of such envy can result in the supervisor feeling that what he offers is superfluous. This accessibility does not mean a contrived openness, which is usually of a defensive nature. For example, a student who changes his perception of what is going on too frequently in an attempt to present a pseudo-flexibility evokes doubt in me as to the quality of his contact with the patient. This can be a reflection of the interaction in the therapy, the result of considerable anxiety in the student or an unconscious rivalry with the supervisor.

For me the most enjoyable part of being supervised was when I said something that made my supervisor pause and contemplate. The point was not necessarily about whether he agreed or disagreed, but more importantly that I had presented something that I hoped might be insightful and it had been given time and space – a few moments in which it had been established and evaluated. In my role as supervisor what has given me satisfaction has been when the supervisee has reminded me of an observation that I had made, a comment sometimes forgotten by me, that has been verified by subsequent events or alternatively has been shown to be inappropriate or irrelevant at the time. The continuity of reciprocity has been kept alive and has been held between us and between the sessions. The response has stimulated me into giving more of myself and into exploring further whatever my inner larder of experience has to offer. This consequently enlarges my experience and causes me to reflect and extend my awareness. Each participant in this relationship needs to stimulate and affirm the role of the other.

Supervision, it seems to me, is about observing the convergence of analytic experience, theoretical teaching and the manner in which the supervisee applies an amalgam of experiences. It is about helping the student to develop a sufficiently reliable internal supervisor which will inevitably include some positive identification with the external supervisor. Alison Lyons used to say that the analyst should be someone whom one wanted to take inside oneself. It could be said that ideally this should apply to the supervisor as well. However, analytic psychotherapy is not about ideal situations. It is about working with what there is and the creativity that can come from this.

Many times it has been said that we do not formally teach how to supervise, the implication being that we should be doing so. Apart from some basic rules and accepting that, as in analytic psychotherapy, it is such an individualistic encounter, perhaps the most enabling contribution would be to offer to supervise the supervisor's supervision? If so, should this be individual or group suspension? Would there be a risk of something akin to line management taking place? Would this militate against originality in what is essentially a personal or even, sometimes, an artistic process?

Although I have maintained the importance of a circumscribed vessel for supervision, the foregoing reflections lead me to the conviction that the process of supervision can be affected by a number of influences, outside the two persons centrally involved, to a greater extent than is usually recognized. Supervision is indeed a dynamic process.

Three Seminars on Clinical Supervision

As a follow-up to the Conference on "Clinical Supervision; Issues and Techniques" (A public conference organized by the Jungian

Training Committee of the British Association of Psychotherapists in April 1988 out of which this chapter was developed) three seminars were arranged for the following November. These seminars consisted of the seminar leader Joan Reggiori and the five persons who had expressed an interest in joining. The following account is a summarized version of what happened.

The seminar leader introduced each seminar with comments on a particular theme before opening up the discussion to all the participants. At the beginning of the second and third seminar she read out a list of the matters raised at the previous one in order to promote continuity Thereafter the leader at promoting an ongoing creative group process by interspersing the discussion with new ideas, observations and comments. These were sometimes challenging or confrontational but were always designed to stimulate further thought and reflection. This could be said to be an important ingredient of the supervisory process itself.

First Seminar

After initial introductions the group used the first seminar to touch on a number of issues. Quite early on the members developed enough confidence in each other and were sufficiently committed to the process to illumine the discussion by sharing their relevant personal experiences.

One of the first items raised was a question about whether certain feeling responses between supervisor and supervisee – not emanating from one particular case – could be termed Transference and Counter-transference phenomena or whether these terms should be reserved only for the responses within the analytic relationship itself. The fact that a particular supervisory relationship existed was not in doubt. The question was whether or not it should have a special name. Another, but related, matter under discussion was the manner in which a supervised case became reflected in the relationship between supervisor and supervisee.

The problem was shared of a supervisor being required by an organization to supervise non-analyzed persons without formal training who were nevertheless conducting therapy with clients. The restrictions and responsibilities inherent were readily acknowledged as problematic.

There was a rhetorical question with regard to the boundaries, of which the sensitive supervisor is well aware, when the supervisee brings their distress, for example by crying, right into the supervision session. To what extent should the supervisor respond in these circumstances?

There was a fair degree of consensus that a supervisee should be allowed to change his supervisor if he felt the supervision was not satisfactory and he had felt stuck with a case for some considerable time. There were, however, differing views as to whether a supervisor, given that he is reasonably experienced, could take the supervisee further than he had been himself.

An indication of the feelings being evoked in this first seminar were shown in the following comments: "Supervisors should not think they are omnipotent." "It should be labeled a hazardous profession." "It's a slippery subject."

Second Seminar

During the second seminar the focus was on fewer issues but these were explored in greater depth. They included challenging the seeming omnipotence of the archetypal supervisor and also that of paternal institution.

The pivotal position in which the supervisee could find himself emerged as an area of some considerable interest. Examples were given of situations when the analyst and supervisee unconsciously split off a negative transference which was then carried by the supervisor, and of situations when the analyst and supervisor had either a close positive relationship or a rivalrous and negative one, both of which had a potential for affecting the supervisee and his supervision. Concern was expressed that if boundaries were not adhered to, the supervisor in trying to "help" the supervisee analytically could begin to exclude the analyst from part of the analytic relationship.

There was discussion about the supervisor and supervisee experiencing a 'clash of personalities' assuming, of course, the problem was not resolvable through analysis. On the whole it was accepted that the supervisee should be allowed to change his supervisor in these circumstances. Whether there were situations when the supervisor could ask for a change of supervisee seemed to be a more complex issue. If both were employed by the same organization the implications could be far reaching. A suggestion which received much support was that there should be a designated Consultant to deal with such problems. He could see each person separately and/or both together.

A query was raised about whether it was helpful or not for the supervisor to assess a potential patient of the supervisee. There was no clear consensus about this. There was, however, unanimous agreement that the supervisee needed to focus on his own internalized figure in subsequent supervision and not on the image formed by the supervisor from his earlier assessment.

The value of having video or tape recordings, as required by some organizations, was discussed. It was agreed that whatever value an organization might place on the teaching aspects of this overseeing method of supervision, concurrent recording of whatever kind limited the therapy. In these circumstances the supervisor was tempted to teach how he would have conducted the therapy himself, after seeing or hearing the recording, rather than concentrating on the inner responses of the supervisee. The presence of a third factor, i.e. video or tape recorder, prevented the establishment of an enclosed therapeutic space, so essential to an intimate creativity. In addition the patient might well withhold information that was socially unacceptable or potentially damaging if disclosed to a third party.

Third Seminar

In the third seminar the acquiring of supervisory skills and the assessment of quality were further explored. Mothering in particular proved to be an enabling theme and the negative aspects of supervision were also raised.

There was a brief discussion about the effect on supervision of the setting in which it took place, e.g. privately or within an institution.

A discussion of whether it was more helpful to teach didactically or to facilitate the 'creative process' led into questions about how decisions were taken as to whether or not a person is qualified to become a supervisor. The comment was made that a good therapist does not necessarily make a good supervisor.

In dealing with the question of whether supervision skills could be taught it was stated that one could teach management but not teach mothering. Mothering was then taken up intermittently as a model for supervising. It was agreed that a supervisor should have a good knowledge of theory and the skill to impart the essence of what is happening. It was also acknowledged that some supervisors were better with less experienced supervisees and others were better with more experienced ones. The supervisor, like the mother, needed to adapt to the stage of development and to stay with the supervisor is through the difficulties and to be available to him. In this way the supervisor is giving back something of his own experience of being supervised. This was likened to the grandmother-mother-child relationship.

There was a query about who should take the initiative to end supervision. Agreed that ideally it should be a mutual decision and not arise unexpectedly, it was also said that it should not necessarily end with qualification. However, the difficulty that could be experienced in breaking the bond with "mother" was mentioned in that there could be a wish not to seem to reject the good "mother." This was compared with the mixed feelings of an adolescent growing up and leaving home.

The example of a supervisor acting as a consultant to a group of persons from different disciplines who met to help one particular patient was given to cite the different yet appropriate use of a supervisor's skills.

There was a brief discussion about the effect on both parties when a supervisee actively dislikes supervision.

At the end there was much enthusiasm for writing up the seminars in some form or other, and a request to arrange another series of seminars.

Comment

The issues that were raised are fundamental and very relevant to an important furthering of professional skills. The above comments are, of course, only a summary of what was discussed. Many pertinent questions were voiced and few were given definitive answers. There was no omniscience but a basic attitude of inquiry – and this to my mind is the essence of learning, and an essential ingredient of supervision. Perhaps certain selected themes could be further and profitably explored in the future?

Notes

1. I hope the reader, for the sake of simplification, will accept that the pronoun "he" includes the feminine and vice versa.
2. Plaut, Alfred (1982) "How do I assess progress in Supervision?" *Journal of Analytical Psychology*, Vol. 27, p. 107 Society of Analytical Psychology, Academic Press, London.
3. Mattinson, Janet (1975) *The Reflection Process in Casework Supervision,* Institute of Marital Studies, Tavistock Institute of Human Relations, p. 13.

Part IV

Assessing Progress in Supervision

[13]

A Symposium: How Do I Assess Progress in Supervision?

[A] Alfred Plaut

In order to assess progress, one has to have an idea of a starting point. When the clinic director's notes on the patient who will become the chief topic of supervision combines with my initial impression of the personality of the supervisee, such a base line or starting point is established in my mind. Parts of this will remain constant, others will vary or change. Among the constants are that I enjoy supervision as part of the day's work when I am free from the analytical responsibility – not to be directly reassuring or critical. I also enjoy the refreshing aspect of seeing analysis with young eyes, to cast my mind back as easily to the days when I was being supervised and saw analytical patients for the first time, as I can recall my adolescence, including the anxiety and general turmoil of one's emotions and the help or hindrance one experienced, in those days, from persons who were senior to oneself. It is important to mention also the variable aspects which can make supervision stimulating; these are represented by the effects of the supervisee and his patient on my fluctuating views of analytical methods and their efficacy.

Against the background of this personal view I should like to put my criteria of progress in supervision in the form of three questions:

1. Can the trainee make use of supervision? The least one can expect by way of a positive answer is that by listening to his own account of what happened between himself and his patient, he will pull various strands together, create a kind of continuity and become

aware of what is lacking. This means recognizing his limitations. I regard this as the monologue state of supervision: the trainee has listened to the patient without having responded in a way that he could easily put into words and he is now trying to make me listen to his (usually written) account in a similar way. Sometimes an attempt to render in full four sessions within one supervisory hour fills it up and at this stage I am more or less silenced.

Further use of the supervisory hour depends on the development of the dialogue between the trainee and his patient on the one hand, and between the trainee and myself on the other, with the eventual result that the patient becomes three-dimensional, like a real living person, to me. When, as sometimes happens, I experience a momentary doubt whether a dream referred to was dreamed by one of my own patients or by the trainee's patient, I know that this stage has been reached and the road is open to further developments within our setting.

2. The converse question is: What are the obstacles which prevent the trainee from making full use of me? As this is not the place to dwell on my own shortcomings, I shall draw attention to the ways in which the trainee's anxiety obviates progress. The major factors are:

(a)   Fear of the supervisor's power;
(b)   Fear of losing the patient;
(c)   Fear of ignorance.

(a) There are two opposite extremes by which fear of the supervisor's power may hold up progress. Let us call the first one 'submission.'

Whatever comment I may happen to make is treated as a pearl of wisdom, and in order to show proper appreciation the trainee may congratulate me on my sagacity and take it down in writing. Alternatively, I may be told that what I had to say was immediately borne out by his patient's behavior or by a dream in the next session. This may, of course, be true, and an identity of viewpoints may be a necessary phase in any learning situation, but one hopes it will pass.

The opposite expression, that of being afraid of the supervisor's power, is the denial that he may have anything to contribute. In its more subversive form it may show itself by the trainee's response to any comment of mine to the effect that he/she had already thought of that, but ruled it out or had found it useless. Or again, he may imply that his own intuitive and spontaneous reaction to the patient does not really brook any further improvement by a third party. The submissive and the denial responses, both indicative of anxiety about the supervisor's power may, of course, alternate.

(b) As regards the fear of losing a patient or even two in a row and the aspersions this may cast on the trainee's analytical potential, this is as understandable as the previously mentioned obstacle. But once it has become an openly acknowledged fear, I feel free to be reassuring by saying that you will now become an analyst until you have lost a patient, and that it is better to stick to an established method and body of knowledge than to become a 'wild' psychotherapist who places his trust in positive transference projections and their short-lived therapeutic effect. The opposite symptom of the same anxiety (losing the patient) may be seen when the trainee is at pains to get the nasty bit out of the way and to enjoy a harmonious relationship with his patient.

(c) Fear of ignorance. I regard it as a part of supervision to go into the trainee's method of looking up and using references, and to keep a watchful eye on whether he is truly digesting what he learns from reading and from seminars. That he should regard his own discoveries as more important than his reading is only natural; that he should regard the writing of pioneers as irrelevant – although nobody would actually say this – is a pardonable narcissistic phase. What really matters in the long run is *whether he can synthesize* his personal knowledge and experience, gained during his life and analysis, with at least some of his reading and knowledge acquired from other sources during his training. We cannot expect a trainee to show more than the beginnings of this synthesizing or integrating process during the period of supervision. As we know, it takes an analytical lifetime to come close to such individuation.

Before this is reached, the question can be broken down as follows: Are the trainee's natural gifts, empathy, sincerity, intelligence, etc. in the process of being blended with a body of knowledge which will nourish and maintain these talents?

3. Finally, how, in practice, do I know – or believe to know – that the requisite progress has been made so that I can recommend the trainee for associate membership? The answer is as subject as it is

brief, and the strength of my conviction depends on my being able to answer three questions in the affirmative. They are in ascending order:

(a) Would I send him a patient?

(b) Would I send him any patient whom I myself would take on for analysis?

And finally,

(c) Would I entrust myself to him or her for analysis?

This last 'criterion' should not be taken to be more than a fleeting thought.

[B] Gustav Dreifuss

I have been a supervisor for many years in the Israel Society for Analytical Psychology and in the psychotherapy section (postgraduates) of the medical schools of Tel Aviv and Haifa. The students of the latter comprise medical doctors specializing in psychiatry, clinical psychologists (M.A.) and social workers (M.A.) with experience in psychiatric hospitals. In contradistinction to that of the trainees of the Jungian group, the program of these University schools is eclectic, and no personal analysis or even personal psychotherapy is required. There are some students who have undergone or are in psychotherapy, but they are in the minority.

It goes without saying that there is a big difference between these two groups, especially with regard to consciousness of transference-counter-transference processes and interpretations of unconscious material.

The evaluation of supervision is as much a highly individual action as is evaluation of analysis. There are of course objective criteria for the profession of analyst, like integrity and empathy, but the evaluation of their relative importance is dependent on the personality of the analyst or the supervisor respectively. A feeling type, for instance, might consider empathy as the most important assessment for the profession, while a thinking type might consider insight (consciousness) of paramount importance. An intuitive type might overvalue the capacity for imagination of the supervisee, while a sensation type might overestimate adaptation to reality.

If we assess *progress* in supervision, we have first to evaluate the supervisee at the beginning of supervision and then assess progress after a period of time and/or hours of supervision. Typology is helpful. Because of my typology and my experience as analyst and supervisor I consider empathy as one of the most important factors for a therapist. If the supervisee has a natural gift of empathy I shall, in the course of supervision, point to the problem of too much empathy whenever it occurs and bring the supervisee to the realization of the shadow of empathy, namely the danger of *participation mystique* and lack of conscious evaluation of the analytical situation.

Let me illustrate my point with some examples:

Supervisee 1: Supervision during seven months; fourteen hours.

A woman psychologist, 54 years old, with many years of analysis. She is a warm and intelligent person and conscious of her strong and weak points; she is capable of grasping the patients 'from their inside,' feels close to them (empathy), but knows the danger of too much acceptance and too little shadow-interpretation. She has a tendency to talk too much, and not to listen enough. She can be too active in her evaluative interpretations. She sometimes ambitiously wants too much were the development of the patient is concerned.

In the supervision we concentrated on her weak points, which showed themselves also in her relationship to the supervisor.

Supervisee 2: Supervision during one year; thirty-four hours.

A woman psychologist, 45 years old, with long analytical (Jungian) experience. She is an introverted intuition type. Her strong sides were empathy, sensing of situations and creating an atmosphere of trust. She was open to let the inner process happen without interference. She was, through her analysis, aware of the danger of over-involvement, over-identification. She knew her tendency to be fascinated by the unconscious material and to be carried away by it.

All these points were carefully discussed in the supervision, and special emphasis was put on evaluating and considering the *concrete outer situations* of her patients. She needed more 'earth' in herself and in her work with analysands.

In the supervision she became aware of her weak points and made considerable progress in overcoming them.

Supervisee 3: Supervision during nine months; twenty-five hours. A psychiatrist, 40 years old, with no analytical experience. He has a highly intellectual and cultural background. He was educated in a medical school in Russia. He has a very positive father-complex: his father was a personality, a successful scientist and medical doctor, and he looked up to him. His orientation at the beginning of supervision was very 'medical' and rational. He had to succeed in his treatment – and rather quickly. He was unaware of the value of his empathic qualities and afraid of them.

In the course of the supervision he became acquainted with psychic processes. He learned to accept his natural empathy and its importance in therapy. He became more patient and mature in his therapeutic relationships. He has now more inner force *to be* with the patient. He can let things *happen* without being too active as a therapist. He is less disturbed by lack of, or slow, progress. He believes more in 'nature' (as he puts it), which means more confidence in the healing function inherent in the psyche itself.

In the supervision with me (he had had one year of previous supervision), he learned not to be in competition with the supervisor, whom he ad put too 'high up' because of his positive father-complex.

This was extensively discussed with regard to transference-counter-transference problems in his treatments and in his supervision. Through an occasional 'glimpse' into the dreams of his patients, he came to an acceptance of the unconscious and the value of dream analysis.

An important experience during supervision was the discussion of guilt feelings of a 70-year-old woman patient who suffered from depressive moods. I had suggested that it was about time for this patient to accept her guilt and to forgive herself, to accept herself with this guilt. (Her son had died in an accident and she connected the death of her son with the lack of care for him during difficult years in her life because of outer circumstances.) This brought about an immediate improvement and the end of psychotherapy. This dimension of psychotherapy had up to then been alien to him, and it furthered his interest in Jungian psychology.

Supervisee 4: Supervision during eight months; eighteen hours.

A woman psychiatrist, 45 years old, with no analytical experience. She is a very rational person, afraid of the unconscious. She was unaware of the positive functioning of her intuitions and feelings in their therapeutic relationship. Because of this she often found herself in situations where her feelings and empathy welled up in her to the degree that she lost her capacity to evaluate the situation she was in. She gained considerable awareness of this point and succeeded in correcting her shortcomings. Through her medical training she had acquired a compensatory feeling of omnipotence because of insecurity and fear of disappointing the patient. She held on to this illusion. In supervision she learned to accept her limits as a therapist in modesty.

Conclusion

Supervision is, besides 'learning' to do psychotherapy, and important tool in becoming conscious. It helps the supervisee to know himself as a therapist and to find his personal style in his work, to feel himself, his psyche, as a therapeutic tool. Progress in supervision is therefore always also a development of the personality of the supervisee. At the end of the supervision I always discuss with the supervisee his estimation of the supervision, by comparing our work with previous supervision if there was any. In this way I also learn about myself and can assess my progress as supervisor in the course of the years.

[C] Michael Fordham

I would like to contribute to the present chapter by making some remarks about the supervision of students in their handling of cases taken in the child analytic training, London.

I have previously stated my position with relation to supervision as a whole (Fordham 1), and a re-reading of that paper does not make me want to alter the essential argument: supervision, in contrast to analysis, should be directed towards the student's performance with his case and not to the student's affective internal world. I have now some further comments to make as to the result of knowledge gained about students, their differing styles of analysis, and how these help in defining the directions in which improvement in their analytical skills might be made.

In view of the various usages of the word analysis I would draw the reader's attention to previous of my writings on the subject (especially Fordham 2), and summarize these by stating that analysis is essentially an attitude of mind which sorts out complex structures with a view to gaining insight into the operation of their more simple components.

The reflections that I shall present are derived from the supervision of child analyses which require a formal setting or framework in which the student sees the child frequently, four or five times a week. The room contains a sink and available water, two chairs, a table, a couch with a rug and cushions. Toys are kept in a cupboard outside the treatment rooms and are those selected by the child with others that the analyst may wish to add. Before the session begins, analyst and child go to the cupboard, the analysts unlocks it and the child takes the toys if he wants them – he usually does. The toys represent a gift by the analyst to the child, and the child can do anything he likes with them, including taking them home or adding to them as he sees fit.

This arrangement maximizes the interactional nature of the analytic process and, hopefully, minimizes the child's capacity to escape into acting out types of play. It has not always been possible to achieve these standards.

Under these conditions the student brings the supervisor his, or her, detailed account of what has gone on in the interview. As might be expected the accounts vary greatly, not only because of the differences in children who are being treated, but also because they reveal the basic styles of the student. Here are two contrasting examples.

The first case is of a boy who had an intellectual inhibition. As evidence accumulated it became rather clear to me that the disorder was due to castration anxiety displaced upwards. The trainee recognized the relevance of my observation, and tried to put it to the boy in her own way. As might have been expected, her patient did not enthusiastically acclaim this insight but became resistant, and the student, noticing that, did not press forward her interpretations. I should explain here that I had left a good deal to the student, avoiding spelling out the interpretation I would have given. Thus I had not said: 'Look, this child is so uncommunicative because he wants to seduce you, but is too afraid of the consequences should he try it on.'

The student went on with her analysis, working sensitively and carefully with the material he produced so that her patient gradually relaxed and became more open with her. Eventually he started attempts at seduction: he became interested in the contents of her room and, in particular, in a cupboard which represented the student's body. He also wanted her to play games with him. The student went along with that but, I thought, extricated herself in time. I understood that the castration anxiety had mitigated through the analyst's careful and sensitive relationship with her patient. Though this analysis was skillful, it was rather passive, and, as her supervisor, I missed penetrative insights into the unconscious processes at work – she tended to wait till they emerged and they did not always do so.

Now to consider a contrasting student. Again the patient was a boy. The student was much more robust and rooted in her body; she soon gave evidence of great capacity for containment.

The boy came each time with an account of the journeys that he had made: he came by London Underground and went well out of his way to get to the clinic. He recorded the stations that he had been to or through, and described his fascination with the train coming out of the tunnel into the station; he would lean over the platform's edge as far as he dared, to see how far down the tunnel he could detect the oncoming train.

The interviews became stuck on these repetitive accounts, so I asked the student what she would say to the boy if neither I nor anybody else could know what she had said. Her reply was somewhat as follows: she thought that his 'geographical' study indicated a sexual interest in her (the student's) body and especially an interest in her genital (the tube) and its contents (represented by the train); he seemed to be asking: would she allow him to look into her genital and the penis inside it? I asked, 'Why not say that?' thereby implying tacit approval of her doing so. I do not remember in detail what she said to the child, but it was in substance what she said to me. From being petrified the analysis became alive – the immediate effect was impressive, and that, in my view, was because she had the capacity to contain the emotional content of the words so that they were neither an attack on the child's consciousness nor a provocation.

It is my contention that during supervision a supervisor should not evaluate or judge the student's capacities, but facilitate the development of what is available. He may evaluate them afterwards, and will need to do so when the student applies for acceptance as an associate member of the Society of Analytical Psychology. Nor is he there to teach in a formal sense, though he may have to from time to time. Thus I did not give either student a theoretical framework into which to fit their observations – that is the function of seminars – I rather tried to convey my experience in the context of the student's emotional and intellectual capacities. To consider how each might improve involves evaluating their work, ant that I will now proceed to do.

Comparing the two examples indicates lines along which development of the students' analytical capacities might go: student 1 needs to increase her capacity for containing and transforming the patient's sexual and aggressive impulses and phantasies. Student 2 could do that, but she needs to pay more attention to the surface data, at which student 1 is adept. Student 2 goes behind or under the surface and gets the analysis going in an intimate interactive fashion, but the surface defensive operations get brushed aside and cause trouble later. The appreciation of the surface can begin by studying with more care the way her patient reacts to her interventions.

My intention in considering these two students is to suggest that lines of development can best be defined from comparative experience rather than from abstract standards. Theory cannot be altogether left out and it is there as a shadow monitoring the interchanges between student and patient on the one hand, student and supervisor on the other. This statement raises questions about the places of abstraction in analytic practice and, also, the ambiguous meaning of experience – after all theory is experience of a kind. I hope, however, my description has been sufficiently clear for it to be understood without further discourse or definition. That belongs elsewhere[2].

References

1. Fordham, M. (1961). 'Suggestions towards a theory of supervision,' *J. analyt. Psychol.*, 6, 2.
2. Fordham, M. (1978). *Jungian Psychotherapy*. Chichester, Wiley.

[D] J.L. Henderson

At the C.G. Jung Institute in San Francisco, a two-year period of control analysis with two different analysts ends with the candidate's presentation of a written case study. Following this, the candidate is examined in an oral interview with six members of the certifying board in a group composed of three from San Francisco and three from the Los Angeles training center. At the last general meeting of the year, the local board announces the new members, and there is usually some discussion concerning the experience of the board members in affirming or criticizing the value of this method of examining candidates in training.

At a recent meeting, someone asked what attitude on the part of the control analyst or the candidate should determine the choice of a case for presentation. I quote a passage from the minutes of that meeting to give some idea of the content of that discussion:

> One member stated he feels there is much ambiguity concerning what sort of case is to be presented. Another said he felt that we should distinguish between a judgment from the soul versus 'bureaucratic hassling.' Still another said he felt it would be inflated to think we can judge the soul, and we should be satisfied with more mundane criteria.

Having been a control analyst for many years, I have gone over these conflicting viewpoints, asking what my attitude in these matters has been, what it is now, and how it may be changing.

Working with a candidate is always an interesting and stimulating experience for me, but there are times when it becomes tiresome, because I do not have a sense of watching two people in a process with symbolic content, but two people in a power struggle where purely psychodynamic 'mechanisms' are being discussed. But this does not mean that I would want my candidates to choose only cases that would interest me. A purely clinical approach is indicated in some cases, but if conducted in such a way that basic resistances are removed with understanding of their inner nature, there is bound to be a sense of working with the 'soul,' as well as with their 'mundane' significance. It is only when both candidate and patient seem to be taken up with the game of analytical interpretation, losing sight of its transpersonal nature, that I lose interest. It is simply because they cease to be real human beings for me, whatever they may be for each other.

I do not like the word 'control' for my work with candidates. At the beginning of our work, I tell them that I am not there to test or examine, but to be available to them as a consultant. They have always responded well to this approach and learn quickly to talk freely of their problems with certain difficult patients other than the case selected for presentation. They also talk about their personal problems from time to time when this seems appropriate. In some cases, I have had to question the validity of using me as a personal analyst instead of a consultant, and in one or two cases it became apparent that the candidate's personal problem was such that he was not ready for control. In general, this does not present a problem; in analytical practice, how can our work be other than personal as well as symbolic or clinical? And I think this is the true reason why the word 'soul' inevitably comes into discussion of Jungian methods. Neumann brilliantly described it, in a paper at the First International Congress in Zurich (1959) as 'the personal evocation of the archetype' (Neumann 3), by which I understand him to refer to an experience which is mutually shared by analyst and analysand, and that it is uncontaminated by programmed responses.

May I now expand my understanding of this ambiguous word 'soul' and its relevance for our work? Although I have always prided myself on my lack of authoritarian control of my candidates in training, I know – and they know – that there is present in the very nature of our meetings a master-pupil aspect to our relationship. Of course, we both make short shrift of the academic nature of this by acknowledging that we are colleagues, but the archetypal layer of the unconscious is not touched by such reasonable interpretations of reality. There is another reality that comes to light over and over again the closer my candidate comes to writing his case presentation, with the impending oral examination to follow. It has been formulated, not by me but by my candidates, and affirmed in the experience of other control analysts, as initiation. This other reality is experienced as a rite of passage from student to full membership in the Institute, and it is verified by most candidates' often-repeated statements that the whole process, even when they had no undue anxiety about being accepted, felt like an initiation.

Now, it happens that I have written a book on initiation, and this is on the recommended reading list for these candidates (Henderson 1). Are they not, therefore, indoctrinated to the idea of initiation and to a suggestion that this might be relevant to their training, and that their examination might be a possible initiation experience? Might they not exaggerate this theme to win my approval? If so, one would expect to find evidence for this – and, so far, I never have. In my book, I maintained that initiation is an archetype, and I gathered a lot of evidence from clinical material corresponding to the myths and rituals of initiation in tribal cultures and in mystery religions. The forms in which this archetype appears are so varied and so unexpected that no one cultural pattern can explain them all. Clinically, I found that however often the patient had learned about these forms, the personal experience of them was felt to be unique and appeared spontaneously in response to a specific need. In a recent paper, Anthony Stevens describes this modern appearance of initiation as a need that is not being met in a social context, which accounts for certain forms of juvenile delinquency or adolescent rebelliousness (Stevens 4). He speaks of these adolescents as having 'initiation hunger,' and this points to the existence of initiation as an archetype.

Still, for many psychologists and anthropologists, initiation is understood only as being transmitted to the neophyte – whether as initiate or analysand – via the culture pattern as a learned response, not an archetypal one, as I found out with dismay from some of the critical notices of my book. That was long ago, and if I had any doubts about my thesis, they have been resolved by my training candidates who have most fully validated my conception of the archetypal origin of true initiation. In each case it was experienced without encouragement to do so, and because the form it took could not have been predicted. Their formulation of it was expressed as if

to say, 'This process I have been going through must be what that
word I have encountered so often, "initiation," must really mean.'

In certain instances, some basic landmarks of initiation could be
seen, such as the ones I had described as 'the ordeal' and 'the trial of
strength.' But these were less marked, being rather primitive or
youthful responses, than the general and more essential experience
of initiation as a state of transition, as transformation, with its new
sense of commitment and surrender of the will-to-power. Not all
these individuals were as smoothly 'initiated' as it may sound.
Whenever a candidate became too sure of a brilliant performance,
and that it would really be the end of all analytical training, the other
control analyst or members of the certifying board invariably chal-
lenged him or her. While this was troubling, at the same time I never
saw these as wounding experiences – merely as exposure of the
shadow inherent in any archetypal pattern, here experienced as a
failure of initiation if too much was expected of it. The so-called
initiation manquée has been known from ancient times as an important part of the rite of passage itself, and is frequently included within
it, as shown in the Grail Legends (Weston 5). Since a personal
evocation of all archetypes has, by definition, an initially inflating
effect upon ego-consciousness, it must be balanced by a strong
tendency to deflation.

In the light of these experiences and their formulation by numerous candidates, I think that a training program of this kind tends to
promote the archetype of initiation as a whole. Starting with an
individual control analyst as master-of-initiation, and ending with an
assessment of growth in accordance with the requirements of the
larger peer group, the candidate learns the dynamics of inflation and
deflation experientially. Finally, the individuation process is sym-
bolically outlined in this whole procedure of renewal and commitment on both levels – the inner subjection one and the outer experience of belonging to a group.

I have focused my attention, so far, exclusively upon the candidate's experience of supervision; but what about the experience of
the patient who is in the control experiment? I expect that every
candidate will inform his patient that his or her material is being
discussed with me, so as to avoid being unduly affected by my
unconscious reactions, or my conscious influence. The reason for

this was strikingly shown to me in a case where the candidate did not tell his patient that he was being used for control, and I had neglected to tell him to do so. Sometime after the candidate had presented his case study and had been duly accepted as a member of our Institute, his patient saw me for the first time at a public event. He exclaimed: 'Who is that man? I must know him'! My candidate then realized that an unconscious form of recognition had been awakened, and the patient's question should have been put the other way round – not, 'I must know him,' but, 'He must know me.'

The sensitiveness of the psyche to such a sharing of a patient's material with another therapist has to be carefully watched during control analysis, and it is not enough merely to ask the patient's permission. He may give it consciously, then find that there are considerable internal resistances. For the most part, I have found that the patients in control are supported by the knowledge that their material is being shown to a more experienced analyst. A number of rather sever problems seem to me to have been solved better than they would be by one analyst alone, whether by my candidate or by myself. This is different from multiple analysis, where the patient may be seeing more than one analyst during the course of his, or her, treatment. Unfortunately, I have not collected enough material to illustrate this convincingly, so it must remain in the realm of supposition rather than proof.

However, there is one area in which I think anyone who has ever done control analysis would agree that both the candidate and his patient must profit greatly from experienced help. This is when dealing with the transference and countertransference as it occurs between the candidate and his patient. Our candidates are clinically-trained psychotherapists, and though some of them are not physicians, they come to us having accepted an ethical code, with its medical requirement to obey the traditional principle that honor both the moral integrity of the doctor and his patient. In the formation of psychoanalysis, this was strengthened and deepened by urging the analyst to respect not only the outward form but the inner content of that integrity. Where transference and countertransference are strongly marked, this integrity is severely tested, since there is borne in the psyche, at times, a strong desire for erotic union which would like to destroy this ethical principle of separateness needed to complete the work on a psychological level. But we assume that, if for no other reason, the professional super-ego will prevent lapses in the maintenance of this moral integrity. It therefore comes as a surprise when every now and then some well-trained and accepted practitioner is found guilty of malpractice in the form of turning the transference and countertransference into a love affair.

Because of this, one cannot be sure that one's candidate in control will not himself or herself some day fail this test and fall into a similar trap. But it is less likely to happen if, in dealing with this problem empirically, one can show one's candidate why – psychologically, not just morally – this is wrong and must be avoided. We live in an age where moral standards are no longer absolute but relative, and it might be understandable that a young psychotherapist might find no moral problem in making love to a woman patient who perhaps has already suffered from being erotically ill-used by men, and her male therapist could conceivably heal her with his tenderness. Or, if the therapist is a woman, what could be more educational than for her to become the *hetaira* who takes a hesitant youth to bed in the hope of making a man of him? Numerous other exceptional, humanly understandable reasons for disregarding medical ethics in this respect may come to the reader's mind, and it becomes difficult for an inexperienced therapist not to be swayed by them. I have, more and more, placed this subject in a central place in my agenda for control work whenever it may come up in the control sessions. In this sense, I give myself permission to depart from my avowed role as consultant and become strongly didactic.

It is *always wrong* for a therapist to expect or to allow a sexual expression of the transference or countertransference – not because of the danger of being exposed in a malpractice suit, and not only for the ethical reasons mentioned above, but because such acting-out makes it impossible to work with the transference and ultimately to resolve it. So I try to indicate to my control candidates that they, as well as their patients, will suffer from a sense of failure in accomplishing the 'great work' if this truth is not respected. This is the basic message of Jung's *The Psychology of the Transference* (Jung 2). The *coniunctio*, in the sense Jung presents it, is not to be thought of as a model for what should take place between doctor and patient. It is a symbol for what can transcend the personal dependence of the patient to the doctor, and to relieve the doctor of any guilt that he may be hurting his patient by withholding his personal involvement. Jung's statement – that the libido that gets into the transference is *always* incestuous – still holds, as far as I am concerned, and I hope to convey this knowledge to my candidates in control. The product of a successful working-through of the transference and counter-transference results in the formation of a symbolic child, or *filius philosophorum*, that can come into being only when the mutual interdependence of doctor and patient has been removed, and this can never take place naturally, therapeutically, if the symbolic process has been turned into a purely personal, human relationship. But a purely clinical warding-off of the danger of stirring up transference feelings is equally to be avoided, and I also try to encourage my control candidates not to fear risking themselves if the patient establishes a transference, no matter how incestuously disturbing it may be at first.

This is expecting a lot from a young candidate, and I respect his or her reluctance to enter into so deep an experience of bonding as the *coniunctio* requires. There are enough patients who, themselves, are unfitted to work through such deep experiences, and whose problems are better understood as needing a strict clinical approach in the area of early object relations. But some of our trainees are in their forties, fifties, and even sixties, and are sufficiently mature and experienced to be ready for a full encounter with the archetypal content of the analytical relationship. For less experienced analysts, this type of learning may come only after formal control work has been finished – and that is why, in San Francisco, we stress the primary importance of a good clinical training and do not expect a highly individuated form of analysis to appear until the candidate has grown up to it in his own time.

References

1. Henderson, J.L. (1967). *Thresholds of Initiation.* Middletown, Conn., Wesleyan University Press.
2. Jung, C.G. 'The psychology of the transference.' *Coll Wks,* 16.
3. Neumann, E. (1961). 'The significance of the genetic aspect for analytical psychology,' in Gerhard Adler (Ed.), *Current Trends in Analytical Psychology.* London: Tavistock.
4. Stevens, A. (1981). 'Attenuation of the mother-child bond and male initiation into adult life.' *Journal of Adolescence* 4, 131-48.
5. Weston, J.L. (1913). *The Quest of the Holy Grail.* London, Bell.

[E] Elie Humbert

This question of assessing progress in supervision brings to mind two experiences which occur repeatedly and regularly in my own practice.

The first concerns those applicants who wish to undergo an analysis and ask me to orient them. I have come to realize that, in order to reply to them, I have to set about making a special kind of assessment (*une curieuse estimation*). After I have tried to discern the nature of their trouble and their aptitude for self-confrontation, I do not try to think of those therapists whom I consider the more skilled or the more knowledgeable, but one, or more, whose personal wound would, I believe, better serve the would-be patient. Such and such an analyst, of excellent reputation, has not, perhaps, been disturbed (*malade*) deeply enough, or perhaps he has been too disturbed, or is as yet insufficiently conscious of it, or is too 'healthy' (*'guéri'*) really to understand what such a patient is suffering.

The standard of judgment applicable to referrals is equally valid for supervision. That is to say, the quality of an analyst, and his progress during his training, are not to be measured in terms of a scale of competence. Certainly, ability and general culture are indispensable. They enlarge personal experience, and without them it would not be possible for an analyst to elucidate and work on illness.

But they are not sufficient in themselves. At the center of the analysis there is the wound of both the analyst and the analysand.

The supervision is charged with attending to those matters. In what way is the wound of the young analyst secretly engaged in his relation to the analysand? The countertransference is analyzed but on condition that we give that term the breadth it has (though it is not mentioned as such) in C.G. Jung's 'The psychology of the transference.'

The analyst under supervision learns new skills and ways of interpreting when he discovers the compensations which come to him in the course of analyzing someone else, the ways in which he protects himself but also the satisfaction he derives from this work. There is progress to the degree that he accepts that the analyses that he is beginning to practice throw his own personal analysis back into the melting-pot, whereas he had imagined a kind of consecration to it; also, to the degree that he is able to realize how the choice and the exercise of his profession are intimately related to his own pathology. In theory this is evident enough; but in practice it is not so easily recognized.

What is at issue behind the taste for working as an analyst and the desire for the persona of an analyst, lies ultimately in the realm of the animus and anima. The encounter within the analytic relationship provides both of those with a preempted arena for projection. They maneuver within it, are nourished by it, and risk keeping possession of the analyst through their infinitely varied activity. Jung admitted as much when he placed the analytic relationship under the sign of the *hieros gamos*, and, furthermore, when he observed that, in our world, analysis is one of the refuges of the endogamous libido. That in itself indicates the danger of remaining just there. From this perspective progress depends on the capacity of the trainee analyst to involve himself in the relationship, but not to live in it.

My second observation concerns the beginnings of the supervision. The future analyst presents his case and discusses it, but nothing happens until the moment when he realizes that he is interpreting in *a priori* terms. It could be, for example, a dream which he has twisted and distorted in order to conserve his own picture of the situation. It is then that the mutual work of supervision engages, and the future analyst discovers what it was in himself that had stiffened his attitudes and his interpretations. Technical work is then begun on the two possible readings and meanings of dreams, on whether or not to interpret within the transference, and the choice between reduction on the one hand and constructive amplification on the other. But in all this it is evident that the issue turns on the effectivity of the analyst and the way in which his own unconscious makes use of his analysis of another person.

In my view, progress is achieved at this stage according to the analyst's own capacity for flexibility, the *Mercurius* factor in him. To what extent is he capable of (a) recognizing the major changes in the unconscious, (b) of passing from one epistemological position to another (the *Einstellung* to which Jung attached so much importance)?

What had been good can become baneful. Integration is like a winding river: it can even flow backwards. Equally, the amplification necessary at one particular time, since it energizes the anima, can become a source of inflation, and then the analyst ought to take up a reductive position and occupy himself with instinctual processes rather than with symbols. Contrary to what is often said, the interpretation of dreams cannot always be relied on to bring about the changes necessary during the course of an analysis.

If the analyst cannot lean on either epistemology or a system of predetermined values, no more will he be able to trust to a single exemplary mode of approach, such as frustration or an understanding attitude to the patient. Can the trainee-analyst empathize and distance himself? I look for those crucial marks of development in his work.

I realize, in conclusion, that the observations which the question, 'How do I assess progress in supervision?' has evoked for me can be summed up in the reflection that in order to be an analyst one must possess an out-of-the-ordinary combination of qualities and defects.

[F] Mario Jacoby

The main topic, 'How do I assess progress in supervision?' seems to me to contain two different questions: namely, how do I assess at all what is going on in an analysis conducted by a trainee; and, what do I understand by 'progress'?

With regard to the first question: even if it were possible to obtain a verbatim account of what has taken place in a session between the trainee and his patient, I am still not sure whether I could assess the situation in all its facets. Is the tone of the candidate's voice, and are his accompanying gestures, the same while he is with me as they were in the actual analytic situation? (The decisive effect of such nonverbal communications is well-known.) The trainee reporting on his work during supervision finds himself in a different field of communication, in a different feeling-climate, colored by whatever transference emotions may be constellated. Once I know a candidate well I can probably distinguish between his report and what may really have happened between him and his patient. Theoretically speaking, the most accurate description of an analytic session is that of a videotape; but in reality the intimacy and spontaneity of interactions are often spoiled by stage-fright and play-acting. So far no trainee has brought me videotapes, though some have wanted me to listen to ordinary tapes of their sessions. An occasional hearing of these tapes has helped me to get a better picture of what had taken place in the hour on which the trainee had merely reported, because I then heard the patient's voice with his specific ways of expression, together with the candidate's interventions, less contaminated by the (mutual) influence of our own encounter. Thus an awareness of whether, and in what way, a transference-countertransference situation between trainee and supervisor may distort the assessment of what is really going on in the supervised analysis seems to me of prime importance. Occasionally it would seem necessary to discuss certain points of this transference situation with the candidate.

The question of a candidate's 'progress' has to be seen within the framework of the curriculum of his training. At the Zürich Institutes candidates begin seeing patients after having passed a set of examinations (Fundamentals of Analytical Psychology, Psychology of

Dreams, Association Experiment and Theory of Complexes, Comparative Theory of Neurosis, Psychopathology, General History of Religion, Fundamentals of Ethnology, Psychology of Myth and Fairy Tales). Thus they have acquired a good deal of knowledge that serves them as a tool in understanding, as well as possible, the language of the unconscious. This, as is well-known, was one of Jung's main concerns. The personal analysis of the trainee is considered to be the heart of the training experience, and there is always hope that his personal experience with the practical side of analytical psychology will increase his introspective sensitivity and his gift of empathy.

Yet, after having seen the first patient, candidates still frequently struggle with the questions – whether expressed or not – 'What am I supposed to do now?' or 'How am I to "apply" what I have learnt about analytical psychology in my work with this patient?' These questions are raised even by trainees who have had previous experience as counsellors or psychotherapists, because they are now supposed to do a Jungian analysis. To me the main 'progress' of a trainee consists in his gradual overcoming of his preponderant concern – 'What am I supposed to do?' The complex comprises such demands as: one *ought* to like one's patient, ought to 'understand' his dreams, ought to know what Jung said about animus-possession or shadow problems and so forth. It is this attitude, that of the 'good student,' which often impedes a true and genuine inner reaction to the patient's problems and demands. As is generally accepted, the quality of an analysis depends essentially on the analyst being connected to himself – this being the prerequisite for an empathy with the patient's psychic world that is enriched by repercussions in his own psyche, be it in terms of dreams, ideas, phantasies, feelings, or sensations. This presupposes honesty and tolerance towards whatever shadowy phantasies and feelings he may encounter within himself, and an awareness of the countertransference in its illusionary and its syntonic aspects. For the sake of this differentiation the candidate sometimes needs a bit of personal analysis from the supervisor.

But how can this increase in, and differentiation of, awareness be used in a fruitful way – how, when, and in what form can it be shared partially or totally with the patient? To my mind this cannot really be taught. The natural gift of the trainee, his flair for symbolic under-standing, and his skill in verbalizing, have eventually to blend with his sensitivity to produce a feeling for the right timing of certain interventions during the analytic session. These interventions only 'sit right' when the responses of the trainee to what is going on have become a part of his own being. In this way he may, gradually, be able to find his own personal style.

When assessing the progress of the trainee, the supervisor has to beware of the traps of his own 'Pygmalion-complex,' namely, his need to form the trainee in a narcissistic way according to his own image and to evaluate the candidate in terms of 'the more he works like me the better.'

[G] A.B. Ulanov

I have done three types of supervision with trainees of the New York C.G. Jung Institute: individual supervision with trainees on cases from their own practice; individual supervision with trainees on their assigned clinic cases; and small group supervision (ideally, just six students) in a clinical seminar required every year in our curriculum where trainees take turns presenting cases. My criteria for assessing a student's progress turns out to be the same in all these kinds of supervision: growth in the student's professional skill and personal identity as analyst. For, finally, I assess 'progress' in terms of the way a student finds and creates his, or her, own personal style of being a Jungian analyst.

In the back of my mind, there always hover the questions teachers and supervisors are asked in our Institute's biannual evaluation of students. We want to know how students relate to and assimilate unconscious material, how they perceive and apply symbolic materi-al, how they relate interpersonally and maintain reliable presence to their analysands. In addition, we evaluate the student's knowledge of the subject-matter of our courses, and comment on what seems to be positive in a student's development, what problem areas turn up, any suggestions we might have to solve these as well as general recommendations.

I find when I review a term of supervision, I always come back to see how a student's professional skills may have developed and his or her personal identity deepened. These questions leave a lot of room for individual variation, a fact I find quite compatible with my main criterion for progress: is there evident an expansion of an individual's personal style of being an analyst? Or does the student instead fall into parroting what I say, or someone else says – like an analyst or an author, including Jung? Or is the student too frightened or blocked by defenses to unfold at all?

Clearly one of the purposes of a supervisor is to impart information and knowledge about the skills of analytical work, and to increase a student's ability to find and use the knowledge of others (see Fordham's "Suggestions Towards a Theory of Supervision," chapter three). In this role the supervisor finds herself situated in the archetypal field of teacher, or even guru, in its deeper sense of passing on not only the tradition but also some of its secrets – a communication of mind to mind as the Buddhists say. So, for example, I may respond to the thorny issue of negative transference in the case a student presents by giving a broad variety of types of responses, of ways this issue can be handled, including my own approach.

Giving several possibilities gives implicit permission to the student to develop his or her own response and mode of approach. I might suggest reading from several points of view, for example Harold Searles's piece "The Dedicated Physician," although I do not altogether agree with his almost exclusive emphasis on countertransference as the key to unlock the case. That singular emphasis is, I think, limiting. Nonetheless, Searles is both wise and useful in observing that a therapist's ardent and conscious dedication to help his patient can also serve to defend him from his own unconscious sadism, negative feelings, and despair over "what to do." He can use his patient's illness to shield him from his own shortcomings (Searles 1979:78-79). Similarly, Winnicott's "Hate in the countertransference" proves helpful in learning ways to hold one's hate, to be fully aware of it, to feel it, and to use it as a clue to what is going on in the patient (Winnicott 1947: 196). On such a subject, I would also be looking out for what is constellated in the room between

student and me around hate and negative transference-countertransference, and asking, can the student tolerate it, and can we, as a
learning-couple, find our place in this immediate field of negative
archetypal and personal interaction? Is there elbow room to imagine
possible scenarios that the analysand's negative transference sets in
motion? Can we hold the opposites in a unitary vision? How does the
analysand's material arrange us vis a vis each other? Do we gang up
on the patient? Or siding with the patient, do we gang up on each
other? Or does the student feel compelled to impose a theory as the
only answer? As Winnicott puts it so bluntly, "If the therapist cannot
play, then he is not suitable for the work" (Winnicott 1971: 54).

Students in supervision are fascinated by the mechanics of the
profession. They want to know all about case management as well as
the odd fact that pertains to a dream symbol. They want to know, for
example, what to do with a person who telephones repeatedly between sessions, how to decide in which order to interpret a dream
sequence, what to do when an analysand instantly eroticizes the
conversation, how to listen for what is not said, what to look for in
assessing ego strength, how to map the precincts of ego and Self.
Students want to find a place for the intangible yet pressing presence
of the anima or animus concept as it arises in sexual transference
(See Ulanov 1979: 108). Should they interpret such material in terms
of archetypal themes or of object relations, and how to include both?
How do diagnostic categories necessary for prognosis, and for insurance forms, coordinate with diagnoses based on the recurrent archetypal symbols and motifs of their analysands' material? (Ulanovs
1987: 18-21). Students want to apply theory to practice. And so I
suggest specific chapters in Jung's *Collected Works* and where relevant articles by contemporary Jungians.

I constantly look for an increase of detailed perception of
analysand in the student-analyst. What is the sequence of conversation in a given session? What specific associations is the analysand
bringing to fantasy and dream material? What particular body pos-
tures, breathing rates, turn of the head as well as of phrase give clues
to the transference, and its changing rhythms from session to session? Is the student gaining a feel for the interplay of archetypal and
personal material, how it arranges the analysand's narrative of his or
her past, as well as the countertransference-transference dynamics in

the present? Are a student's interpretations not only correct but well-timed? Can a student hold an interpretation – *not* say it – but wait for the client's arrival at this insight? Kohut's words come to mind about the necessity of "creative observation" that "is always interwoven with theory..." (Kohut 1978: 388; see also Kohut 1962: 319-336; Kohut 1984: 160-171). Does a student suddenly go blank about concepts and is that because he or she needs to do more work to assimilate them, to own them? Or, does the blank occur because of unacknowledged affect between supervisor and student? Does the student feel sadistically judged by the supervisor and resort to a panicked dumbness to evade the blow? Does the supervisor miss the particular bent of the student's mind? Is the supervisor behaving like a know-it-all, or is the supervisor unduly modest? or ungenerous in sharing knowledge? Above all else, is the supervisor-supervisee couple usurping center stage, forgetting that the benefit of the treatment to the analysand endures as the main criterion of the "progress" of their work?

Another major purpose in supervision, I believe, is to convey an attitude of mind, or perhaps better, a habit of personality, which will inform and influence analytical work in unmistakably positive ways, giving confidence to the student and tangible evidence of that much sought growth in the student-analyst. This attitude or habit might best be described as appreciation of psychic reality. The wonder that the psyche exists and has so much to express; the amazement that the unconscious *is* and is *un*conscious; the astonishment that when we bend our ear to its murmurings, it will respond not only in kind, but in peculiarly apposite ways; the growing conviction that out of our conversation with this reality meaning will accumulate, get constructed, and yet appear to arrive – does the student experience any of this? Does the student feel its shock? its gift? its presence? If not, things will not go well. If so, regardless of wounds, the student will thrive.

Wounds are part of treatment and part of supervision. Each analyst must respond to each analysand out of the totality of his or her own personality – literally everything that is there. This must include, then, weaknesses as well as strengths, all of one's limitations as well as talents. Humbert's idea of the necessity of the match of wounds in analysand and analyst is a most helpful insight here, as well as the balancing idea Winnicott expresses when he says, "One would rather have a really suitable person for doing, this sort of work than an ill person made less ill by the analysis that is part of psycho-analytic training" (Winnicott 1971: 1-2; Humbert 1982: 121).

To learn to accept our wounds' part in the treatment, neither denying them nor inflicting them on the analysand, requires in the supervision an attitude of receptivity and attentiveness to the person of the student. This is different than the procedures of analysis with a student, because the main goal – and there is a main goal – always points to the analysand, the person under the student's care, and, by once-removed, under the supervisor's care. So the focus, the purpose of uncovering a wounded place in a student, is to facilitate treatment of the analysand. Is the analysand benefiting? That is the reference point around which supervisor and student always circle and find their bearings.

It is too extreme, I believe, to exclude this sort of analytical focus from supervision. The student's psyche is the instrument of treat-ment, so the student's afflictions must appear in the supervisory work and be noticed and attended to. Blocks in taking in material, fear to enter psychic reality which act as focal points in personal disturbance will turn up as well in the student's treatment of the analysand. For the sake of the analysand, these problems must be addressed in supervision. Though, at the opposite extreme supervi-sion is not analysis, nor should it be. The temptation always exists to turn it into analysis – for reasons to do with the supervisor's wounds sometimes, but also the much simpler wish to evade the hard labor of doing supervision. For here is a large synthetic task – to marshal theories, observation, budding personal style, the passing of knowl-edge from mind to mind, let alone to eschew all the temptations to lecture, to know better, to craft a disciple out of the student. No wonder supervisors may want to duck this job by doing a sort of analysis that is not really an analysis because the supervisor can always start talking and explaining! The reference point that guides the supervisor and student in the handling of the student's own complexes is always the treatment of the analysand. Discussion of the student's complexes centers on how they interfere with the case.

Practically, supervision means creating an atmosphere where stu-dents will bring their mistakes, their clumsiness, their dullness in the handling of a case, as well as their insight, their inspiration, their talent. Here they will say to the best of their ability where they are stuck, or confused, or bewildered, or know they are avoiding issues. And they will say where they suddenly got the picture, made the mutative interpretation, took a risk, won through to the analysand's heart and received in kind in their own heart. This atmosphere of supervision means students can own up to terrible anxiety, to violent intrusions of personal complexes into the treatment of an analysand, to the thrill of an inspiration that hit the mark. It means they can risk experimenting with theory, growing their own ground plan that will accompany them into the "unknown territory of the new case" (Winnicott 1971: 6). If the supervision gives a safe enough space, students will be surprised in trying to communicate by being communicated to unexpectedly from something deeper in themselves.

I have always been comforted by Leslie Farber's very funny account of his supervision with Harry Stack Sullivan. Using the first two sessions to illustrate how consistent Sullivan's practice was with his theory – that the self gets born in anxiety – Farber recounts how Sullivan deliberately provoked anxiety in him as part of the supervisory process. Farber managed, just barely, to survive it. Having taken months to arrange the first session, Farber felt Sullivan showed not the "tiniest interest" in his account of his patient, merely responded to his seeking advice with "a tired wave of his hand," asked an inscrutable question, and dismissed him. At the next meeting Sullivan asked if any thoughts had occurred since the last session. Farber confessed that he had not been up to thinking; he had been so anxious, he had simply gone to bed. To which Sullivan replied, "Well, that's rather promising. I hadn't really expected so much" (Farber 1976: 24). Any of us remembering our training days will feel summed up here all the squirming we did in the presence of an admired supervisor, all the anxiety flooding through us, all the deadening insecurity.

Progress in supervision goes well beyond increase of skill. Evidence of an evolving personal analytical style must appear. For example, students become less defensive, more able to say what they do not know and need to learn, from and with each other as well as in relation to the supervisor. In small group supervision, students will become more direct about the question they want others to focus upon, and blunt about their needs for support and able and willing, then, to accept a matching brusqueness in confrontation with their colleagues. A student growing in this way will be less preoccupied with a supervisor's evaluation and more concentrated upon taking in all that is available, no matter from whom, no matter how it comes. Training issues take second place to learning issues. An appetite for the material grows: the reality of psychic reality captures the imagination. Good supervisory sessions, both small group and individual, generate excitement and shared passion, so that all of us present experience energy zinging around between the material, what the students put in and what the supervisor contributes. Each enhances the other. Everybody learns something valuable that could not be learned all by themselves. Such moments generate gratitude for dependence that is met and fed, and allows one to thrive and become creative.

In such an atmosphere students may be able to see how their countertransference reactions interfere with responses to an analysand. They can admit this to themselves, hear what the supervisor or their peers in the small case supervision class have to say about it, and take the matter back with them into their own analytical work, neither turning supervision into substitute analysis, nor avoiding the relevance of the comments for their own personal growth. Students will show an increase of empathy toward themselves as well as toward their analysand. They will begin to discern which archetypal constellations predominate in their style of work. They will be able to imagine how their own style of analyzing can develop. Their personal style will move from the precincts of persona into those of person.

A major criterion in assessing students' progress in supervision, I believe, rests on whether or not they show themselves to be trainable. Can they make use of what the supervisor has to offer, what the books can tell, what their peers say to enlarge their knowledge and develop their own style of working? Or do they experience learning as humiliation? Do they enjoy the work, or does it unduly fatigue and depress them? Do they possess elbow room to play with ideas and different modes of perception and apperception? Or is the supervision a clenching of teeth, a scattering of affect, a scanning of the supervisor to see "how am I doing?" The ability to be trained is the graduating mark of achievement. Not to please, not to placate, not to defend, not to prove, not to defeat or compete, but to learn and be glad in it. To get fat on the feeding and enjoy the taste. For what we hope for in the end, really, is more than a well-equipped person, more than a display of skill. We want students who are alive in their work, who delight in it, in a most personal way. Sometimes a student, even one of considerable talent and a great deal of knowledge, may prove untrainable. The basic defensive pattern may be set in rigid ways. No change may be possible – except disintegration and rebuilding from the ground up – and the price seems too great and is resisted at all costs. Then, for me at least, the supervision has failed.

When supervision succeeds, it grants to all participants an increased psychic space. I feel more free to elaborate, to imagine, to reflect on my own analytical style. I may, for example, imagine being an analysand of this student, or try to see the way I might work with the analysand the student is presenting, and compare that with the student's actual handling of the case. Seeing where the student and I vary in approach as well as agree is instructive for us both. I like great analytical spaces in which it is possible to look from all angles at the psychic reality manifest in this particular person's life. Students permit this when they permit themselves to be themselves as they acquire knowledge and find their own styles of analytical being. That is why some of us continue to look forward to our supervisory sessions. For we know, some of the time at least, we will find in them an experience of being alive and real, involved in a profession that, when it works, makes us feel alive and real and glad to be so. Jung summed up the risk and the joy when he advised, "Learn your theories as well as you can, but put them aside when you touch the miracle of the living soul. Not theories, but your own creative individuality alone must decide" (Jung cited in Baynes 1928:36).

Note:

This article originated in my being asked, along with others, to respond to the question: How Do I Assess Progress in Supervision? This symposium was published in *The Journal of Analytical Psychology*, 27, 2, 1982:105-131. I have expanded it slightly in this revision.

Bibliography

Baynes, H.G. and C.F. (1928). *Contributions to Analytical Psychology.* London: Kegan Paul Trench Trubner.

Farber, L.H. (1976). *Lying, Despair, Jealousy, Envy, Sex, Suicide, Drugs. and the Good Life.* New York: Basic Books.

Fordham, M. (1961). "Suggestions Toward a Theory of Supervision." *Journal of Analytical Psychology*, 6, 2.

Humbert, E. (1982). "How Do I Assess Progress in Supervision?" *Journal of Analytical Psychology*, 27, 2.

Kohut, H. (1962). "The Psychoanalytical Curriculum." *The Search for the Self, Selected Writings of Heinz Kohut 1950-1978*, Vol. 1 of 4, ed. Paul H. Ornstein, New York: International Universities Press.

— (1978). "Introductory Remarks to the Panel on 'Self Psychology and the Sciences of Man.' *The Search for the Self, Selected writings of Heinz Kohut 1978-1981*, Vol. 3 of 4, ed. Paul H. Ornstein, Madison: International Universities Press.

— (1984). *How Does Analysis Cure?* Chicago: Chicago University Press.

Ulanov, A. (1979). 'Follow-up treatment in cases of patient/therapist sex,' *Journal of the American Academy of Psychoanalysis*, 7, 1, 101-110.

Ulanov, A. and B. (1987). *The Witch and the Clown: Two Archetypes of Human Sexuality.* Wilmette: Chiron.

Winnicott, D.W. (1975). *Through Pediatrics to Psycho-Analysis.* New York, Basic Books, pp. 194-204.

— (1971a). *Therapeutic Consultations in Child Psychiatry.* New York: Basic Books.

— (1971b). *Playing and Reality.* London: Tavistock.

[H] H.-J. Wilke

Until now little has been written on the central importance of supervision in the training of analysts. Nor, in my view, has it been subject to much methodical research. This is not so much a shortcoming as a demonstration of how much analytical psychology, a modern discipline which is still striving to establish itself on a scientific basis, is traditionally dependent on direct verbal and non-verbal communication, and to development within that tradition. So this discussion of supervision can change nothing since the crucial factors, in the supervision process as it develops, are personal experience and communication: critical reflection increases an awareness of that developmental process.

The terms 'supervision' and 'control analysis' seem to me to obscure rather than to elucidate the process. Both words indicate a standpoint beyond that of the events taking place; they allocate a superior position to the supervisor, make him into a super-ego, or controller. To some extent the trainee does experience his supervisor in that way, but, to my mind, this makes it possible for the supervision to fail in its essential purpose. I should like to amplify these remarks under three headings.

Supervision as Assistance

The beginner in the field of professional analytical psychology is inexperienced and consequently anxious. He needs help, (a) in understanding the dynamics of the patients, (b) in the use of therapeutic methods, and (c) in coming to a valid estimate of his own role and finding out how he (with his complexes) is integrated into the analysis of the patient.

In all this the supervisor plays the part of an assistant, like the senior surgeon who hands the beginner the correct and required 'instruments' (ideas, amplifications and so on), thus helping both patient and trainee. It is through the supervisor that the patient will be better understood by his therapist. The supervisor contributes additional insights and amplifications for the understanding of the patient, and so assumes a partially interpretative function as regards the patient's unconscious whenever he intuitively succeeds in participating correctly in the therapeutic process. But should he fail to do so, and should his insights not meet the immediate therapeutic situation but embrace contents which will perhaps only later be constellated and actualized in the patient, then the trainee leaves his supervision and goes back to the therapy rather poorly advised.

In Latin, *assisto* conveys a sense of helping and supporting, as 'assistance' does today. As regards supervision, therefore, assistance signifies, true to its original meaning, the providing of help for both therapist and patient. To this the supervisor, in his helping function, brings his professional experience as well as his experience of life, his 'personal equation,' his complexes and his problems. On the occasions when the supervisor has lost contact with the content of the analysis and is following his own dynamic, the trainee will be able to tell him so, if the relationship between them is a non-authoritative one.

Supervision as Seconding

The word 'second' derives its meaning from duelling and fencing. In certain forms of fencing, which was partly a sport, partly a kind of initiation rite (and, moreover in the eighteenth century, was regulated by the authorities), the second played a protective role: he was permitted to crouch down near at hand, and with his own weapon, intercept those blows prohibited by the rules of duelling. It is reported in the Encyclopedia that the ship that protected or accompanied the flag officer was termed *secundant*, or *secund*. The Latin word *secundus* designates the second place in a temporal sequential or numerical order, but it later acquired the sense of encouraging and approving, and also meant 'fortunate,' or 'going according to plan.'

From this etymological outline emerges the important idea of the protective function of seconding, and of the second place. The therapeutic encounter is between trainee and patient, and the supervisor should always take second place to that. We know how fatal it is if, in the mind of the trainee, that relationship is reversed, and he makes the therapy serve the needs of the supervision to gain approval by means of interesting dreams or other material. The center of events then shifts from the therapy to the supervision. Admittedly this occurs only seldom, but there is the danger of a diadic situation becoming a triadic one. For this reason the first thing almost every analyst does the moment he is qualified is to give up the supervision, and only take it up again later if he finds he needs to.

The secondary, subservient, role of the supervisor is demonstrated most clearly by the fact that he is never up to the minute as regards the treatment. I know about the therapy only in so far as the trainee informs me. Only if he has too little understanding of his material am I in an advantageous position through my own understanding of the analytic context, and I can then only intervene on the basis of my (false or apparent) superior position. This means that I am not strengthening the confidence which the trainee should gradually acquire through supervision, but am in danger of confirming his feelings of inferiority. It is important for the supervision, therefore, that I retain my secondary role and interpret events from 'below' not from 'above.'

Along with the supervision as seconding, and assisting, I also see in it an important protecting function. Protection is of value for both the trainee therapist and the patient. Both need safeguarding from what are, in boxing terms, those inadmissible and dangerous blows 'below the belt,' and help is needed to work through them when they have become unavoidable.

The protective function is there because of the threat (often emphasized by Jung) arising from the unconscious dynamic of the complexes, the infection of the psychic illness, against which neither the consciousness nor the ego of the therapist confers sufficient immunity. To see it as a concession would be a misunderstanding, since it can only become effective when it is needed and called for, and because the therapist must, at all times, be conscious of what help he needs, and of his own weakness and inferiority. Also, it always leads to that weak spot in our experience and professional practice that is difficult to bear, not only for the beginner, but for everyone. There is then a chance for an increasing colleague relationship to develop. Eventually it will become clear to the trainee that the superiority he experiences from his supervisor derives, to a great extent, from the supervisor's role, and that it is an advantageous standpoint. He can then be given it, and benefit from it.

The Supervisor as Adjunct

The word 'adjutant' evokes military associations. Since the days of Freud military terms have established themselves in analytical imagery and indicate an inner and outer conflict which often takes place in the field of the transference. The military adjutant is a desk, not a field officer and is a purveyor of information in the central military command. This conveys very precisely the special part the supervisor plays in analytical training in Germany, where, I would add, ruefully, we have to sigh forms and pass them on to insurances and institutions to which the candidate is not yet accredited.

The function of the military adjutant has a distinct bearing on supervision in the sense that the collecting of manifold information (from case studies, the literature and professional experience, comparable to the adjutant's reports to his superiors) provides those amplifications which the supervisor supplies for the trainee to work through with his patient.

Here, too, Latin provides us with meanings more far-reaching than those military ones. I find it interesting that *adiuto* denotes primarily someone, or something, which supports devotedly, encourages and assists. It might be seen as the assiduousness of a subordinate military officer; but in respect of the analytic situation it can be thought of as that liveliness, inner interest and emotional and intellectual value which the supervision assures for both sides. Thus, I frequently overrun my prescribed time during supervisory sessions.

Further Thoughts

This commitment, which applies to supervisor and trainee, indicates a process which does not relate to the cognitive functions alone. It ensures the personal transmission of professional norms and standards, our living tradition that is not codified and which, in its fullness, scarcely admits of codification. For during training the trainee gradually gains his professional identity as a Jungian analyst. The supervisor, over the years, gains his identity as a professional educator.

In all this there is, in my view, a decisive parameter of success for both patient and therapist. The increasing stabilization of the professional identity of the trainee I take as an important precondition for the success of the analysis of the patient, at any event as regards intellectual and cognitive development. Behind that positive developmental process occur those errors in method and technique which can run parallel with it, and those misinterpretations and neurotic interventions in the handling of the patient which are always subject to further correction. That process, observable in the supervision, is the continuation of what began in the personal analysis; it develops further, even after the training analysis is over, through the analysis of the patient, and helps the professional identity of the trainee to become part of his personal identity. It prevents the development of a professional persona that is separate or split off from the rest of the personality. It is the process which over and above the training accompanies us throughout our professional lives.

It is not surprising that, in such circumstances, the therapy of a patient can founder while the training and the supervision run a successful course. I have found it an interesting and important observation that a trainee whose case presentation has had a markedly skeptical reception is seen, as a result of later discussions, as most likely having had more of an eye to his own development than to that of the patient.

For the supervisor the discordant development of patient and therapist is difficult to detect. I think it occurs infrequently but that may be due to my taking the trainee's development to be a parameter of that of his patient.

Naturally there are any number of parameters by which the success of the therapy, for both patient and therapist, can be estimated. To consider the supervisor in his role as helper and protector and in terms of his emotional commitment will yield certain criteria. If the protective function of the supervisor is being called upon unduly, then the case can produce special problems and difficulties – for example, there are suicidal crises, or the therapist has serious difficulties, overanxiety, lack of insight, or inadequate experience of life. If the helping function is being unduly required, this can be an indication that the trainee has made too little effort as regards knowledge of theory, the literature and method. What causes me most problems is when I do not succeed in making an emotional commitment either to the case or to the difficulties of the trainee. When this happens I suspect that it reflects a disturbance within the supervisory relationship that also exists, as a problem, within the therapy itself. All estimates of the supervision must change during the course of it, and be subject to a development which, even when quite precarious, can serve as a standard by which to assess the therapeutic situation of the patient.

Development on the part of the supervisor during a long supervision indicates creative processes at work in both patient and therapist. For me a supervision usually begins with a kind of chaos. Out of that emerge, first, the picture of the trainee, then with, and behind it, the picture of his patient. While we work at the picture of the patient that builds up between us, imperceptibly and to a greater or lesser degree, the pictures we have of either other also change. We learn how to deal with each other sensibly and productively, both to recognize our weaknesses and to respect each other: we become colleagues. That relationship is the factor that later integrates the professional group, and gives a common intellectual basis to our national or local one, on which the training establishment is centered. And that, too, reflects the success of our supervision.

Part V

Phases in a Supervisor's Life

[14]

The Transition from Training Candidate to Supervising Analyst

Paul Kugler

The period of time immediately following the completion of analytic training through the assumption of the responsibilities of a supervising analyst may be emotionally turbulent as the recent graduate works to build up an analytic practice and undergoes acculturation into the professional community. Generally it is assumed that an analyst needs to wait a certain number of years, usually five, following graduation before engaging training candidates as a supervisor. To better understand the role of this transitional period in the development of the identity of the analyst, I would like to explore some of the psychological and social dynamics encountered during this transition from training candidate to supervising analyst. We have analyzed in great detail the development of our patients' identities, their intrapsychic and inter-psychic conflicts, past and present, as well as, their personal and cultural contexts. Traditionally we have assumed that the analysis of the other half of the therapeutic dyad takes place during the analyst's training analysis. And to a certain extent this is true. But, only to a limited extent. A significant amount of the identity of the Training Analyst develops only after graduation and often takes place outside of the context of personal analysis.

The transition from training candidate to supervising analyst is a complicated psychological process about which little has been written. Recently graduated analysts carry a heavy burden of expectations which they may not be immediately equipped to fulfill. Often new analysts encounter a certain pressure to maintain a presence of maturity, stability, authority and confidence that may not necessarily coincide with their actual psychic reality. In addition, there are unconscious institutional dynamics around issues of training and professional rivalries confronting new analysts. And rarely are these dynamics in the development of the analyst's identity made conscious or spoken about directly at the institute level.

The Stages of Professional Development

Essentially there are four phases in the professional life of a psychoanalyst. The first is the period of Training Candidacy during which the person receives formal education at a Training Institute. During this period we acquire experience in personal analysis, participate in case conferences, are supervised, and attend didactic seminars. Then, at some institutes, there is the writing up of clinical cases, a thesis and the examination process.

The second phase extends through the five or so years immediately following the completion of the Diploma. During this period the analyst is often referred to as a Recent Graduate or Junior Analyst and may be restricted from participation in certain aspects of training. This phase involves becoming integrated into the professional community and further developing their professional identity and personal style of analysis.

The third phase begins roughly five years after graduation. Analysts at this middle stage variously are referred to as Supervising Analysts, Training Analysts, and Senior Analysts. This period involves, for some, active participation in the training of candidates and opens up many new facets of individuation. There is an increased focus on didactic and pedagogical issues. We may write more. We may teach more. Attention to the existential concerns associated with the everyday running of a Training Institute may increase. As the Senior Analyst confronts the difficult realities of training, the process is less idealized and more realistically approached. There is increased focus on the dynamics of the Training Institute as a whole, working to resolve complicated professional conflicts and ethical problems which require a subtle holding of the tension between candidates' desires, analysts' ideals and the Institute's practical realities. Senior Analysts also assume the fiduciary responsibility to maintain economic solvency in the Institute, weighing the balance between student and faculty needs and financial realities.

During this phase we have the opportunity to develop our clinical capacity to supervise and run case seminars. Our attention is focussed on training analysis, analytic technique and the process of conceptualizing the clinical case and conveying this capacity to candidates in didactic seminars. More importance is placed on the quality of the training process as a whole – admissions interviews, didactic seminars, examination procedures, supervision, case conferences, and where required, the writing of thesis and clinical cases. Essential to the successful chairing of these committees is a precise understanding of the training requirements, along with a combination of psychological maturity, common sense and good will. Through their work to develop the highest possible quality of the various facets of training, the Senior Analyst works to ensure the future quality of the profession itself.

There is a fourth and final phase in the analyst's professional life which involves retirement from training activities and clinical practice. Analysts in this phase might be characterized as Elders of the analytic community. Our profession is one in which retirement from analytic practice is almost unheard of except in cases of health problems or the development of a different vocation. Simply retiring from private practice at age 65 or 70 is the exception, not the rule.

The focus of this chapter will be primarily on the second phase, the period immediately following the completion of formal analytic training through the assumption of the responsibilities of a supervising analyst. This transitional period can be emotionally turbulent as the new graduate works to build up an analytic practice, undergoes acculturation into the professional community, transforms the perspective on analytic training from candidate to analyst, and begins to develop the necessary analytic, didactic, and clinical skills to function as a supervising analyst. Perhaps by becoming more conscious of the intrapsychic and interpsychic tensions encountered during this transitional period we may provide for a more integrated experience in the process of becoming a supervising analyst.

The Transition from Training Candidate to Analyst

The first issue I would like to review is the effect receiving the Diploma has on the patients of the new analyst. When I was Director of Admissions I observed that every year there would be two or three applicants to the training program who were in analysis with recently graduated analysts. Often these applicants were ill prepared psychologically and their applications for training were usually unsuccessful. When asked during admissions interviews why they had decided to apply for training, often there was an uncomfortable moment when these applicants replied that their analyst had encouraged them to pursue training, or had interpreted a particular dream as "a calling to become a Jungian analyst." I often asked myself whether it was the applicant's desire to become an analyst motivating the application or was it *their analyst's desire to become an analyst*? Recent graduates may project aspects of their still partially unconscious analytic identities onto clients, especially those who have activated an idealized countertransference, and look for "analyst material" in their analysands. An unconscious confusion results between their own developing analytic identity and the personal identities of their analysands. While the new graduate has objectively received the Diploma and is an official member of the professional community, on the subjective level, assumption of the analyst identity may take many years.

Differentiation from the Student Image

The new analyst has spent many years with their identity firmly intertwined with the image of being a student. This identification does not end immediately upon graduation. The recent graduate's identity and its relationship to the archetypal syzygy of student-teacher may take various forms. After receiving the Diploma, the analyst may remain partially identified with the student pole. When this happens the new analyst tends to become over-identified with candidates still in training and assume the role of "candidate advocate," siding with students in conflict with the training committee.

Many years have been spent by recent graduates with unconscious aspects of their identity interwoven with various portions of the training program. Prior to graduation the candidate's relation to other students, teachers, personal analysts, and supervisors is infused with unconscious contents ranging from shadow material to Self projections. This allows for a powerful and rich psychological experience during training. Personal analysis and supervision provide a container to differentiate and integrate this psychic material, but upon graduation the new analyst, like the young adult leaving home, must either introject these psychic contents or find new places to house them in other interpersonal relationships.

Separation from the Training Program, while providing relief from having to meet outer requirements, presents a different set of issues. Suddenly the new analyst is on his / her own and often is confronted with a disquieting anxiety about competence and analytic ability. To compensate for self-doubt and insecurity about professional capabilities, the beginning analyst may look for security and certainty in a particular school of thought or mentor. Either or both may function as an idealized Self-object, providing a sense of security, cohesion and direction. The community of analysts connected by a common ideology or mentor replaces the student "family" lost upon graduation. Eventually a healthy degree of disappointment may surface as the Self projection is withdrawn and the school of thought or mentor is viewed more realistically.

Another reaction to the student-teacher syzygy may be for the recent graduate to disidentify with the student pole and over-identify with the teacher. In this case, the graduate has a strong desire to immediately teach, do supervision, and assume all the training responsibilities that until only recently have been carried out by their training analysts and supervisors. The movement out of the student image and into the assumption of the analyst identity is also often accompanied by a reactivation of unresolved adolescent conflicts. New analysts may find themselves acting out old family patterns. This is sometimes experienced in exaggerated needs to idealize or repudiate "parental" figures in the profession in order to individuate and achieve an analytic identity.

Boundaries and Training

As the new graduate works to establish a psychological relationship to a Training Institute many dynamics will be encountered. There are the usual institutional transferences, the struggle between the so-called clinical and symbolic perspectives, the question of standards for admission into Training Institutes and professional societies, and the potential for generational conflicts between the older more established analysts and the recent graduates needing to find their own individual voices and authority.

During this period immediately following graduation, many complicated boundary issues are also encountered. For example, how "friendly" might the new analyst be with students who only a short time ago were colleagues? When the new analyst speaks to candidates their comments are now colored with the "analyst image," its power and authority. This is not such a problem when the analyst graduates from a foreign institute and returns home, but it is a problem where the recent graduate continues to be involved with their Training Institute. When the new analyst begins to sit on admission and evaluation committees, teach, and give exams, other boundary issues arise. For example, should new analysts teach candidates known during their student period? What discussions should recent graduates absent themselves from in training meetings. Should they participate in evaluations of candidates who were in training with them? Or, should the recent graduate wait four or five years for a new generation of students? These concerns are complicated and need to be carefully balanced between the value of the training experience for the new analyst and the need to respect the boundaries of candidates.

Assimilation of the Analytic Identity

Often during this period of dis-identification with the student image and the assimilation of the analytic identity, the recent graduate may experience emotional fluctuations between feelings of inflation and those of insecurity and inadequacy. When inflated there is a strong desire to teach, or maybe even to form a new institute. There is an overconfidence in analytic capacity and the feeling of knowing much more than past teachers and supervisors. New analysts may feel the Institute's entrance requirements for training are not high enough, or clinical experience of applicants not extensive enough, or the requirements for the completion of the diploma not strict enough. Tensions may emerge between the outer requirements as defined by the Institute and the newly developing inner identity of the analyst. Until the professional identity is firmly established accompanied by an integrated sense of individuality and uniqueness, the analyst may feel threatened by outer regulations used to define "Jungian Analyst." During this phase the analyst's identity may still be unstable and vulnerable, and look for confirmation through an outer reification of its image in Institute requirements.

On the other hand, when deflated feelings surface, the new analyst may question the choice of vocation, capacity to practice as an analyst, and may fear being discovered for all he or she does not know about the theory and practice of psychoanalysis. Dreams appear in which the analyst has failed the final exams or forgotten to complete all the requirements for the diploma. *Integration of the analytic identity involves meeting not only the outer institutional requirements, but also the requirements of the psyche itself.* These inner requirements are often more difficult to achieve than those objectively spelled out in The Institute's Guide to Training. As we struggle to discover and fulfill our own requirements to be an analyst, it becomes more and more apparent that these are not necessarily the same as those formalized on the Institutional level. No longer are the "judges" located on the Admissions Committee, the Evaluations Committee or the Examinations Committee. Gradually in the process of developing our analytic identity these historical figures transform into psychic functions, inner figures, aiding in the process of psychological judgment, personal admissions, and self-examination. When these figures are left in projected form, we may try to institutionalize them, creating the outer Institute and its requirements in our own image. If we are able to differentiate our inner requirements from the outer institutional ones, we will be better able to lobby hard in professional discussions for our unique point of view, while also being able to accept modification or rejection of our proposals without feeling narcissistically wounded. More psychological differentiation of inner requirements from outer ones may lead to less institutional splitting and more tolerance of differences and individuality in analytic training.

Summary

There is a period of time immediately following the completion of the Diploma in Analytical Psychology through the assumption of the responsibilities of a supervisor, in which the analyst's professional identity is being integrated. During this period of acculturation into the analytic community, we may experience more inflation, deflation, rigidity, anxiety, zeal, vulnerability, and inferiority than during other periods in our professional life. Awareness of the possibility of these intrapsychic and interpsychic tensions may allow for a more conscious and less turbulent passage through the phase of professional development immediately following graduation and leading up to the assumption of the role of supervising analyst.

[15]

The Education of the Supervisor

Marga Speicher

Supervisors play an important role in the professional development of an analyst: they teach, facilitate, oversee; they provide support, suggestions, critique; they function as role models. As faculty members they are full participants in the educational process for the next generation of analysts. But how does an analyst prepare to become a supervisor, clinical teacher, faculty member? What are the components of the educational process through which an analyst becomes a supervisor? Such questions are repeatedly raised in the Jungian training community and call for extensive exploration by those engaged in analytic training.

An educational process always extends over a substantial period of time – typically a lifetime. To be effective it must reach and affect the whole person, touching conscious and unconscious dimensions. Education always calls for experiential, emotional, intellectual and spiritual awareness and knowledge as well as the ability to apply one's knowledge in practice. Since ancient times educational endeavors in crafts, business, arts, professions have begun on a simple model of learning in an apprenticeship. As a given field expanded, such educational endeavors developed into programs of structured study and learning.

Becoming a Jungian Analyst

The process of becoming an analyst has moved from the apprenticeship model in the first half of this century to the current model of structured training programs with three major components:

1. The candidate's personal development is fundamental and includes an immersion into an analytic process that precedes training and continues throughout the training years. This process is expected to lead to an analytic stance towards oneself that continues throughout life.

2. Study in relevant fields of knowledge aims toward an understanding of human nature as manifest in body and psyche, emotion and intellect, spirit and soul; in society, culture, history; in the arts, myths, and traditions of religious practice. Candidates study intrapsychic and interpersonal dimensions of the analytic process from the clinical, developmental and archetypal perspectives in lecture series, seminars and workshops.

3. Analytic practice under supervision is the final phase in the analyst's preparation. In the supervisory hour, personal development and theoretical knowledge come together as candidate and supervisor focus on the student's work with analysands.

In most institutes the candidate is expected to write a final paper (thesis) to demonstrate the capacity to integrate the knowledge and understanding gained in training. This final paper shows the fruits of their immersion in the didactic and analytic process and provides an opportunity for the articulation of their experience. The thesis has experiential, descriptive, reflective, and cognitive components.

Becoming a Jungian Supervisor of Candidates

Supervision of analytic candidates serves several functions: (a) teaching of analytic practice, (b) overseeing the candidate's work with analysands, (c) attention to issues of personal development in the candidate,[1] when such issues affect her work with analysands, (d) evaluation of the candidate's capacity to work analytically with clients that includes fairness to the candidate, the institution, and the candidate's future analysands. There is considerable diversity and discussion amongst faculty members about the relative importance of and interplay amongst these functions.

The term supervisor stresses the second of the above functions. I hold the view that all four are significant and consider supervisors to be members of an institute's faculty and an integral part of the institute's overall teaching process.

The process of becoming a supervisor builds on the process of becoming an analyst and goes beyond, calling for the acquisition of additional experience, reflection, and study. To this day, an analyst becomes a supervisor in the apprenticeship model: The analyst has had experience of being in supervision as a candidate and often in the years following graduation. As a member of the professional community the analyst has observed the institute faculty, heard (or overheard) senior analysts' comments regarding supervisory dilemmas, and gradually become a participant in discussions about matters of training. At some point the analyst becomes a supervisor. Between 1990 and 1992 I conducted a survey for the *Workshop on Supervision* at the XII International Congress for Analytical Psychology in 1992 in Chicago, IL., about the practices related to supervision in Jungian training programs. The results of the survey were presented during the *Workshop on Supervision.*[2] I will summarize points of the survey that have direct bearing on this essay.

Respondents to the survey concurred that functioning as a supervisor builds on qualities and skills of being an analyst as well as requiring knowledge and skills extending beyond those of analyst. Differences arose about how institutes should address issues pertaining to professional development of supervisors:

1. One group of institutes holds the position that continued training beyond receiving the diploma is the sole responsibility of the analyst. While they acknowledge the value of self-directed further development leading to the designation of some analysts as supervisors, these institutes speak for intentional absence of institutional standards, recommendations, and criteria.

2. Another group of institutes reports discussion and questioning regarding the development and designation of supervisors. They require a number of years experience (typically five years) beyond receiving the diploma to provide for a period of transition following training. During this time the analyst can consolidate an identity as analyst and become a full member of the professional community.[3] Institutes named various qualities which a supervisor needs to demonstrate. The responses, however, did not give details about what such demonstration entails nor how it is evaluated. The list of qualities included: (a) personal and professional maturity, (b) ability to pursue analytic work in depth, (c) ability for analytical reflection, (d)

capacity to tolerate the uncertainties inherent in the analytic process and, therefore, to reduce the tendency to compensate by pseudo-certainty, (e) capacity to reflect on and work with the interpersonal dynamics between analysand and candidate as well as between candidate and supervisor, (f) capacity for integration of theory and analytical practice which might be demonstrated in the form of papers or public lectures, (g) demonstrated ability to teach, (h) participation in a series of workshops or lectures dealing with issues specific to supervision. – The responses in their entirety show that senior analysts in most institutes are thinking about and struggling with issues related to the professional development of supervisors.

My concern with the issues pertaining to professional development of supervisors came to the forefront during the years (1987-1992) when I served on the Board of the C.G. Jung Institute of New York,[4] initially as board member and later as Chairperson (1989-1992). During that period the Board considered whether to have articulated guidelines for the professional development of supervisors.[5] Those discussions and the involvement in the *Workshop on Supervision* at the Chicago I.A.A.P. Congress led me to engage intensively in personal reflection and thinking about my experience as candidate and supervisor, review the professional literature on supervision in depth psychology, engage in discussion with colleagues across disciplines and learn how other institutions have dealt with the issues around supervision.

In my review of the literature and discussions with colleagues I have come upon descriptions of experiences from many theoretical perspectives that were valuable and easily integrated into Jungian thinking and practice.

Professional Development of Supervisors in the Psychoanalytic Field

In many metropolitan areas in the United States structured programs for psychoanalytically oriented supervisors have come into existence. These programs[6] are open to graduate analysts and offer a part-time course of study for one or two years focusing on the theoretical and practical aspects of the supervisory process. Reading, lectures, discussion seminars, observation of live supervisory sessions, viewing of videotapes, supervision of a student's work in supervision, preparation of a paper – these are some of the means by which the educational process facilitates the transition from the practice of analysis to the teaching and supervision of analysts.[7]

Professional Literature on Supervision

The professional literature on supervision has been growing steadily. When the C.G. Jung Institute of New York devoted a Faculty Retreat to discussion of supervision in 1991, we compiled a list of articles by Jungian analysts as background reading.[8] We also put together a short list of recent writing by analysts of various theoretical orientations.[9] Reviewing the literature with colleagues was rewarding and stimulating.

Becoming a Jungian Supervisor: A Further Perspective

In the Jungian training community, discussion about the process of preparation for supervisors is alive. Two quite different viewpoints were articulated in 1992: (a) need for a formal preparation to become a supervisor and (b) informal preparation, but no formal requirements. A basic question, then, arises: How do we attend to the process of becoming a supervisor? Is it necessary that the training community attend to the process? What are the archetypal dynamics that may lie behind the process which leads to a transition in professional life from analyst to supervisor? For me, the process of initiation serves as the archetypal dynamic energizing the process of becoming a supervisor of candidates.[10] The process of initiation contains several aspects: (a) the applicant must possess certain qualities that make her eligible to proceed to another phase; (b) entry into a process that has conscious and unconscious components – tasks to be performed, steps to be taken, new attitudes to become manifest; (c) designation of the moment when the community confirms the applicant has completed the process.

When we look at the process of becoming a supervisor from this archetypal perspective, it becomes the task and responsibility of the training community to direct and facilitate the process. The fulfillment of the responsibility calls for a level of care analogous to the process of preparation of analysts. When the training community takes such a perspective, connection to the archetypal energy is facilitated for current and future supervisors carrying the responsibilities of the position: to be co-initiators (together with all faculty) for the next generation of analysts.

What form might a preparation of Jungian supervisors take? I will offer thoughts that have grown out of my own experience with the intent and hope of stimulating reflection, thinking, and discussion in the training community. My views rest on the following assumptions:

1. A graduate analyst who wishes to become a supervisor and teacher of candidates is seeking to enter a new phase of professional life within the training community. The entry into this new phase stands under the archetypal image of initiation.

2. The training community carries responsibility for delineating the qualities the applicant needs to possess, the steps and tasks involved in the preparation, and the moment that designates the supervisor in her new position.

3. The energy which the training community devotes to the preparation of supervisors brings multifold returns in its impact on the training process: it enhances, enriches, deepens, and supports the process.

Towards a Model of Preparation for Supervisors

As the training community moves towards developing a model of preparation for supervisors, senior faculty in training programs need to review and articulate their stance toward the preparation of new faculty and supervisors. They must decide whether to follow the apprenticeship model or to develop a more structured model. Responsibility and authorship for a program of supervisory preparation rests fully with senior faculty in each training program.

The process of preparation to be a supervisor has several major components:

1. Capacity to work as analyst is the foundation for preparation to be a supervisor. Graduation from a Jungian training program is essential and should be followed by a period of time (typically five years) in which the analyst more fully moves out of her identity as candidate, brings to further resolution the transferential ties to the

institute faculty and consolidates her stance as analyst. Such consolidation includes: continuation of the analyst's pursuit to do analytic work in depth over a period of time (long-term analytic work) coupled with ongoing reflection, study, reading, collegial discussion about issues of analytic practice. Regular participation in programs with professional content sponsored by Jungian societies as well as organizations in the analytic field in general provide a forum for exchange with colleagues. The analyst thus establishes for herself a pattern of ongoing self-directed professional study analogous to the continued personal exploration following dyadic analytic work.

2. An analyst has to have the desire and interest to become a faculty member, supervisor and clinical teacher. Not all analysts wish to be supervisors. But if and when an analyst desires to move toward supervision, she needs to engage in the relevant preparation.

3. Direct preparation for work as a supervisor can take place during or following the period of consolidation of the analyst's professional identity. A very good medium for the preparatory work is the formation of small study groups to provide a container for the process. Depending on the size of the training community, such study groups could form on the local or regional level. They would meet periodically under the leadership of experienced supervisors and center their work around: (a) reflection on the experience of supervision while a candidate; (b) theoretical study and discussion of the relevant literature; (c) observation of supervisory sessions; (d) issues pertaining to the evaluative component in supervision of candidates within a training program. The period of preparation might conclude with the writing of a paper addressing some aspect of the supervisory process. The paper would provide a medium for review and integration of experiential, descriptive, reflective, and cognitive understanding of some aspect of the supervisory process.

Reflection on the Experience of Supervision. Reflection on one's personal experience of being supervised leads to increased awareness of the supervisory process[11]. It is a consciousness-raising endeavor. Questions to be explored might include: What were the styles of my supervisors? Which style of supervision was the most useful (least useful) to me at what point in training? Why? What were the gaps in my supervisory experience as a candidate? How would I wish to fill them? What functions of supervision were most relevant in the training process: focus on learning needs; focus on practice, clinical understanding, combining of theory and practice; understanding the analysand, the analytic process, the intrapsychic and interpersonal dynamics, the personal and/or archetypal aspects, the transferential field, issues of personal development that affected the analytic field? What was my experience of the interplay between the teaching and the evaluative aspect of supervision? Were evaluations fully discussed? If not, why not? How would I have liked to see them handled? – As prospective supervisors review and discuss their experiences, awareness of important components of the supervisory process will increase.

Theoretical Study of the Relevant Literature. The Jungian literature on supervision could be studied almost in its entirety. The essays in this volume probably cover much of the existing Jungian literature. The relevant literature in the analytic field at large is, however, more extensive. Any study group can easily build a bibliography that serves to raise innumerable questions for discussion. I recommend Clinical Perspectives on the Supervision of Psychoanalysis and Psychotherapy (see note 8.2) as a good starting point; the contributors to that volume provide a variety of viewpoints on the supervisory process and references to additional sources. Extensive references also can be found at the bibliography at the end of this book.

A list of important issues for fruitful study will quickly become very long indeed. It seems essential, though, that matters related to the process of learning and teaching be considered. These are the areas where there are substantive differences from the analytic stance. A prospective supervisor needs to find a supervisory stance which fits her personality and which takes into account the different ways in which candidates learn best. Where the supervisor's theoretical-analytic interest is at the moment, will affect her selection of the point of focus on the candidate's work. It may or may not coincide with the point of focus most significant for the candidate's learning. Questions of legal and ethical responsibility need to be addressed.

Issues more directly related to teaching range from instruction on how to take an analytic stance for the beginning candidate to the facilitation of sensitive attunement to the transferential field, archetypal dynamics and early life traumas. How do we foster the development of an empathic stance and of the ability to hold firm? How do we stimulate a sense of curiosity and engagement towards discovery? How do we assist candidates towards the development of an analytic field in which understanding, insight, development can arise? How do we clearly differentiate the dynamics between supervisor and candidate from those issues between candidate and analysand which emerge as parallel process between candidate and supervisor? How do we deal with personality issues in a candidate that repeatedly intrude into the work? Where is the boundary between analysis and supervision and where do the two zones overlap? How do we assist beginning candidates in dealing with anxieties stemming from lack of analytic knowledge? Also important is differentiation of anxiety associated with being judged from anxiety stemming from characterological sources that may result in avoidance of certain areas with analysands.

The literature on supervision addresses such issues and we can learn from the experience of senior supervisors. Discussion amongst colleagues with an openness to new ideas can lead to greater awareness of the gaps in our knowledge and the nature of our biases.

Observation of Supervisory Sessions. Study groups benefit greatly from observing live supervisory sessions followed by open discussion. The discussion may touch on a variety of areas: supervisory style and emphasis, supervisee's learning needs, selection of point of inquiry for the supervisory session, dynamics between supervisor and supervisee, etc. An experienced supervisor might hold a supervisory session with one of the study group members or a study group member could hold a supervisory session with another study group member. In the established supervisory training programs videotapes of supervisory sessions have been made and it may be possible to obtain them. The literature on supervision contains transcripts of supervisory sessions[12] which are useful to study. The group might also invite experienced supervisors to discuss their style of supervising.

The Evaluative Component in The Supervision of Candidates. The supervisor carries responsibility to evaluate the candidate's

work openly, directly, and fairly. Responsibility involves both time-
ly feedback to the candidate as well as evaluations to the institution.
Ultimate responsibility is towards analysands who may come to this
future analyst. Supervisors inevitably face conflict amongst these
functions: teaching and facilitating the candidate's development versus evaluating achieved capacity; concern for the candidate versus
concern for the public versus concern for the institution. Early in the
supervisory career, an analyst is especially vulnerable to being
pulled by opposite sides of the conflicts. For example, she may be
dominated by evaluative responsibility to the institution or may
defensively avoid such responsibility focusing instead on the facilitating aspect.

4. The analyst's preparation toward becoming a supervisor might
conclude in a meeting with a small committee of senior faculty (e.g.
a committee of three). That meeting would be devoted to a collegial
discussion of the analyt's preparation, the themes in supervisory
practice she considers significant, the analysts paper about some
aspect of the supervisory process. The committee could conclude
that (a) the analyst is ready to become a supervisor; (b) there are gaps
in the analyst's preparation that need to be filled in before becoming
a supervisor; (c) the analyst's approach to preparation is quite flawed
and she needs to reevaluate her direction.

When the analyst has demonstrated to the training community a
serious study of the supervisory process, the training board would
formally designate her a supervisor and member of the faculty.

*How would a program of preparation for supervisors be devel-
oped, designed, and implemented?* I favor an approach that provides
some structure and leaves considerable freedom for individual initiative. Training programs might develop a framework that suits the
local circumstances and leaves to the study group the freedom to
determine the specifics.[13] The essential point is that analysts undertake a process of preparation through individual and group study
involving discussions with peers and experienced supervisors.

Responsibility and authorship for a program of supervisory development rests fully with senior faculty in each training program.
However, as a given faculty clarifies its position and outlines its
framework, it may join with programs that hold a similar view and
develop with them study opportunities for potential supervisors on a

regional or national level. Further, symposia and workshops at national and international conferences can be designed to offer programs not available locally.

A Current Dilemma

No one in the training community has undertaken a formal period of preparation to become a supervisor but many have engaged in considerable private study and sought out opportunities for collegial discussions. Should the next generation be asked to do more preparation than we have done? How do we bridge the gap?

In regard to preparation for supervision we are at the same point where the field was in regard to preparation of analysts in the middle years of the century when analytic training programs were being developed (London in 1947; Zurich in 1948). Our work toward development of training in supervision will evolve as the training in analysis has evolved. We must, however, demand of ourselves that we invest as much effort in our continuing education as supervisors and teachers as we expect of the next generation in their preparation to become supervisors and teachers. As institutes develop a framework for training in supervision, the efforts of senior faculty engaged in that work will raise the awareness of all in a given community. The study groups that are formed certainly should be open to active supervisors and teachers who would contribute from their experience and benefit from collegial exchanges. With such participation, current supervisors will engage in parts of the process which we propose for the next generation.

An educational process always extends over a substantial period of time. Our education to be supervisors begins with our personal analysis, continues with our training to become an analyst, builds upon the capacity to work as analyst and requires that we acquire knowledge, understanding and skill in the supervisory process. A process of continuing education extends over the entire professional life of an analyst requiring ongoing reflection, study, and collegial discussion about matters of psyche, analytic practice, and teaching.

Notes

1. Candidate or supervisor, of course, can be a woman or a man. When I use pronouns in this essay, I will use the feminine pronoun rather than the linguistically awkward mix of *she/he*.

2. Marga Speicher, "Selection and Training of Supervisors," *Proceedings of the Twelfth International Congress for Analytical Psychology*, ed. Mary Ann Mattoon, Einsiedeln, Switzerland: Daimon, 1993, pp. 536-539.

3. Paul Kugler addressed issues pertaining to this transition period in his paper at the IAAP Congress, "From Training Candidate to Supervising Analyst," ibid., pp. 528-535, reprinted in a revised form as chapter fourteen of this book.

4. The Board makes policies and decisions governing training and is equivalent to the Training Board or Training Committee at other institutes.

5. A weekend retreat of the Board and Faculty was devoted to discussions of supervision in 1991. It led to the requirement that an analyst who wishes to serve as supervisor must have five years experience working as an analyst following completion of training. Further, a Committee on Continuing Education in Supervision was established by the professional society (NYAAP) to discuss and formulate guidelines for the preparation of supervisors.

6. In New York City three psychoanalytic training institutes offer structured training in supervision: National Institute for the Psychotherapies; Postgraduate Center for Mental Health; Washington Square Institute in Psychoanalysis and Psychotherapy.

7. Representatives of the programs at National Institute for the Psychotherapies, James L. Fosshage, and at Postgraduate Center, Mary Beth Cresci, discussed their respective programs at the Annual Conference of the International Federation for Psychoanalytic Education (IFPE) in 1992. A supervisory training program in San Francisco was also discussed at that Conference by Claire Allphin, a Jungian analyst in San Francisco. These three papers were published in the IFPE Newsletter, Volume II, Spring 1993. The Newsletter is circulated only to IFPE members but I can provide a copy upon request.

8. Most of the Jungian articles selected for the Board Retreat are reprinted in this volume.

9. The committee that prepared the materials for the Retreat recommended two publications:

   (1) *The Journal of the Postgraduate Center for Mental Health* devoted the Spring/Summer issue in 1990 to supervision. The issue is entitled "Supervision of the Psychoanalytic Process" and contains eleven essays by the faculty of the Postgraduate Center. *Psychoanalysis and Psychotherapy*, Volume 8 Spring/Summer 1990, New York: Brunner/Mazel.

   (2) The volume Clinical Perspectives on the Supervision of Psychoanalysis and Psychotherapy, edited by Leopold Caligor, Philip M. Bromberg, James D. Meltzer, published by Plenum Press in 1984. It contains sixteen essays by senior supervisors of the William Alanson White Institute in

New York. Each writer presents his/her understanding and style of supervision with examples from supervisory practice. In the Preface the editors review the establishment and the work of a Study Group on Supervision at the White Institute in 1979. This Study Group organized a series of programs for the William Alanson White Professional Society in 1980-1981 in which five senior analysts supervised a candidate in front of the Society in much the same was as they would in their offices. The ensuing interest in discussion of the supervisory process led to the establishment of supervisory peer study groups and to the compilation of the articles in the volume. A few are reprinted from journals; most are original publications.

A committee member prepared a bibliography of recent articles on supervisory issues in psychoanalytic journals. Further, we had a computer search done in Psychology Abstracts, searching under "supervision": it yielded an annotated bibliography of 132 entries published between 1966 and 1991, not all of them related to psychoanalytic supervision.

10. I addressed this issue at the "Workshop on Supervision" in Chicago. See Marga Speicher, "Selection and Training of Supervisors," op. cit., pp. 538-539.

11. In work with beginning supervisors it has been observed that new supervisors whose personal experience has remained unexamined tend to work reflexively in the manner of their favorite supervisor or in the manner opposite to their least productive supervisory experience. Examination of the experience of being supervised, therefore, is essential as foundation for supervisory work directed to a supervisee's learning needs.

12. Roy Shafer, "Supervisory Session with Discussion," *Clinical Perspectives on the Supervision of Psychoanalysis and Psychotherapy*, op. cit., pp. 207-230.

13. Analysts working out such a framework may find useful considerations in a paper by Joan Fleming, "The Education of a Supervisor," given in 1979 in Chicago at a Symposium on Supervision, sponsored by the American Psychoanalytic Association, reprinted in *The Teaching and Learning of Psychoanalysis: Selected Papers of Joan Fleming*, ed. Stanley S. Weiss, New York: The Guilford Press, pp. 143-165. The paper focuses on the need to foster in supervisors development of the capacity to teach. Fleming describes pitfalls and obstacles to such teaching, reviews efforts made toward educational support for supervisors, and outlines significant components of an approach towards education for supervisors on the local level.

[16]

The Aging Supervisor

H.-J. Wilke

The Over-aging of the Old Sage

Adolf Guggenbühl-Craig[1] has expressed doubt about the essential connection between "old and wise" in the archetype of the Old Sage. While the myth of old age is itself not destructive, our use of it can be. Guggenbühl-Craig considers our use of the myth of the Old Sage corrupt and prejudicial, helping instead to repress the reality of the weakness of old age. Biology and medicine teach us that the final and latest onto- and phylo-genetic acquisitions are also the most vulnerable, easily damaged and diminished. Many abilities necessary for analysis and supervision are acquired later in life and therefore are more susceptible to being damaged or diminished by the aging process. According to my observation, there are three abilities specifically used for analytic training and teaching which, if impaired or destroyed by the process of aging, strikingly affect the supervisor's performance and self-esteem.

1. The ability for self-critical perception and reflection which is especially cultivated during the analytic process.

2. The ability to monitor with a preverbal sensibility the social interactions in analysis and supervision with a special attention to a sense of shame and tact. This ability is a part of the sensation function and it enables us to perceive and respect the other's threshold of shame, avoiding embarrassment.

3. The ability to cultivate and maintain an extroverted interest in the particulars of the outer, concrete world. As we age, this ability often gives way to a more introverted attitude and an interest in more basic and general concerns.

The process of aging is difficult to anticipate for young people because they have no personal experience of the process and limited perception of aging in the elderly. The generation gap may already begin with the difficulty in communicating about the biological and psychological limitations of youth and old age. To avoid or defend against the painful and sometimes tragic aspects of this gap, both the old as well as the young, often grasp at methods that appear at times ridiculous: the young become aware of the Old fool hiding behind the mask of the Old Sage, and the Puella / Puer aspect of the trainee is easily transformed, under the moral burden stemming from the Old, into ignorance and levity. The destructiveness of such interactions is well known and has been graphically depicted by Goethe in the dialog between Mephisto and his pupil.

Baccalaureus:
> *... Admit, the things through many ages known*
> *Are safely to be called not worth the knowing.*

Mephistopheles:
> *I've thought as much. For I was stupid once.*
> *And now I feel a superficial dunce.*

Baccalaureus:
> *Hear, hear, good sir! Why, now you're talking sense,*
> *The first old man to show intelligence.*

Mephistopheles:
> *I thought to light on wealth of hidden gold,*
> *And wretched charcoal lumps were all I found.*

Baccalaureus:
> *Confess then, that your cranium, bald and old,*
> *Equals in worth these skulls that lie around.*

Mephistopheles (good-humoredly):
> *Think you, my friend, that rudeness is your right?*

Baccalaureus:
> *In German only liars are polite.*
> *... An ague is old, in which you freeze,*
> *A frosty and fantastical disease.*
> *A man with thirty summers on his head*
> *Has seen his best, and is as good as dead.*

It would be best to have you put away.
...This is the noblest call for youthful soul!
The world was not, until I made it whole...

Mephistopheles:

Go, my original, your glorious way!-
How truth would irk you, if you really sought it;
For who can think of truth or trash to say,
But someone in the ancient world has thought it?
...Poor babes, I will not be your scolder:
Reflect, the Devil, he is old,
To understand him, best grow older.[2]

Experiences

All of us know from personal educational experiences, whether in elementary and high school or at the university or during postgraduate analytic training, how certain older teachers may appear a little ridiculous. Certain aged faculty are easily made fun of and their capacity to accomplish their pedagogic functions if often restricted. These common experiences allow for the creation and maintenance of certain stereotypical reactions of the elderly teacher by students.

Today, after almost 25 years as a Supervisor, I sometimes notice how trainees become slightly amused when they have succeeded in arousing my interest in a subject important to me. I then proceed to talk about the subject at some length and suddenly realize I have come to the edge of ridiculousness. Two or three decades ago, I would have felt humiliated by such a realization, but today I am able to cope with these feelings. Often I refer to Seneca, who judged even the "great genius" as follows: *Nullum magnum ingenium sine mixtura dementiae*, a judgment which is usually more disavowed by the admirer of the "great genius" than by the genius him / herself.

The decrease in the threshold of shame in the elderly, may perform a vital life serving function. Without it the suicide rate in the elderly would perhaps be significantly higher and general life-expectancy reduced. The mistaken idealization of old age benefits neither the young, nor the old.

As regards my understanding of the situation with trainees, the following discrepancy is significant: I share only in a limited way the interest of the trainees, their fascination with new theories of neurosis, the mind, and human beings. At this point in my life, I am more interested in general, unvarying, constant factors; expressing simple things in a clear way; finding expressions and formulas in language which simply summarize a whole variety of things. At this stage of life, my point of view bundles the "whole variety" into simple formulas. The trainee may consider such simple formulas in our profession as no more than a verse from the "Maxim of the People." But, perhaps such formulations are an essential part of the meaning and world view of this stage of life. Perhaps such simple formulations will help our trainees better understand the psychological life of the elderly.

My learning period had a long and lasting effect on me. As I look back, I assimilated many of the subjects taught by older teachers with a certain lack of judgment. Consequently after years, things came back to my mind, which only now I am able to grasp in their real significance, relying on my extensive life experience and professional knowledge.

Learning from Authorities and Learning in the Peer-group

Traditional learning shows that knowledge and know-how is handed down from the old to the young. Even today, as a rule, teachers are older than their pupils. In some fields, however, this fact could be reversed. Today, for example, I am informed about new trends in science from much younger researchers. Margaret Mead[3] was probably the first person to make the public conscious of this reversal of direction in the learning processes in modern societies.

Not only does the process of learning take place between student and teacher – authority, but it also may take place in groups of contemporaries. Usually children have to learn "cultural techniques" from older people or their parents. However, all the simple "survival techniques," such as defiance, compliance, to defend or hand over property, to hide or to flee, children learn in play groups and among contemporaries. This observation raises an interesting question about the didactic role of peer groups later in life: What is the relation between the contents and skills acquired in our peer-groups during analytic learning and the ones we were taught by teachers? Of course, this depends on how authoritarian or liberal the structure of the educational institution is.

Reflecting on my own experience during of high school, the university and my analytic training, at that time I was quite oriented towards those in authority. But, I also improved considerably my knowledge through the various group interactions with colleagues and friends. Only with peers did I start pondering over various topics during endless nights of discussion. Out of the combined influence of my teachers, peers and personal analysis, I finally developed my own understanding of Analytic Psychology. The importance of peer group discussions for training, I have only just come to recognize and appreciate.

Two Recommendations

1. As to the social competency of analysts – often being considered in rather poor shape – we need to place more importance on learning taking place in the candidate's peer groups. An already existing and well operating example for this type of education is the case supervision group, which in the past has not been given enough support and value. As a rule, group supervision starts with 3 to 4 trainees, more or less oriented towards a group leader. This peer group might evolve into a leaderless group, a group more or less free of authority and continue working together after training, leading to a stable relationship of colleagues and friends. It might be possible to institutionalize towards the end of the training this model of peer supervision, which may naturally evolve after graduation into the so-called "supervision of colleagues," peer supervision in the community of analysts. A model which has been positively practiced through out our working life is based on the natural and reciprocal exchange between friends and colleagues.

There are certainly still other institutional structures in which the peer tutorial model could be realized. It is my conviction that teaching and training patterns using peer groups compensate the potential of conflicts which originate from the training with the authority-oriented model. The purpose of training should never be to create a location exempt from conflicts. But, by complementing the student-teacher field of conflict by another, the peer group field, we may eventually create a healthier educational climate.

2. The larger professional organizations (for example, the International Association for Analytical Psychology) might exert a subtle influence over local institutes and departments by establishing some clear, simple, and flexible policy regarding aging and professional practice. A certain common agreement regarding the particular responsibilities of training analysts and supervisors might be established. In many disciplines, professional functions defined with particular responsibilities are linked by age. In other fields, for example, Business and Industry, where these rules are not practiced, we can observe how important Industrialists in old age begin to destroy their own business. I presume that such a destructive dynamic may also be observed, rather frequently, in analytic communities, especially in relation to aging and degeneration processes. I am not suggestion having an age limit fixed for training analysts, supervisors and instructors by an international association. This I would not be prepared to accept. One of the reasons I am reflecting on the topic of the aging supervisor is to develop a better understanding of the psychological issues associated with training responsibilities and the aging process. Through this understanding, perhaps we can find a common ground to discuss how to deal with issues involving aging analysts. Any regulative decision by an international association would concern me and many of my colleagues and friends as well as many institutions. I would like to suggest the following statement as a possible heuristic principle: "The International Association recommends to all of their recognized training analysts and supervisors, as well as to the Institutes, to check at regular (periodical) intervals, if those who have surpassed the usual pension-age can still rely on, make use of all their functions necessary in training, and being able to do so with sufficient security, competency and life perspective." If, however, my self-critical potential should not be sufficient enough for such an examination, I truly hope to be able to understand and endure the advice given to me by a friend or even the institution. The training analysts of the C.G. Jung-Institute Berlin had many discussions about this problem and finally introduced this principle into the institute through a paper defining "functions and duties of training analysts."

In my opinion, the lack of understanding between the generations concerning aging, and in anticipation of dying, raises more problems for younger people, than problems for those who are immediately affected by aging. Perhaps in our selection of training analysts and supervisors, we sometimes have ideals which are too high and a mistaken sense of rigor, leading to an over-aging of the teaching staff. The easiest and most natural compensation might be for Training Institutes to have a sufficient number of supervisors, training analysts and instructors at their disposal. On the other hand, achieving a sufficient number of faculty is at times prevented by demands for higher standards in qualification and experience. Understanding and mutual respect between the young and the elderly might also be complementary: the young in mild embarrassment out of being inexperienced and, the elderly behaving with moderate reserve about experience which burdens us with prejudice.

Summary

Denying the natural process of aging with the help of the archetype of the Old Sage can produce a generation gap, through which understanding and interaction may be impeded. In supervision most problems of aging are produced by the reduction of self-critical perception and reflection, a reduced threshold of shame and the increase of introversion. In order to reduce the resultant conflict dynamic, the authority-oriented-learning experienced during training might be compensated by introducing learning in peer-groups. Through the guidance of our International Association, problems of learning modalities might be kept more conscious. In addition, guidelines regarding aging professionals might be formulated within a larger discussion of the process of aging and age-limit relative to supervisors and training analysts.

References

1. Guggenbühl-Craig, A.: Die närrischen Alten. Betrachtungen über moderne Mythen. Schweizer Spiegelverlag AG. Zürich 1986.
2. Goethe, *Faust / Part Two*, Penguin Classic, *1950, pp. 96-99.*
3. Mead, M.: *Der Konflikt der Generationen, Jugend ohne Vorbild.* Olten, Freiburg i.B. 1971.

Part VI

Supervision and Institutions

[17]

Supervision, Training, and the Institution as an Internal Pressure

James Astor

In this chapter I contrast supervision which is part of the training of psychotherapists and analysts and supervision which is sought by the practitioner as part of their own development but independent of any training requirement. I have used the Society of Analytical Psychology as my model for the institution, but my reflections are not exclusive to this organization. My preparatory reading for this chapter has included the two volumes of essays by Isabel Menzies Lyth, *Containing Anxiety in Institutions* and *The Dynamics of the Social* (Menzies Lyth 14, 15). Additionally, I have had many discussions with friends and colleagues whose trainings have been with organizations other than the Society of Analytical Psychology. My work as a supervisor and teacher brings me in contact with students from the London Centre for Psychotherapy, the British Association of Psychotherapists, and the Association of Child Psychotherapists.

Introduction

Just as there is nothing more unchristian than the history of the Catholic church to a Protestant, so there is nothing more unanalytic than the institutional history of analysis to an analytical psychologist. But the practice of analysis is enthralling. Supervision and training involve the relationship of the individual to an institution as well as to their own development. The focus of my thoughts and ideas revolves round the difficulties of keeping faith with the beauty of the analytic process in the context of institutional pressures.

Psychoanalysis was once revolutionary, just as Darwinism had been *vis-a-vis* religion. So unacceptable was it to individuals, so challenging to the 'basic assumptions' – their unexamined attitudes – that the dominant establishment – the collective expression of these attitudes – and its organs, the institutions, campaigned against it.

At first it was condemned, then it was denied; eventually it was modified, changed, and developed. All these were, and are, attempts to restrict it. In the beginning, the doctors attacked psychoanalysis for looking beyond the hysterical symptoms to the interpersonal relations of the individual. Next, the philosophers, the psychologists, and the academics, whose province had traditionally been the mind, condemned it for its inexactitudes, illogicalities, and use of metaphor. Some of these so called criticisms are now our credentials. The mind feeds on emotional truth and atrophies on lies and self-deceit. We may express our discoveries in the language of science but it is our imaginations which gather in the material. In order to help organize our thoughts and to generate hypotheses, clinical practitioners have produced theories which evolve over time and are then modified by new evidence.

Theory and Institutional Mentality

Jung, who had many theories, did not want to start a school or a movement for Jungian analysis. In setting up the Society of Analytical Psychology (the first institute to offer a training in analytical psychology) our founders were in a sense going against his wishes, although he did agree to become the first president. Schools can develop bodies of knowledge, theories, which can become orthodoxies, and so destroy the spirit behind their inception. Perhaps one reason why Jung distrusted setting up institutions for analytical psychology was that, like theories, they can be used to restrict the revolutionary nature of the discoveries of the work group. This is because theories tend to reduce experience and observation to conscious knowledge. Jung, as we know, valued uncertainty, the irrational, and the struggle that accompanies individuation.

One recognized difficulty with institutional teaching is that it is based on theories. These theories are often incompatible but they are taught as the basis for so many of the conscious exchanges we have with our patients. Choice of training, like choice of analyst and choice of supervisor, is often a neurotic one. The training process might be likened to the trainee arriving in a fragmented state, being taught the ideas that underlie the profession's organized fragmentation and then being expected, as a trainee, to integrate what the trainers have failed to integrate themselves. These points of view are well known (and have been discussed by Dr. Robert Hinshelwood (Hinshelwood 7). They present only one aspect of the 'shadow' of our institution. Another is the way language is hijacked in such a way that it no longer has an agreed meaning. This has been taking place in analytical psychology. 'Active imagination is misused when it refers to imaginative activity (Fordham 3). Transference no longer seems to refer to those obstacles in the way of communication and understanding which have an infantile origin. Projective identification no longer means what Melanie Klein had in mind when she derived the term from Freud (Klein 10). To say how these words are used is difficult because their use has become too idiosyncratic, but I can give a general instance, Fordham's pioneering work on countertransference is now cited by some New York analytical psychologists as the basis for their confessions to their patients, that is, as if their abandonment of analytic method at these moments is an expression of syntonic countertransference!

Part of my thesis is that the danger to analysis is to be found within those very institutions which profess to train and prepare the fledgling analyst for the flight of their lives. Historically the source for this can be traced back to Freud who began the rot when he started a movement which had no room for dissidents, as Jung found out. But as analytical psychologists we, too, are part of a movement. One of the problems with a movement is that it requires a propaganda, in the religious sense of the word – a congregation for propagating the faith. This poses a problem for individual development. Part of training for the apprentice analyst consists of the struggle not to be an institutional gosling imprinted on an institutional mother goose, banning our dissident thoughts by virtue of this unconscious process. It is as well to be mindful of Bertrand Russell's witty caveat, 'If you want to start a propaganda, you need to propagate with a proper goose' (told to the author by Michael Fordham).

These concerns underlie the question of how best to run a training compatible with its conscious motive, namely the desire to get better at what we do, without turning an analytic training into a general psychotherapy training. While I recognize that analysis is a specialization within psychotherapy there remains a fundamental difference. Fordham distinguishes analysis and psychotherapy as follows:

> A therapist has a therapeutic goal controlling his activities, which may be anything from the removal of symptoms to an alteration of character in a desirable direction, such as fostering greater adaptation, increasing consciousness, and so forth. An analyst, though not indifferent to 'improvements' in his patient, is primarily concerned to define, in the simplest terms possible, the patient's state of mind in relation to himself. He does his best not to have goals for his patient but, by sustaining his analytic attitude, he lets the patient define his own goals. (Fordham 6)

In psychotherapy patients are told what the psychotherapist is conscious of. This usually consists of making constructions, staying within bounds of received ideas, usually archetypally colored, often about mothers and children or models of family life and history as a natural order. This is not analysis in the way Jung conceived it, that the practitioner should not know before hand, eschewing memory and desire as Bion expressed it (Bion 2). What analysis requires is the capacity to tolerate being a beginner, not just during training but every day of your life, every session you work. The problem with psychotherapy is that the patient can become the embodiment of the psychotherapist's theory and the psychotherapist then becomes objectified, that is, loses his true subjectivity. By this I mean that the psychotherapist, by treating the patient's communications as a metaphor of his own theoretical model, is using his 'knowledge' (another metaphor) as a barrier to subjective experience. When this barrier exists he is no longer listening to the patient. In professionalizing this work we institutionalize it. Menzies Lyth quotes Fenichel as writing that 'social institutions arise through the efforts of human beings to satisfy their needs, but then become external realities comparatively independent of individuals that never the less affect the structure of the individual.' (Menzies Lyth 15)

The risk to the individual from the institution is that in its teaching and training functions it develops the individual's exoskeletal skill acquisition, a 'learning about' from the outside, rather than the endoskeletal learning from the suffering on the inside. This endoskeletal learning is what Margot Waddell described in one of her recent papers on George Elliot, as 'suffering and moving on rather than explaining and looking back' (Waddell 18). Institutional learning is often of the explaining and looking back kind, clinging to the safe story telling of reconstruction.

Meltzer, following Freud, suggested that perhaps analysis will increasingly become a method for investigating states of mind but not necessarily a treatment (Meltzer 12). This provocative statement, directed, in my view, at discouraging one from searching for the 'correct' interpretation, is contradicted in the numerous clinical examples in his books which show the changes that analysis engenders. But if analysis is an art then psychotherapy is at risk of becoming a *treatment* and the proliferation of psychotherapy trainings is an indication that this is already happening. Psychotherapy can be taught, and you can now even get a master's degree in it at London University. The way it is taught is mainly through the study of theory as explanation of behavior. Problems are made bearable for the patient and psychotherapist by finding causes for them, usually historical. Meltzer writes:

> The tendency of psychoanalysis as a social organization has been to see itself, in Bion's terms, as a Basic assumption Fight-flight Group, always in the process of fragmenting itself while waiting for the next Messiah. The quest for respectability and the unmentionable economic factors in the lives of its practitioners have always served to tighten the hold of this organizational level on the so called training. Since any organization must select its candidates for obedience rather than creativity, the policy to train practitioners rather than educating interested people has always been followed. The result has been a rapid spread, but, like an oil slick, very thin. Its guild structure has always been "the enemy of promise," claiming a nonexistent monopoly of its all too public 'mysteries.' On the other hand the work group functions have continued to make progress over nearly a century. Their development has remained largely unknown to the critics of psychoanalysis who seem, almost to a man, to be content with reading early Freud. (Meltzer 13)

The task facing the institution is how to run a training which embodies the principles of 'the work group' (Bion 1). Development as part of the continuing professional and personal life of the Society of Analytical Psychology analyst is curiously absent from the soci-

ety's institutional structure. When the training is 'complete' no further systematic or supervised study is included in the progression
through the gradations of the analytic hierarchy, from associate
professional member to professional member to training analyst.
Nowhere, therefore, is the ethos of 'the work group,' as a necessary
part of individual development, fostered by the institution.

Supervision as Part of a Training

Plaut (Plaut 17), Newton (Newton 16), and Fordham (Fordham 4)
in the Society's 1960 symposium on training (published in 1961)
made distinctive contributions to our understanding of the problems
of supervision. Plaut pointed out that the trainee's introduction to the
society, the initiation, came through the supervisor and, in a topo-
graphical model, he sketched out the complexity of the relationship,
student / analyst / supervisor / training case / pioneer-founders, not
forgetting to point out, in inimitable fashion, that no one had trained
the trainers when he sought training and that successive generations
make it harder for the next generation to qualify. Newton's contribution was equally characteristic in that it focused on her interest in the
integration of theory and practice, and in particular that theory,
unrelated to a student's practice or clinical experience, could be
persecutory. Among other persecutory elements constellated in the
training situation she drew our attention to an ideal that she felt was
covertly present in her day, namely that the trainees' analysts must
not display any residual neurosis, and concomitantly that the training
analysts were themselves, of course, free of any neurosis. Fordham's
contribution gave the reasons for the historically important decision
to separate training and supervision and he went on to discuss the
transference / countertransference problems that arise in the supervision of candidates. The reason for the separation was that it was
thought important to keep the analyst tree from the assessing role of
the supervisor who had to give an opinion as to the candidate's
suitability for membership of the society. In the old days analysts
also used to report to the professional committee on their analysands.
The potential problems are legion in this area and it has been discon-
tinued. But when the society was starting as a training organization
this reporting by the analyst enabled the quality of the analyst's work

to be monitored by his colleagues. The motive at that time was to keep up standards and to a limited extent, the Institute of Psycho-Analysis still continues this reporting requirement within their training. It is worth summarizing Fordham's views as expressed in 1961 since what follows develops from them.

The effect of training is to interfere with the transference the candidates have to their analysts: a) by the subtle shifting of transference phenomena into the training group; b) by the candidate projecting into the control cases and then developing a transference to the supervisor; c) by the increase in real knowledge of the analyst arising from the training situation, that is, by the matching of projections against direct perceptions. He also states categorically that candidates must be treated as junior colleagues, that their countertransferences to their patients should be pointed out but not analyzed, and that the supervisor should refrain from manipulations like 'I think you should take that to your analyst.' The corollary of this is that analysts should refrain from expressing opinions about supervisors chosen by their patients. Underlying Fordham's reflections is his awareness of how the triangular relationship of candidate, analyst, and supervisor can stimulate competitiveness and rivalry, destructive to the development of the candidate's own skills. Fordham stresses the need for supervisors to facilitate the candidate's deliberate aim of acquiring knowledge. It is necessary for the supervisor to put to one side awareness of the candidate's residual neurosis and to refrain from thinking that the candidate's analyst is not doing a good job. Fordham's final observation, which is as true now as it was then, was, 'Candidates are put under greater stress than is any trained analyst and so we need to find out how to diminish it' (Fordham 4). I find nothing to disagree with in these three contributions all of which refer to supervision as part of training and could be the basis for the development of supervision as a process whereby the apprentice defines his own goals, acquiring knowledge in an endoskeletal manner. But problems abound in training supervisions and some of them that I am going to describe may also contribute to the absence of a postgraduate 'work group' ethos in these trainings.

Difficulties in Cooperating in Supervision During Training

Never far away during training is the internal pressure arising from the evaluative presence of the training committee. Present too is the compatibility or incompatibility between the way the supervisee was analyzed and the way the supervisor is showing them how to analyze. This can cause conflicts of loyalty. Occasionally it can stir up the supervisee's residual neurosis. This can show itself in the defensive reporting of the work, in such a way that it is impossible to understand what is really happening in the analysis. Equally obstructive is writing down what the supervisor is saying during the supervision. This can be a process of taking over the supervisor's knowledge without thinking about it first. In the early stages of supervision this can look like learning. It is a projective defense since the supervising analyst's mind is taken over by projective identification.

For instance, it has been my experience that a conscientious supervisee, notebook in hand, has taken down and applied my ideas to the material of their supervised case. By so doing they have demonstrated to me how little I knew and how foolish my ideas were. The diligent application of these ideas without understanding demonstrated their clinical ineffectiveness. The supervisee came week after week, reported the interviews in detail, and made notes from what I said. Superficially it seemed that an analysis was in progress but at best the patient was having some psychotherapy and at worst none of us was doing what we were being paid for. Fundamental character problems remained unchanged. The patient kept on enacting the transference, the psychotherapist, among other difficulties, kept on treating the infantile as the erotic and part-objects as whole objects; this was a convincing example both to them and to me of exoskeletal learning. We recovered from this when we stopped all note-taking during the supervisions and focused instead on the minutiae of the emotional climate that existed between therapist and patient. This has led gradually to greater candor about their feelings and ideas on the part of the supervisees which I was then able to affirm as having value and use as the basis for interpretations of their interactions with their patients.

A different but common supervision problem within training occurred recently when a supervisee came without any notes, stating that he had left the patient behind. There then followed an account of how the patient had responded well to the last week's work, which had incorporated much of the previous week's supervisory insights. We had therefore constellated in the supervision a negative therapeutic reaction. I waited to see whether this was present in the patient. The supervisee then told me how the subsequent session with his training case also showed evidence of the patient resenting the trainee's knowledge, just as he had resented mine. From this it was then possible to connect the notes that had been left behind with the trainee's identification with the patient. The supervision in this session was proceeding by my analysis of the transference /countertransference of the trainee to me but in a projected form, leaving the trainee to recognize the identification rather than pointing it out myself. I made no interpretations of this. I must emphasize I am not analyzing the trainee but using my analytic understanding to discuss their case. I am, for instance, not saying anything about the relationship of the trainee to me in the context of the patient's relationship to him, that there is a difficulty with father, although I am mindful of this.

Projection, Identification, and Training

Underlying the difficulties that exist in the supervision of other therapists' work within a training are the reasons for the trainees doing the work in the first place. If, as might be the case, they are engaged in some sort of personal reparative work, under the archetype of the wounded healer, then the borderline between creative empathy and identification with the patient's omnipotence can become blurred (see Hinshelwood 7), particularly if the supervisee is demoralized by the supervisor's knowledge, thereby making the problem worse. (This is because it is fairly unusual to begin psychotherapeutic working life with treatment successes. A good outcome is not only difficult to define but is often not apparent until some time after the ending of the work.) From my own experience of being supervised during training and of supervising, I have been both fed up with supervision and with my supervisor and been on the receiving end of this feeling.

During my child analytic training I was analyzing a psychotic boy, who would fill me with his crazy world and the impossibility of understanding it. There gradually built up in me a feeling that my supervisor was useless. Week after week I talked about what was happening, what I was feeling, but not, significantly, about my despair at the supervision. This was an expression of the transference to the child. Eventually I exploded, told my supervisor that they were useless, knew less than I did, and had not had a good idea in weeks. What a relief! The supervisor, being a mature and experienced person with a real capacity to bear uncertainty, received my explosion with discomfort but tolerance. It was not thrown back at me but was accepted without grudge or bitterness. Gradually I could then discover the unconscious nature of the projective identification I was in the grip of. This was an experience that left us both feeling very uncomfortable, but we survived it and it greatly increased my capacity to work with this psychotic child. To behave in the somewhat unexpected manner (for a trainee) that I did on that occasion reflects the trust and safety I felt with my supervisor, that there would be no retaliatory consequences.

I am also concerned here with the pressure on the supervisees, in particular their feelings of worth as analysts. For at the beginning of a training supervisees are caught between the patient's criticism of them on the one hand and the feeling that the supervisor is also telling them they are not doing it right. The corollary of this for the supervisor is that he has to be able to bear the feeling that he has not been much use to his supervisee. The supervisee, as Fordham recommends, must be treated as a junior colleague, as I was by my supervisor with whom I had this outburst. I wonder if one way of incorporating the recognition of this junior colleague status into the fabric of the training might be to allow trainees to be involved in the selection, under supervision, of training cases, as Barry Proner has suggested (in a verbal communication).

Supervision, Perceval's Problem, and the Role of the Hermit

Perceval had a problem of initiation into his quest for the Grail in much the same way as trainees have problems becoming analysts and being apprentices. Zinkin summarized Perceval's progress in his paper on the Grail quest (Zinkin 21). Perceval's problems are similar to those I have described which arise from the interaction of institution and individual. Towards the end of Perceval's struggle (his training) he discovers the hermit. The importance of the hermit is significant in the comparison I want to make. He has something of the wise old man about him, is facilitating and nonjudgmental. He represents the move away from the search for the 'correct' interpretation to 'negative capability' (Keats 9).

> Perceval begins with the idea that the way to get what he wants is to take it. Indeed, he is advised by his mother that if he fancies a girl's ring he should take it from her finger, and soon after doing just that he kills the Red Knight to get his armor. He does so not by following the rules of combat but by demanding that he be given the armor. When the Red Knight becomes angry and strikes him with his staff, Perceval hurls his javelin at him and kills him. All this is at a very early stage of his career and he subsequently has to learn the rules, to acquire courtesy and respect towards both ladies and enemy knights. He has to acquire a proper place at the Round Table before he is eligible for the Grail question. Later, he has to grow beyond it, and in fact it is his misplaced courtesy which leads him not to be too inquisitive, not to ask the vital question the first time he reaches the Grail Castle. He then looses sight of the Grail, and only after many years of privation does he find it again. During these years he not only has to give up his regressive longings for his mother and for his wife but has to learn through a hermit the true nature and history of the Grail and the meaning of Good Friday. All this constitutes a long and arduous training to make him worthy of the Grail (Zinkin 21).

The parallels with the training of analysts can be seen here. The crude beginning, the need for training, the requirements of conformity, the loss of initiative and curiosity that trainings produce. The recovery from this, which involves giving up the regressive longings for more analysis, is then followed by the discovery of the hermit and a new learning.

Until quite recently potential trainees were actively discouraged from working with patients prior to starting their analytic training. Now the reverse is the case. Potential trainees are encouraged to get some experience of psychotherapy before applying. It might, therefore, be argued that by the time candidates arrive at the analytic training institution they are ready for the hermit. But do our trainees come for a new learning? It has been mooted in the discussions within the Society of Analytical Psychology that trainees, for instance, come to us for Jung. Further it has been suggested that this is a choice, presumably arising from their study of Freud's pioneering clinical studies and Klein's inspirational work on projective identification, the paranoid schizoid and the depressive positions. But my experience of trainees and post-trainees is that their appreciation of, and by, the society derives primarily from their potential for development. I am suggesting that the choice of an analytic training is rarely a choice that has arisen from the study of the pioneers of analytic thought (Freud, Jung, Klein, Bion, Fordham, Meltzer). Further, it is not my experience of post-trainees' work that they are confident in either a psychoanalytic conceptualization of their patient's material or an analytical psychological one.

Some bewilderment has been expressed as to what sort of psychological species the graduate of the Society of Analytical Psychology is at the end of his training, a statement which encapsulates the absence of training in the training. Now if this is so, that our training is not in fact a training so much as an attempt to promote the development of people interested in the clinical application and development of Jung's ideas, then a measure of bewilderment is a small price to pay for what is otherwise thought to be a good training. It could be, however, that we are in danger of not grounding our students well enough in basic dynamic psychology for them to be able to appreciate that understanding and loving Jung can be expressed in its most inspirational way in the beauty of thinking within the transference (usually associated with psychoanalysis). In much the same way loving Mrs. Klein can be expressed in the study of literature or the painting of a picture (as well as working within the transference). In the microcosm of our own society an outstanding issue is the part psychoanalysis plays in our training, as a necessary ingredient in the internal structure we aim to provide for our trainees. There cannot be any real doubt as to the necessity of it, if we are offering a clinical training, but the amount is under review. Might we not be making false opposites in setting psychoanalysis against analytical psychology? The competition, surely, is for the time available? This inevitably means discussing what we consider essential to our psychological equipment. A good grounding in object relations theory, for instance, and its post-Kleinian developments, in my view, is basic. If analysis involves, in part, reducing complex structures to their simplest, then the application of this involves the reduction of archetypal behavior to its infantile bodily representations (see Fordham 6 on this issue). No one who practices psychotherapy and its specialization, analysis, would argue against an understanding of more than one point of view. A more rigorous clinical training than ours would involve the trainees presenting their training cases to different clinical seminar leaders as well as to their supervisor. This would expose them to the experience of the different emphases analysts bring to their understanding of the patient-analyst interaction. There are those, however, who favor more study of Jung's work in the training. I would not disagree with this but would ask whether this might not be made better use of after studying character development and psychopathology within an object-relations model of the mind. More Jung might then be like the necessary immersion of the interested practitioner, who is free of the constraints of training, in a new learning but one based on clinical experience. In practice what this would mean is that the training of adult analysts would follow the historical pattern evolved by Fordham (Fordham 6).

To return to Perceval's problem: I suggested that the stages Perceval has to go through can be compared to those of the apprentice analyst. The initial taking of the ring and the armor I liken to the too swift taking up of the supervisor's ideas and knowledge, which are then applied without conviction, not followed up but die. They do not originate from assimilated experience on the part of the supervisee but from the too hasty adhesive identificatory processes activated by 'wanting to be able to analyze like the other person.' Supervisees need to take their own time to assimilate their supervisor.

Preparation for eligibility for the quest is equivalent to the initiation into the society, coming to meetings, seeing your analyst in another light, starting seminars, making new friends. The diminution of originality and interest referred to is equivalent to a basic assumption mentality which seeps in during training. This is what Fenichel cautioned against, the inevitability of the institution becoming an internal structure affecting the individual (see also Bion 2): The actual manifestation of this is to be found in the corporate mentality expressed by the phrase 'the comforts of institutionalization.' This is most evident in the various edicts which link professional advancement to committee work done for the society. The basic assumption here is that the member who is to be advanced must be 'one of us.'

The difficulties of learning to acquire a proper place at the round table are also to be found in the students' response to the conformity demanded of them when it comes to the training requirements. Expediency can replace truthfulness and rules take the place of interest, for example, counting the hours not the changes in the patient. Strictly speaking, this is a perversion of the learning process where perversity is understood as a negativistic and caricaturing function 'under the aegis of a destructive part of the self ... devoted to distortion and attacks on the truth' (Waddell, Williams 20). Training requirements become a chore, and this can foster a rebellious attitude, often dressed up as real independence. In supervision this can appear in the student's irregular attendance, or, when they do come, presenting too much material for the time available. The supervising analyst is then left excluded as if the supervisee is saying that he does 'the real work' and that the supervisor is similar to the caricatured disengaged analyst who relies on his authority propped up by his intellectual defensiveness. Another extreme form of this, which most supervisors have encountered at some time or other, are those whose reporting is more of themselves than of observations of the patient, that is, they are presenting themselves not the patient.

The 'regressive longings' which Perceval suffers from I understand to be similar to the feeling in the trainees that if only they had had more analysis then they would be better analysts. What this means, assuming that the trainees have had a good analysis, especially of their sexuality, is that when they are feeling demoralized in supervision they have stopped thinking analytically. They have ceased to think about their supervision in the way in which they would think about difficulties which arise in work with their patients.

Of special interest to me is Perceval's experience of the hermit's teaching, which l liken to seeking out your own supervisor once the experience of the training and its limitations and virtues have been assimilated. This could be a person, or possibly a group, or for some it comes from immersion in the published work of Jung. Perceval's development, like the analyst's, needs this whole process from its naive beginnings, through the arduous apprenticeship to the eventual recognition of the value of the hermit in maintaining the search for the Grail. This is the picture linearly expressed. As we all know, we shift in and out of these states of mind in periods lasting for a few seconds to days and weeks. One phase does not replace another. This second kind of supervision with the hermit has no goal; there is only a direction. In place of pass or fail is change as a process, independent of value judgments. This change can be recognized both in the supervisees, in their patients, *and in the supervising analyst*. Supervision becomes a chewing over, reflecting on, and scrutinizing of the interactions in the session with the opportunity of having the material listened to by another analyst as if it was their own (see Meltzer 11). It is as if the supervisor is saying, to paraphrase Margot Waddell, 'This is how I see it in my way; does this help you to see it more clearly in your own way?' (Waddell 19). It is almost as if the material presented is a dream and the supervisor makes it his own for the purposes of his understanding. Important in this process is that the presenting analyst omits their own comments from the reporting (see Meltzer 11).

It is like looking over the shoulder of an artist as he paints a picture. Like an artist you have to do it, to learn how to do it, and sometime during this struggle you realize that what you thought was yet another beginning is in fact the arrival; you are an analyst, your work has its own integrity.

Creative uncertainty ensures that rigidity is constantly battled with to prevent priestly ossification, the dangerous monopolizing of public truths. Essentially what is required in being able to develop as an analyst is to enjoy being a beginner. Unless truly psychotic, most patients of students improve, not because the students are necessarily skillful but because they are interested. The tendency of trainings is to squash the initiatives which accompany this interest; instead the function of supervision should be to foster these initiatives. The hermit becomes an internal object and analysis works because of the method which allows the patient's objects to meet the analyst's objects. In other words, as analysts we are presiding over a process Compare our all too frail humanity with the intense transference affects of our patients to us, yet most improve, find the experience interesting even if we do not always succeed in doing as good a job as, retrospectively, we would have liked. This inner world of objects is truly a great mystery and is our enduring Grail quest.

Summary and Conclusion

So have we come full circle? Did Jung, in not wanting Jungian institutes, know what I am hoping to raise for discussion in this essay, namely that his particular contribution to our understanding of the soul cannot be taught as a training. A training in analytical psychology at best is a training based initially on a thorough personal analysis, which is followed by the study of the great discoveries of psychoanalysis linked to the attitudes and original ideas of Jung. As the practitioner becomes experienced these ideas then begin to take shape in his mind. The institution's valuable function must be to attempt to provide the rigor, discipline, standards, and regulation of a new profession, but this can create difficulties in the individual in relation to the vocational aspects of analytic work.

When training is over, a period of recovery is necessary. But once this has occurred, it has been my experience both as a supervisor of graduates' work and as a supervisee, taking my own work to a supervisor, that this second supervision and concomitant immersion is where individual development can lead to the discovery of your own analytic voice. We all need supervision to counteract the dead hand of inner institutionalization. In our quest for the Holy Grail it is necessary to work on the edge of a constant creative tension where work and one's heart's desire merge imperceptibly.

Postscript

In Jung's letter to Bernhard Lang on belief and God in which he discusses the Buber/Jung controversy her writes:

> I start with the confession of not knowing and not being able to know; believers start with the assertion of knowing and being able to know. There is now only one truth and when we ask the believers what this truth is they give us a number of very different answers with regard to which the one sure thing is that each believer announces his own particular truth. Instead of saving: To me personally it seems so, he says: It is so, thus putting everybody else automatically in the wrong.

Later in the same letter he writes:

> How could I have any communication at all with a person if I approached him with the absolutist claims of the believer? Though I am

sure of my subjective experience, I must impose on myself every conceivable restriction in interpreting it. I must guard against identifying with my subjective experience. (Jung 8)

This can be learnt through experience, it cannot be taught.

References

1. Bion, W.R. (1961). *Experience in Groups*. London- Tavistock.
2. — (1970). *Attention and Interpretation*. London. Tavistock.
3. Fordham, M. (1956). 'Active imagination and imaginative activity.' *Journal of Analytical Psychology* 1,2.
4. — (1961). 'Suggestions towards a theory of supervision.' *Journal of Analytical Psychology 6,2*.
5. — (1989). 'Some historical reflections.' *Journal of Analytical Psychology* 34, 3.
6. — 1991). 'The supposed limits of interpretation.' *Journal of Analytical Psychology 36, 2*.
7. Hinshelwood, R. (1985). 'Questions of training.' *Free Associations*, 2
8. Jung, C.G. (1957). 'Letter to Bernard Lang,' *C.G. Jung Letters*, Vol. 2. London: Routledge & Kegan Paul.
9. Keats, J. (1817). 'Letter to his brothers' (No. 32), in *Letters of John Keats*, Ed. M.B. Forman. Oxford University Press, 1960.
10. Klein, M. (1946). 'Notes on some schizoid mechanisms.' *International Journal of Psycho-Analysis 27*, pp. 99-110.
11. Meltzer, D. (1967). *The Psychoanalytical Process*. London: Heinemann.
12. — (1973). Sexual States of Mind. Strath Tay: Clunie Press.
13. Meltzer, D., Harris Williams, M. (1988) The Apprehension of Beauty. Strath Tay: Clunie Press.
14. Menzies Lyth, I. (1988) *Containing Anxiety in Institutions*. London: Free Association Books.
15. — (1989). *The Dynamics of the Social*. London: Free Association Books.
16. Newton, K. (1961). 'Personal reflections on training.' *Journal of Analytical Psychology* 6, 2.
17. Plaut, A. (1961). 'A dynamic outline of the training situation.' *Journal of Analytical Psychology, 6, 2*.
18. Waddell, M. (1989). 'Experience and identification in George Eliot's novels,' *Free Associations 17*.
19. — (1990). 'The vale of soul making.' Unpublished public lecture.

20. Waddell, M., Williams, G. (1991). 'Reflections on perverse states of mind,' *Free Associations 2, 2.*
21. Zinkin, L. (1989). 'The grail quest and the analytic setting.' *Free Association 17.*

[18]

A Model of Clinical Supervision

Jean Carr

Clinical Supervision is a process between the supervisor and supervisee. However, this relationship is only part of a wider system, which can be used to provide the framework within which various aspects of the supervisory process can be examined. Supervision is an essential component in all training and ongoing professional development. There have been various contributions looking at parts of the total system. This chapter presents an overview of the system, within which these contributions can be placed.

Outlined below is a model for the supervision system, outlining the various components and the relationships between them.

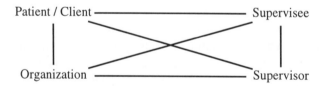

The participants in the system are:

1. *The Supervisee* who can be training in psychotherapy: employed in an agency and subject to various agency requirements for supervision; attached in some way to a hospital or clinic, etc. There are many examples, probably the least common is the Psychotherapist, working privately, who goes for supervision purely for her own development, without any requirements from an agency or training body.

2. *The Organization* which is the Social Services Department, hospital, clinic, voluntary body, etc. or the training body with its

234   *Jean Carr*

requirements. Also to be included here is the whole edifice of "psychotherapy." This is related to as a set of theories, behaviors, training etc. which will have different meanings for each individual. For one person it may be a rather exclusive "club" which she wants, but fears, to join, for another a form of professional haven, where [he or she] can integrate and develop the many strands of [his or her] life and professional work.

3. *The Supervisor* can be employed in the same agency as the Supervisee, who can have a limited choice of Supervisor. In a training body, the Supervisee can choose [his or her] Supervisor, and they may know each other in various contexts outside the supervision setting. The Supervisor is seen in various ways, realistic and otherwise, e.g., an acclaimed expert, someone on a pedestal at whose feet one can sit. Alternatively, parental and teacher transferences are very likely to develop.

4. *The Patient/Client* whose treatment is at the core of the system, but whose treatment is by no means the sole motivating source in the system.

If the therapist is in personal analysis, this brings in yet another party which influences the system, but this will be excluded as it creates yet another set of relationships.

This model outlines a system of dy- and triadic relationships, each with its own characteristics, and each exerting an influence on the total network. The factors involved in each can be on a rational level and also determined by unconscious processes. Each has its own transference and countertransference components, its own combination of ego and shadow, individual and collective, ritualized behaviors, its own set of overt and covert needs, alliances, etc.

Most importantly, what happens in relationship (1) is influenced by, and influences, the rest of the system. Looking at the system from the viewpoint of the supervisee, various relationships can be identified and examined.

Looking first at (1)

The Supervisee brings to this, as to any other learning situation, hopes and fears about him or herself, the teacher, the outcome of the learning. This relationship will include the conscious, rational responses that are against work, development and change. A useful discussion of these processes is contained in "The emotional experience of learning and teaching."[1] The Supervisee brings from her past, and especially from parental relationships, various fears and expectations. There may be the belief in the "all-knowing teacher," the source of all knowledge and goodness, a pattern frequently seen, maybe even exacerbated, by psychotherapy organizations. The student on the other hand feels she knows nothing. Psychotherapy supervision, by the very nature of the work and the intimacy and depth of the learning situation, can especially activate elements that are there in all teaching/learning situations. The various discussions about how does psychotherapy help, what are the curative factors, what part does the personality of the therapist play, all can lead to intense doubts in the Supervisee about herself and her work. One can have difficulties, even fail, in grasping physics theory or a literature text without the intensive feeling of real damage to the self that can be associated with learning in the psychotherapeutic process. On the other hand, over time, the intensity and privacy of psychotherapy supervision can act as a strong container, and minimize fears that could be more difficult in a more open group or classroom situation. This fear of being judged, whether one is "good enough," can lead to Supervisees being oversensitive to critical comments, thus influencing their work with the patient or to simply not hearing it, and even adopting the "know how to do it anyway, without my Supervisor." In other professional trainings, it is possible to get by without too much exposure and being 'touched' by the work, this is not so in psychotherapy.

The Supervisee can also experience high admiration for the Supervisor, but this admiration must inevitably be linked with some degree of envy. This can lead to positive learning through identification, but also to idealization and, almost, hero worship. Envy, if uppermost, can lead to attacks on what is offered and destruction of the Supervisor's comments. Some students, to avoid struggling with these issues, assume that they can simply be what is desired and experience supervision as part of the process to be gone through, but without real commitment.

Triangle 1, 2, 6

One factor in this network is the number and complexity of the triangular relationships that are formed. Some of the dynamics in this particular triangle are explored by J. Mattison in *The Reflections Process*.[2] The main thesis of this is that "The processes at work in the relationship between the client and worker, (2) are often reflected in the relationship between worker and Supervisor (1)." It is necessary to note how relationships (2) and (1) influence each other, and in turn are influenced by the Supervisor's 'relationship' (6) with the patient. Although the Supervisor will most likely not meet the patient, a strong relationship to the 'imagined' patient can develop.

One issue that is often discussed is whether the patient should know that her therapist is in training and has someone supervising her. Without answering that question, it is useful to examine the way this knowledge can influence the process of therapy and supervision. If the patient knows about the Supervisor in the background, this can lead to a powerful oedipal transference. For the patient there is a figure in the background who has power, knowledge, but with whom contact is forbidden. The patient can split off bad feelings on to the Supervisor, leaving the therapist good. For example, the view that "You, my therapist, would be more helpful, loving, etc., if not for the authority in the background telling you what to do." The patient can fear that the therapist and Supervisor have a relationship that is more interesting and exciting than his with his therapist, from which he is excluded. Alternatively, I have found that if a triangular relationship like this exists, some more borderline patients can feel more 'held' by these two people, and there can be useful work initiated in this recreation of the family situation.

A triangular relationship of a very different nature is 1, 5, 4.

The training organization is a powerful, ever present force influencing the relationship between Supervisor and Supervisee. Both can feel judged in different ways, with their work in supervision, not only the work of the Supervisee under examination. The Supervisee can feel there is a strong bond between his Supervisor and the training body, and he is excluded from this like a child is excluded from relationships between the adults. Difficulties can sometimes arise between Supervisee and the training body, in which the Supervisee can seek to involve the Supervisor in a collusive relationship against the training body. Supervisors can over-identify with their students and perhaps we are familiar with the Supervisor, all of whose geese are swans. In this section focusing on the Supervisee, relationship 5 is a complex relationship, which has a dynamic that reverberates through the rest of the system. The Supervisee is grateful to be on the course, she is dependent on it for professional development and recognition, and has possibly committed money, and certainly time and energy to the process. This situation must, at times, activate some anger and rebellious thinking or behavior. A Supervisee can want to "do her own thing," to be free of constraints, but having to remain within the boundaries of the training, which at other times can be experienced as supportive and containing.

Within this relationship are contained the ritual elements of "becoming a psychotherapist" that contain a dimension that goes beyond the learning and assessment process. In each organization, there is a process that students must go through, elements that must be completed. All of which while quite rational, and work-oriented, also contain elements of more primitive "rites of passage." Some of these issues are identified by D. Meltzer,[3] who looks at psychoanalysis as a social organization, using Bion's description of work groups and basic assumption groups.

Looking at the system from the viewpoint of the Supervisor, relationship (1) can be experienced very differently from the Supervisee. An eminent Freudian analyst said that he never ceased to be amazed that patients and colleagues came to him for help and advice, without realizing the extent to which he felt inadequate and still "a little boy inside." Supervisors also will at different times in their personal and professional lives, be more or less vulnerable, in different situations, to the stresses and dynamics of supervision. This is especially so for new Supervisors who, in the relationship (4) can feel on display, being assessed themselves by the training organization, and maybe even the Supervisee's own training analyst, discussions from which the Supervisor is excluded. The Supervisor may have varying opinions on the standards of training, depending on whether it is in her own organization or not, and varying levels of commitment to it and views on acceptable standards of practice for the Supervisee. How the Supervisor sees the agency requirements will influence the perception of the type of work expected and the trainee's competence.

Although the Supervisor would usually, not always, have no direct contact with the patient, a detailed picture builds up. The Supervisor works with her own "imagined" patient.

It is an inexorable fact that judgments are being made about the Supervisee's work, especially in training organizations, but also in various agencies where there are requirements that the worker will meet the standards of work set by the agency. If there are difficulties, the Supervisor can often hang on, so to speak, hoping things will get better and trying to make the best of it. The question can be asked "who fails?" Is it the trainee, who has been unable to grasp the theoretical and practical issues in psychotherapeutic work? Is it the Supervisor who "can't teach," has a personal conflict with the Supervisee? Alternatively, is it the patient in some way? Can the patient be scapegoated as "borderline," "difficult," etc. when the difficulties are to be found in the supervisory relationship, unacknowledged or difficult to handle, and projected outwards on to the patient.

The focus in this paper has been from the viewpoint of the Supervisor and the Supervisee. There are many other influences that could be explored in building up the framework within which two people, the Supervisor and Supervisee meet to talk about and try to understand the work that is going on with a third person, the patient. Despite the difficulties identified, supervision usually works, and people can be helped to practice psychotherapy within this myriad of influences. Perhaps the most important thing is while trying to understand as much of the dynamics as possible, and their influences on the supervision, it is advisable to set limits, and aim at some personal definition of whether the Supervisee has acquired sufficient knowledge and skill to undertake psychotherapeutic work.

References

1. Salzberger-Wittenberg, G. Henry and E. Osborne (1983). *The Emotional Experience of Learning and Teaching,* London: Routledge and Kegan Paul
2. Mattinson, Janet (1975). *The Reflections Process in Casework Supervision,* Institute of Marital Studies, Tavistock Institute of Human Relations.
3. Meltzer, D. and Williams, M. Harris (1988). *The Apprehension of Beauty.* Strath Tay: Clunie Press.

[19]

Supervision: The Impossible Profession

Louis Zinkin

I imagine that most people who read this book have been at some time or other, either a supervisor or supervisee. Whichever role we adopt, we know that supervision can be a delight, but may often be a torment. Which of us has not experienced a certain sinking of the heart when after exchanging a few pleasantries and waiting in quiet anticipation, the supervisee begins to open his notes? And which of us cannot recall a sense of despair when we go to a supervisor, gaze at our notes, relieved to find we have not left them at home, and begin to wonder how on earth we are going to use these comments to explain the analytic encounter to the satisfaction of our supervisor. In the meantime, our supervisor looks toward us, looking perhaps ever so kindly and encouraging, but seems, nevertheless, to be expecting something from us that we have no hope of providing? We all, of course, approve of supervision and agree there is probably no better way of learning the trade, the art, the science of psychotherapy. But at the same time, we need to admit our sense of torment.

Let us acknowledge that our traditional teaching method may be the best available, but it is not really adequate. In fact, it is much better to clear the air and admit that it is impossible. This acknowledgment need not create despair. We can still make good use of the situation. In fact, it may cease to be a torment and we may even thoroughly enjoy ourselves once we realize that, although for want of a better name, we have evolved something in analytic institutes which we call "supervision." One partner is called the "supervisor" and the other is called an even worse name, the "supervisee." The trouble with the term "supervisee" is that it suggests that the object of supervision is the other person, rather than the work of therapy. In spite of using this language, we do not really come close to what supervision means in any other context. It is not, for example, in the least like a driving lesson. That may also be a torment, but we do know that our driving, however good or bad, is being supervised. I should like, therefore, in this final contribution to a book on supervision to help us better understand the impossibility of our task.

A good way to start is to ask a difficult, rather than an impossible question. What makes a good supervisor? This is an important question for four groups of people: (1) for training committees who appoint supervisors in the first place, (2) for the trainees who look for the right supervisor to approach, (3) for the analysts who are asked to take on the responsibility of recommending a supervisor to his or her training patients and (4) for the supervisors themselves.

All four of these groups are hampered by enormous disadvantages in *assessing who is a good supervisor*. To begin with, Training Committees bear a heavy responsibility, especially as the candidate's supervisors are usually appointed for life. Unlike practically any other job, supervisors are chosen without any convincing demonstration that they are capable of doing the job. Nobody trains the supervisors. Training Committees are good at voting, but what the voters have to base their decision on is pitifully inadequate. They reach statistical decisions that give yes or no answers in much the same way that the trainee is judged ready to be certified as a therapist. Determining the readiness of a therapist is difficult enough, but at least therapists are trained and their work is scrutinized throughout their preparation. Such a training has relatively clear criteria that can be applied to the potential therapist. This is not the case with the institutional appointment of the status of supervisor.

The second group that needs to know how to assess a good supervisor is the group of trainees who may be asked to choose one. Candidates assume that supervisors are all judged competent by a training committee. What then might be looked for by the potential supervisee? A famous figure with a great therapeutic reputation? Perhaps a supervisor who has written books and papers? Would such an analyst be a good teacher or even a good communicator? Might the potential supervisee look for someone kindly and supportive who will give them an easy time or someone demanding and challenging, setting high standards? These are just a few of the questions confronting the potential supervisee. Other issues involve the relation of the supervisor to the personal analyst. Should the supervisor be someone like their analyst or someone quite different? Should candidates for supervision be allowed to shop around? And are the supervisors and supervisees free to turn each other down if they don't feel suited?

Whatever the potential supervisee's ideas are on these questions, they have precious little to go on. At worst, potential supervisees will be influenced by gossip and hearsay. At best they will go to someone whose seminars they have enjoyed.

We can dispose of my third group quite easily. This group consists of the personal analysts who are asked by their analysands to suggest a supervisor. After agonizing trial and error, I have come to the conclusion that the analysand should resist asking their personal analyst to recommend a supervisor. Such a request may cause untold damage to the analysis, not just because the analyst is compromised if drawn into a discussion of the relative merits of colleagues, but because even in what might seem to be an ideal matchmaking position, one often makes a hopelessly wrong decision.

But, of course, the candidates difficulties do not end with the selection of a supervisor. My fourth group consists of the supervisors themselves. When I am supervising, I try to be as good a supervisor as possible. The main factors which guided me when I started, were the supervisors valued during my training. But while I had training as an analyst, I had no training to become a supervisor. Reflecting about supervision over the years, which I do particularly when I encounter difficulties with a supervisee, I have come to the conclusion that in doing supervision we are actually trying to do the impossible. The difficulty arises at the precise moment when we think that what is needed is supervision – a super-vision that allows us to see the actual patient being discussed – and forget that this is not possible. The difficulty arises when we think the supervisor's role is to put right what, based on the clinical notes, appears to be wrong in the supervisee's therapy. The problem arises when we forget that only the therapist can correct the situation because only the therapist knows what actually happened.

If we cannot supervise then what can we do? We may have, after all, a great deal to teach. And through the process we learn something of the way the particular supervisee works. We also have access to some of the patient's material, such as a dream and the patient's associations. We may suggest interpretations, and personally, I do make a point of putting the interpretations into exact words. We may pick out a theme that runs through a session. We might bring a new perspective to the case material with a discussion of transference issues, or a myth, or a reconstruction of the past. We may observe the interaction taking place between the two participants, something always difficult for the therapist who is caught up in the analytic process. We might teach about technique, such as how and when to intervene, how to use the countertransference, how to frame interpretations, how to deal with the mechanics of case management, such as holidays, fees, waiting rooms, noise, canceled sessions, etc. We might pick up subtle forms of acting out and suggest ways of working with it. We can support and reassure the trainee who does not understand what is going on and help to tolerate uncertainty, ambiguity and confusion. When problems arise, we might refer the supervisee to the relevant literature. And above all, by our general demeanor, we act as a model which the trainee can introject. The list of valuable functions the supervisor may perform ranges from teaching the "tricks of the trade" to inspiring the supervisee with the sheer beauty of the analytic process.

Why then do I call supervision an impossible profession? The reason is that what we think we are doing is literal supervision. We cannot really supervise the work of analysis because to do so, we would have to sit in the actual room. If we were to do this the therapeutic process would no longer be an analysis. Nor will any mechanical device, such as audio or video recording or one way screens, solve this problem. *Analysis simply cannot be supervised.* Our mistake is to think that our present method is literally supervision. Our error is in assuming that the supervisee, whom I shall now refer to as the *so-called supervisee*, can repeatedly write notes about what goes on in therapy and report these case notes in supervision. The mistake is in assuming that by supervising these notes we can supervise the analysis. I am not simply pointing out the well-known difficulties of remembering accurately what has been said, or the impossibility of conveying to the supervisor the atmosphere in the room, the many subtle nonverbal interactions, the intuitive hunches and so on. We all freely grant that what we are supervising is only a grossly impoverished approximation of the "real thing." I am suggesting, rather, that a supervised analysis is not an analysis, which is a private two-person affair, but something else. The supervisor is, all the time, both present and not present – which is impossible.

Recently I was approached by a so-called supervisee, who requested supervision on a private case because being "only a trainee" he could be insured against malpractice claims only if the case was supervised. The insurance company was using the medical model where a consultant supervises a registrar. But the consultant may at any time see that patient himself, may look at reports of X-rays or blood samples. The consultant has access to the same material which the registrar has and can at any time take over the treatment. None of this is true of the analytic supervisor who, in most cases, has never seen the patient and would be most reluctant to do so. It is like an apprenticeship, but normally the apprentice, say a car mechanic, is working on an object, a car, which the master mechanic can also see and work on.

I cannot say I am always fully conscious of the importance of these differences in supervision, but every now and again I am forcefully reminded of them. At present I am supervising, in my hospital work, the analytic psychotherapy of a young woman, whom I had seen myself for an initial assessment. As I began hearing about her in supervision, I had an uneasy feeling that this was not the same patient. I could picture the patient being described and as the weeks went by my picture of her became more and more vivid. But my mental image of the woman in the case presentation was not the same as the patient I remember having seen. At times I began to wonder if I had misperceived her. My diagnostic formulation might have been quite wrong. After all, I had only seen her once and could have easily been misled. The fact remained that I had been able to establish a good rapport with the girl in the assessment interview, but was now having the greatest difficulty in establishing a rapport with her image as reported by the therapist.

Normally when supervising I try to imagine the patient, try to listen to the client through the words and actions reported to me by the therapist. But in this case, I found it impossible to do so. Gradually, however, I found I could imagine the patient, but only by forgetting that I had ever seen her myself. By putting aside my original memory of her, I was able to make room for a new picture of her. This was not only the picture of another woman who looked different and sounded different, but this imago required a different diagnosis from the one originally made. Yet, I am convinced that if I were to see her again, my original image of her would return.

This experience caused me to question the practice at analytic institutes of having an assessor evaluate the suitability of the potential case for the trainee. As I look at the intake analyst's assessment report and imagine the candidate's presentation of the patient as the analysis unfolds, I sometimes wonder if the assessor and the therapist have both met the same person. It may be that it is not that the assessor has "got it wrong," nor that the therapist who may be a beginner has not understood the case, but that a person cannot be viewed out of the context of relating to another person.

A similar experience occurred when a supervisee started to present tape recordings of her session. I had been supervising the therapist for about eighteen months. She was a gifted, very able therapist and quite experienced. She had the most remarkable recall and could give me what sounded like verbatim accounts of the sessions without notes, including what is often left out – a detailed account of what she said to the patient. In spite of all this, she and I felt stuck. The patient too felt he was making no headway. After a good deal of discussion, the therapist began making audio recordings. We would listen to the tapes together. Within minutes of listening to the patient on tape, I had the same strange experience. This was not at all the patient I had imagined. I quite liked him and realized that previously I found him irritating and felt unempathic towards him. Had I unconsciously been picking up the therapist's negative counter-transference? If so, it was unconscious on her part too. I could tell that his talk, if transcribed, would read very much as she had previously reported it to me. So what was different? Did it lie in the nonverbal sphere, in the nuances of his tone of voice, in the hesitations, the silences between words. I quickly picked up on an odd sound. "What's that cough?" I asked. "What cough?" she replied. What I actually heard was a slight clearing of the throat, which sounded quite loud on the tape. This turned out to be a nervous mannerism. He did this whenever he was touching on some anxiety, and specifically was communicating aggressive thoughts and fantasies. The therapist had simply never noticed it and, therefore, had not reported it.

On a tape the supervisor also hears how differently the therapist sounds from what had been imagined, sometimes more or less confident, more or less empathic, more or less confused, more or less articulate. The whole interaction sounds quite different. I am not arguing for the use of tape recordings. Rather, my point is that even if physically in the same room, or interviewing the same patient, one can never get into the position of the consultant doctor in charge, or of the master mechanic with his apprentice. It is simply impossible.

Should one, therefore, give up the idea of supervision or call it something else, like consultation? One trouble with the word "supervision" lies with the metaphor of vision, that the supervisor "sees" the analysis. Another problem is with the prefix "super-," the idea that the supervisor is looking down from a superior position, a master to a pupil. The supervisor is certainly supervising something, but he is certainly not supervising the analysis.

Nevertheless, it does seem to me that when the time comes to assess candidates for acceptance by the institution which claims to have trained them, by far the best guide is the experience of their supervisors, rather than the candidate's performance in seminars, their ability to write papers, the view of the training analyst or the candidate's own. Although nobody can really know how the trainee works analytically, as they would if it were possible to be invisibly present during the trainee's sessions with the client, the person who has the best overall idea is the one who has, over time, heard the trainee's account of the sessions and examined them with him / her. By being given the responsibility for making this judgment, the supervisor is a supervisor (in the sense of overseeing the trainee) and not just a kindly, friendly helper, as a sympathetic colleague might be later in professional life.

However, as all training committees know, supervisors may sharply disagree about the same candidate and such disagreements are inevitable and undecidable.

The supervisor who tries to be teacher, friend, father, mother, the old wise man or woman, the reflecting mirror, counsel for the defense and for the prosecution, judge and jury, not just one, but all of these things, is in an untenable position, one for which there is no training. For better or worse, he or she, poor devil, is practicing an impossible profession.

Postscript

After completing this chapter, I realized a possible answer to the problem raised. What I suppose we shall go on calling "supervision" is actually a shared fantasy. The process is the result of the trainee trying to imagine what he and his patient have been doing together and the supervisor trying to imagine it too. Supervision works best if both remain aware that what they are jointly imagining is not true. But both can profit enormously. Both can enjoy the experience as well as suffer the difficulties. And also, there is teaching and learning to be found in this joint imaginative venture. Of course, I intuitively knew all this before writing this chapter, but having given myself the task of consciously addressing the topic, I now know it a little better.

Selected Bibliography

Books

Alonso, A. The Quiet Profession: Supervisors of Psychotherapy. Mcmillan, New York: 1985.

Caligor, L., Bromberg, P. and Meltzer, J. *Clinical Perspectives on the Supervision of Psychoanalysis and Psychotherapy*, Plenum Press, New York: 1984.

Dewald, Paul. *Learning Process in Psychoanalytic Supervision: Complexities and Challenges: A Case Illustration.* International Universities Press, Madison, Connecticut: 1987.

Fleming, Joan and Benedek, Therese. *Psychoanalytic Supervision*, Grune & Stratton, New York: 1966.

Papers of Joan Fleming, M.D., Guilford Press, New York: 1987.

Hess, A.K. *Psychotherapy supervision: Theory, research, and practice*, John Willey & Sons: New York: 1980.

Lane, Robert. *Psychoanalytic Approaches to Supervision*, Brunner/Mazel, Publishers, New York: 1990.

Langs, R. *The supervisory experience.* Jason Aronson: New York: 1979.

Lewin, B.D. and Ross, H. *Psychoanalytic Education in the United States.* Norton, New York: 1960.

Meisels, Murray and Shapiro, Ester. *Tradition and Innovation in Psychoanalytic Education*, Lawrence Erlbaum Associates, Publisher, Hillsdale, New Jersey: 1990.

Wallerstein, R.S. *Becoming a psychoanalyst: A Study of psychoanalytic supervision.* International University Press: New York: 1981.

Weiss, Stanley, Ed., *The Teaching and Learning of Psychoanalysis.*

Articles

Ackerman, N.W. (1953). Selected problems in supervised analysis. *Psychiatry* 16, 283-290.

Anderson, A.R. & McLaughlin, F. (1963). Some observations on psychoanalytic supervision. *Psychoanalytic Quarterly,* 32, 77-93.

Angel, Valerie (1990) Discussion. *Psychoanalysis and Psychotherapy, Special Issue: The supervision of the psychoanalytic process*, 1990, 8 (1), 46-50.

Arkowitz, Sydney (1990). Perfectionism in the supervisee. *Psychoanalysis and Psychotherapy, Special Issue: The supervision of the psychoanalytic process*, 1990, 8 (1), 51-68.

Arlow, J.A. (1963). "The supervisory situation." *Journal of the American Psychoanalytic Association*, 11, 576-594.

Aronson, Marvin (1990). A group therapist's perspectives on the use of supervisory groups in the training of psychotherapists. *Psychoanalysis and Psychotherapy, Special Issue: The supervision of the psychoanalytic process*, 1990, 8 (1) pp. 88-94.

Atwood, Joan (1986). Self-awareness in supervision. *Clinical Supervisor*, 4 (3), 79-96.

Bagarozzi, Dennis (1980). Wholistic family therapy and clinical supervision: Systems, behavioral and psychoanalytic perspectives. *Family Therapy*, 7 (2), 153-165.

Balint, M. (1948). On the psychoanalytic training system. *International Journal of Psychoanalysis*, 29, 163-173.

Beckett, Thomas (1969). A candidate's reflections on the supervisory process. *Contemporary Psychoanalysis*, 5 (2), 169-179.

Berger, Simmons, Gregory, and Finestone (1990). The supervisors' conference. *Academic Psychiatry*, 14 (3), 137-141.

Bernstein, A.E. and Katz, S.C. When supervisor and therapist dream: The use of an unusual countertransference phenomenon. *Journal of the American Academy of Psychoanalysis*, 15 (2), 261-271.

Bibring, E. (1937). Methods and technique of control analysis: Report of Second Four Countries Conference. *International Journal of Psycho-Analysis*, 18, 369-372.

Blitzsten, N.L. and Fleming, J. (1953). What is a supervisory analysis? *Bulletin of the Menninger Clinic*, 17, 117-129

Blomfield, O.H. (1985). Psychoanalytic supervision: An overview. *International Review of Psycho-analysis*, 12 (4), 401-409.

Bromberg. P. (1981) The supervisory process and parallel process. *Contemporary Psychanalysis*, 18, 92-111.

Bush, George (1969). Transference, countertransference, and identification in supervision. *Contemporary Psychoanalysis*, 5 (2), 158-162.

Caligor, Leopold (1981). Parallel and reciprocal processes in psychoanalytic supervision. *Contemporary Psychoanalysis*, 17 (1), 1-27.

Carifio, M.S. and Hess, A.K. (1987). Who is the ideal supervisor? *Professional Psychologist*, 18 (3), 244-250.

Cohen, Larry (1980). Behavioral and analytic supervisees' evaluations of the desirability of certain characteristics in the ideal and typical supervisor. *Dissertation Abstracts International*, 41 (4-B), 1496.

Cohn, Odette (1992). Analytic candidates' experiences: Internalization and supervisory styles. *Dissertation Abstracts International*, 53 (6-B), 3150.

Cole, Phillip (1989). The impact of an empathic orientation in a psychoanalytically oriented supervisory role on the accuracy and depth of the evaluative process. *Dissertation Abstracts International*, 49 (9-B), 3997.

Cook, Harold (1990). Countertransference in psychoanalytic supervision. *Psychoanalysis and Psychotherapy, Special Issue: The supervision of the psychoanalytic process*, 1990, 8 (1), 77-87.

Cooper, A. and Witenberg, E.G. (1983). Stimulation of Curiosity in the supervisory process of psychoanalysis. *Contemporary Psychanalysis*, 19, 249-264.

Davidson, Leah (1987). Integration and learning in the supervisory process. *American Journal of Psychoanalysis*, 47 (4), 331-341.

DeBell, D.E. (1963). A critical digest of the literature on psychoanalytic supervision. *Journal of American Psychoanalytic Association*, 11, 546-575.

Deutsch, H. (1983). On supervised analysis. *Contemporary Psychoanalysis*, 19 (1), 67-70.

— (1983). Control analysis. *Contemporary Psychoanalysis*, 19 (1), 59-67.

Dewald, Paul (1969). Learning problems in psychoanalytic supervision: Diagnosis and management. *Comprehensive Psychiatry*, 10 (2), 107-121.

Doehrman, M. Parallel processes in supervision and psychotherapy. *Bulletin of the Menninger Clinic*, 40, 3-104.

Emch, M. (1955). The social context of supervision. *International Journal of Psycho-Analysis*, 36, 298-306.

Epstein, L. (1986). Collusive selective inattention to the negative impact of the supervisory interaction. *Contemporary Psychoanalysis*, 22(3), 389-409.

Felner, A.H. (1986). Discussion: Collusive selective inattention to the negative impact of the supervisory interaction. *Contemporary Psychoanalysis*, 22(3), 389-409.

Feixas, Guillem (1992). A Constructivist approach to supervision: Some preliminary thoughts. *International Journal of Personal Psychology*, 5 (2) 183-200.

Fiscalini, John (1985). On supervisory parataxis and dialogue. *Contemporary Psychoanalysis*, 21 (4), 591-608.

Fleming, Joan and Weiss, Stanley (1978). Assessment of progress in a training analysis. *International Review of Psycho-Analysis*, 5 (1), 33-43.

Frayn, Douglas (1991). Supervising the supervisors: The evolution of a psychotherapy supervisors' group. *American Journal of Psychotherapy*, 45 (1), 31-42.

Frijling-Schreuder, E.C.M.; Isaac-Edersheim, E.; and Van Der Leeuw, P.J. (1981) The supervisor's evaluation of the candidate. *International Review of Psycho-analysis*, 8 (4), 393-400.

Frijling-Schreuder, E.C.M., (1970). On Individual Supervision. *International Journal of Psycho-Analysis* 51, 363-370.

Galler, Roberta (1990). Thoughts on the impact of psychoanalytic theory. *Psychoanalysis and Psychotherapy, Special Issue: The supervision of the psychoanalytic process*, 8 (1) pp. 37-45.

Gaoni, Bracha (1974). Supervision from the point of view of the supervisee. *American Journal of Psychotherapy*, 28 (1), 108-114.

Gediman, H. and Wolkenfeld, F. (1980). The parallelism phenomenon in psychoanalysis and supervision: Its reconsideration as a triadic system. *Psychoanalytic Quarterly*, 49 (2), 234-255.

Glenn, Jules (1987). Supervision of child analyses. *Psychoanalytic Study of the Child*, 42, 575-596.

Grinberg, L. (1970). The problems of supervision in psychoanalytic education. *International Journal of Psycho-Analysis,* 51, 371-383.

Grossman, William (1992). Comments on the concept of the analytic instrument. *Journal of Clinical Psychoanalysis*, 1 (2), 261-271.

Harris, Adrienne (1985). "The rules of the game": Discussion. *Contemporary Psychoanalysis*, 21 (1), 17-26.

Isakower, Otto (1992). The analyzing instrument: An illustrative example: A student's account of a period of analysis and supervision: "The Mona Lisa Theme." *Journal of Clinical Psychoanalysis*, 1 (2), 209-215.

Issacharoff, A. (1982). Countertransference in supervision. *Contemporary Psychoanalysis*, 23, 407-422.

Jackson, Jonathan (1989). Supervision and the problem of grandiosity in novice therapists. *Psychotherapy Patient*, 1989, 5 (3-4), pp. 113-124.

Josephs, Lawerence (1990). The concrete attitude and the supervision of beginning psychotherapists. *Psychoanalysis and Psychotherapy, Special Issue: The supervision of the psychoanalytic process*, 1990, 8 (1) pp. 11-22.

Kavaler-Adler, Susan (1990). The supervisor as an internal object. *Psychoanalysis and Psychotherapy, Special Issue: The supervision of the psychoanalytic process*, 8 (1), 69-76.

Keiser, S. (1956). Panel Report: The technique of supervised analysis. *Journal of the American Psychoanalytic Association.* 4, 539-549.

Lambert, M.J. & Arnold, R.C. Research and the supervisory process. *Professional Psychology*, 18 (3), 217-224.

Lane, Robert (1985). The recalcitrant supervisee: The negative supervisory reaction. *Current Issues in Psychoanalytic Practice*, 2 (2), 65-81.

Langs, Robert (1982). Supervisory Crises and dreams from supervisees. *Contemporary Psychoanalysis*, 18(4), 575-612.

Langs, Robert (1994). Supervision in training institutes. *Contemporary Psychoanalysis*, 30 (1) 75-82.

Langs, Robert (1989). Reactions of supervisees (and supervisors) to new levels of psychoanalytic discovery and meaning. *Contemporary Psychoanalysis*, 25 (1), 76-97.

Lawner, Peter (1989). Counteridentification, therapeutic impasse, and supervisory process. *Contemporary Psychoanalysis*, 1989, Vol. 25 (4), pp. 592-607.

Leavy, Stanley (1985). The rules of the game. *Contemporary Psychoanalysis*, 21 (1), 1-17.

Lebovici, S. (1983). Supervision in French psychoanalytic education: Its history and evolution. *Annual of Psychoanalysis*, 11, 79-89.

— (1970). Technical remarks on the supervision of psychoanalytic treatment. *International Journal of Psycho-Analysis*, 51, 385-392.

Lederman, Selwyn (1982-83). A contribution to the theory and practice of supervision. *Psychoanalytic Review*, 69 (4), 423-439.

Lesser, Ruth (1983). Supervision: Illusions, anxieties and questions. *Contemporary Psychoanalysis*, Vol 19, 1.

Levenson, Edgar, A. (1982). Follow the fox: An inquiry into the vicissitudes of psychoanalytic supervision. *Contemporary Psychanalysis*, 18: 1-15.

London, Alana (1989). Unconscious hatred of the analyst and its displacement to a patient and supervisor. *Modern Psychoanalysis*, Vol. 14 (2), pp. 197-220.

Lubin, M. (1984-85). Another source of danger for psychotherapists: The supervisory introject. *International Journal of Psycho-Analysis and Psychotherapy*, 10, 25-45.

Martin, Gary; Mayerson, Peter; Olsen, Homer; Wiberg, Lawrence (1978). Candidates' evaluation of psychoanalytic supervision. *Journal of the American Psychoanalytic Association*, 26 (2), 407-424.

Mendell, Dale (1986). Cross-gender supervision of cross-gender therapy: Female supervisor, male candidate, female patient. *American Journal of Psychoanalysis*, 46 (3), 270-275.

Moulton, Ruth (1969). Multiple dimensions in supervision. *Contemporary Psychoanalysis*, 5 (2), 146-150.

Newman, Carl (1986). Psychoanalytic supervision and the larger truth. *American Journal of psychoanalysis*, 46 (3), 263-269.

Olivieri-Larsson, Rudolf (1993). *Group Analysis*, 26 (2) 169-176.

Paidoussi, Rea (1969). Varied experiences in supervision. *Contemporary Psychoanalysis*, 5 (2), 163-168.

Pedder, Jonathan (1986). Reflections on the theory and practice of supervision. *Psychoanalytic Psychotherapy*, 2 (1), 1-12.

Rilton, Annastina (1988). Some thoughts on supervision. *Scandinavian Psychoanalytic Review*, 11 (2), 106-116.

Robiner, William and Schofield, William (1990). References on supervision in clinical and counseling psychology. *Professional Psychology*, 21 (4), 297-312.

Roazen, P. (1983). Introduction to H. Deutsch's "On Supervised analysis." *Contemporary Psychoanalysis*, 19(1), 53-59.

Salvendy, John (1993). Control and power in supervision. *International Journal of Group Psychotherapy*, 43 (3) 363-376.

Schlierf, Christa (1982). A critical remark on supervisory technique. *Psychosomatic Medicine*, 2 (2), 48.

Schneider, Stanley (1992). Transference, countertransference, projective identification and role responsiveness in the supervisory process. *Clinical Supervisor*, 10 (2), 71-84.

Searles, H.F. The informational value of the supervisor's emotional experiences. *Psychiatry*, 18, 135-146.

— (1962). Problems of psychoanalytic supervision. In H.F. Searles, *Collected Papers on schizophrenia and related subjects*. New York: International University Press.

Shechter, Roberta (1990). Becoming a supervisor: A phase in professional development, *Psychoanalysis and Psychotherapy, Special Issue: The supervision of the psychoanalytic process*, Vol. 8 (1) pp. 23-28.

Sloane, P. (1957). Panel Report: The technique of supervised analysis. *Journal of the American Psychoanalytic Association*, 5, 539-547.

Solnit, A.J. (1970). Learning from psychoanalytic supervision, *International Journal of Psycho-Analysis*, 51, pp. 359-362.

Spotnitz, H. (1976). Trends in modern psychoanalytic supervision. *Modern Psychoanalysis*, 2, 210-217.

— (1982). Supervision of psychoanalysts treating borderline patients. *Modern Psychoanalysis, 7 (2), 185-213.*

Springman, Rafael R. (1986) Countertransference: Clarifications in Supervision, *Contemporary Psychoanalysis*, 22: 253-277.

Szecsody, Kachele, Dreyer (1993). Supervision: An intricate tool for psychoanalytic training, *Zeitschrift für Psychoanalytische Theorie und Praxis*, 8 (1) 52-70

Szecsody, Imre (1990). Supervision: A didactic or mutative situation. *Psychoanalytic Psychotherapy*, 1990, vol 4 (3), pp. 245-261.

Teitelbaum, Stanley (1990). The Impact of psychoanalytic supervision on the development of professional identity: Introduction. *Psychoanalysis and Psychotherapy, Special Issue: The supervision of the psychoanalytic process*, Vol. 8 (1) pp. 3-4.

— (1990). Aspects of the contract in psychotherapy supervision, *Psychoanalysis and Psychotherapy, Special Issue: The supervision of the psychoanalytic process*, Vol. 8 (1) pp. 95-98.

— (1990). Supertransference: The role of the supervisor's blind spots. *Psychoanalytic Psychology*, Vol. 7 (2) pp. 243-258.

Treese, Gary (1990). The phenomenon of shame in supervision and its role in the development of professional identity in psychologists. *Dissertation Abstracts International*, 51 (1-B), 445.

Weiss, Stanley and Fleming, Joan (1975). Evaluation of progress in supervision. *Psychoanalytic Quarterly*, 44 (2), 191-205.

Widlocher, Daniel (1983). The supervisee and the supervisor: Interpretations and interventions. *Annuals of Psychoanalysis*, 11, 91-98.

Windholz, E. (1970). The theory of supervision in psychoanalytic education. *International Journal of Psycho-Analysis*, 51, 393-406.

Wolstein, Benjamin (1972). Supervision as experience, *Contemporary Psychoanalysis*, 8: 165-172.

Wolstein, Benjamin (1984). A proposal to enlarge the individual model of psychoanalytic supervision, *Contemporary Psychoanalysis*, 20: 131-155.

Yerushalmi, Hanoch (1992). Psychoanalytic supervision and the need to be alone, *Psychotherapy*, 29 (2), 262-268.

Zaphiropoulos, M.L. (1983). An appraisal of H. Deutsch's "On supervised analysis." *Contemporary Psychoanalysis*, 19: 67-70.

Index

Alphabetical List of Authors

Alan McGlashan
Gravity and Levity
The Philosophy of Paradox
162 pages

This book heralds a breakthrough in human imagination, not a breakthrough that may take place in the future, far or near, but one that has already occurred – only we may not have noticed it. Life, as the author shows, is open-ended and full of paradoxes. Its principles cannot be understood by logic and causal reasoning. We can only come to terms with life if we accept that there is no final answer to it and that adjusting to life's natural rhythm is the key to finding release from the horrors and problems around us.

TALKING WITH ANGELS Budaliget 1943
A document transcribed by Gitta Mallasz
474 pages, revised second edition
Budaliget 1943: A small village on the edge of Budapest. Three young women and a man, artists and close friends are gathered together in the uneasy days before Hitler's armies would destroy the world as they knew it. Seeking spiritual knowledge, and anticipating the horrors of Nazi-occupied Hungary, they met regularly to discuss how to find their own inner paths to enlightenment.

For 17 months, with the world locked in a deadly struggle for survival, the four friends meet every week with the spiritual beings they come to call their "angels"; Gitta Mallasz takes notes, the protocols which form this book, along with her commentary. The angels' message of personal responsibility is as meaningful and as urgent today as it was for its initial recipients half a century ago.

I am deeply touched by the dialogues with the angels.
Yehudi Menuhin

I could read it over and over again and never get tired of it.
Thank you, thank you, thank you for sharing this book with me.
Elisabeth Kübler-Ross

Hayao Kawai
Dreams, Myths and Fairy Tales in Japan
The well-known Japanese author, university professor and Zürich-trained Jungian analyst, Hayao Kawai, presents here the long-awaited second of his works in English. Originally presented as lectures at the historic Eranos Conferences in Ascona, this book describes five Japanese fairy tales, insightfully examined from Eastern and Western vantage points by an author intimately familiar with both. (158 pages, illustrated)

Rainer Maria Rilke
Duino Elegies
Translated by David Oswald

The *Duino Elegies* are one of the twentieth century's great works of art. In the space of ten elegies, presented here in a bilingual edition, an impassioned voice struggles to find an answer to what it means to be human in a world torn by modern consciousness. (128 pages)

C.A. Meier
Personality
The Individuation Process
in the Light of C.G. Jung's Typology
Carl Gustav Jung never produced a systematic treatment of his own work – he was always moving forward. His assistant-of-many-decades, Carl Alfred Meier, made it his life-task to gather and present in detail the various aspects of Jung's far-reaching discoveries. This final volume of Meier's work addresses the human personality in its encounters between consciousness and the unconscious, a process referred to as *individuation*. In describing such encounters, the author extensively explains the notion of Jung's *psychological types*. (192 pages)

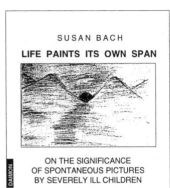

SUSAN BACH

LIFE PAINTS ITS OWN SPAN

ON THE SIGNIFICANCE
OF SPONTANEOUS PICTURES
BY SEVERELY ILL CHILDREN

DAIMON

Susan Bach
LIFE PAINTS ITS OWN SPAN
On the Significance of Spontaneous
Paintings by Severely Ill Children
with over 200 color illustrations
Part I (Text): 208 pp., part II (Pictures): 56 pp.
Life Paints its own Span with over 200 color
reproductions is a comprehensive exposi-
tion of Susan Bach's original approach to
the physical and psychospiritual evaluation
of spontaneous paintings and drawings by
severely ill patients. At the same time, this
work is a moving record of Susan Bach's
own journey of discovery.

Susan Tiberghien
Looking for Gold – *A Year in Jungian Analysis*
The author relates an experience that belongs to everyone – the experience
of soul, of tapping the depths of the unconscious. Here is the search for
wholeness, for bringing together the visible and the invisible. The author calls
it "seeing with her eyes closed."
Susan Tiberghien shares one year of dreams, analysis, daily life. A writer,
mother, woman in love, she enters her inner world, experiencing vertigo and
breathlessness until she lets the light and darkness fuse within her.
Each of the sixteen chapters marks a turn, with a dream and an epiphany. Thus
they build upon one another, as the reader comes into cyclical time, discover-
ing that dreams, too, have their seasons. (192 pages)

Forthcoming: A Festschrift for Laurens van der Post
The Rock Rabbit and the Rainbow

The Rock Rabbit
and the Rainbow
A Tribute to
Laurens van der Post

edited by Robert Hinshaw
Authors from around the world have combined
their talents in a tribute honoring this one-of-a-
kind writer, soldier and statesman, a man of his
time. Contributions include: Joseph Henderson:
"The Splendor of the Sun"; Alan McGlashan:
"How to be Haveable"; Ian Player: "My Friend
Nkunzimlanga"; Jean-Marc Pottiez: "Rainbow
Rhapsody"; T.C. Robertson: "A Triad of Land-
scapes – a Day in the Veld with Laurens"; and
numerous other essays and works by Aniela
Jaffé, Jonathan Stedall, Harry Wilmer, Jo Wheel-
right, C.A. Meier and many others.
(ca. 240 pages, illustrated)

ENGLISH PUBLICATIONS BY DAIMON

Susan Bach – *Life Paints its Own Span*
E.A. Bennet – *Meetings with Jung*
George Czuczka – *Imprints of the Future*
Heinrich Karl Fierz – *Jungian Psychiatry*
von Franz / Frey-Rohn / Jaffé – *What is Death?*
Liliane Frey-Rohn – *Friedrich Nietzsche*
Yael Haft – *Hands: Archetypal Chirology*
Siegmund Hurwitz – *Lilith, the first Eve*
Aniela Jaffé   – *The Myth of Meaning*
                  – *Was C.G. Jung a Mystic?*
                  – *From the Life und Work of C.G. Jung*
                  – *Death Dreams and Ghosts*
Verena Kast   – *A Time to Mourn*
                  – *Sisyphus*
Hayao Kawai – *Dreams, Myths and Fairy Tales in Japan*
James Kirsch   – *The Reluctant Prophet*
Rivkah Schärf Kluger   – *The Gilgamesh Epic*
Rafael López-Pedraza   – *Hermes and his Children*
                  – *Cultural Anxiety*
Alan McGlashan – *The Savage and Beautiful Country*
                  – *Gravity and Levity*
Gitta Mallasz (Transcription) – *Talking with Angels*
C.A. Meier   – *Healing Dream and Ritual*
                  – *A Testament to the Wilderness*
Laurens van der Post – *A «Festschrift»*
R.M. Rilke – *Duino Elegies*
Susan Tiberghien – *Looking for Gold*
Ann Ulanov – *The Wizards' Gate*

Jungian Congress Papers:
Jerusalem 1983 – *Symbolic and Clinical Approaches*
Berlin 1986 – *Archetype of Shadow in a Split World*
Paris 1989 – *Dynamics in Relationship*
Chicago 1992 – *The Transcendent Function*

Available from your bookstore or from our distributors:

In the United States:

Atrium Publishers Group
3356 Coffey Lane
Santa Rosa, CA 95403
Tel. (707) 542 5400
Fax: (707) 542 5444

Chiron Publications
400 Linden Avenue
Wilmette, IL 60091
Tel. (708) 256 7551
Fax: (708) 256 2202

In Great Britain:

Airlift Book Company
26-28 Eden Grove
London N7 8EF, England
Tel. (607) 5792 and 5798
Fax (607) 6714

Worldwide: Daimon Verlag
Hauptstrasse 85
CH-8840 Einsiedeln Switzerland
Tel. (41)(55) 532266
Fax (41)(55) 532231   *Write for our complete catalog!*